WELFARE STATE AND DEMOCRACY IN CRISIS

T0272004

Welfare State and Democracy in Crisis

Reforming the European model

Edited by

THEODORE PELAGIDIS
Panteion University of Athens, Greece

LOUKA T. KATSELI
University of Athens, Greece

JOHN MILIOS
National Technical University of Athens, Greece

LONDON AND NEW YORK

First published 2001 by Ashgate Publishing

Reissued 2018 by Routledge
2 Park Square, Milton Park, Abingdon, Oxon OX14 4RN
711 Third Avenue, New York, NY 10017, USA

Routledge is an imprint of the Taylor & Francis Group, an informa business

Publisher's Note
The publisher has gone to great lengths to ensure the quality of this reprint but points out that some imperfections in the original copies may be apparent.

Disclaimer
The publisher has made every effort to trace copyright holders and welcomes correspondence from those they have been unable to contact.

ISBN 13: 978-1-138-70241-7 (hbk)
ISBN 13: 978-1-138-70264-6 (pbk)
ISBN 13: 978-1-315-20356-0 (ebk)

Contents

List of Contributors

Guglielmo CARCHEDI, Faculty of Economics, University of Amsterdam.

Dimitris CHRISTOPOULOS, Minority Groups Research Center, Athens, Greece.

Frank DEPPE, University of Marburg, Germany.

Dimitris DIMOULIS, Univeridade Bandeirante Sao Paulo, Brazil.

Michael DUNFORD, School of European Studies, University of Sussex, UK.

Jean-Pierre GARNIER, Centre National de la Recherche Scientifique, France.

Christina GIANNOULIS, Universität des Saarlandes, Germany.

Jörg HUFFSCHMID, Institute of European Economy and Economic Policy, University of Bremen, Germany.

Louka T. KATSELI, Department of Economics, University of Athens, Greece.

John MILIOS, Department of Humanities and Social Sciences, National Technical University of Athens, Greece.

Leo PANITCH, University of York, Canada.

Theodore PELAGIDIS, Institute of International Relations, Panteion University of Athens, Greece.

Amartya SEN, Nobel Laureate in Economics, 1998. Cambridge University, UK.

Klaus SIEVEKING, Zentrum für Europäische Rechtspolitik an der Universität Bremen, Germany.

Kostas VERGOPOULOS, University of Paris VIII, France.

Richard D. WOLFF, Department of Economics, University of Massachusetts-Amherst, MA 01003-7510, USA.

INTRODUCTION

1 Welfare Decline and the Crisis of Democracy

THEODORE PELAGIDIS
LOUKA T. KATSELI
JOHN MILIOS

1. Two decades of restrictive austerity policies in Europe have influenced every aspect of social life. The privatization of the welfare state, the downsizing of government, the emergence of new forms of social exclusion, the increasing unemployment and the fall or even polarization of wages, the "orthodox," "free-market" delivery systems for health, education, and welfare, are changes which affect not only the economy but also the politics of developed capitalist societies.

Yet, no alternative has been created to this "new" way of managing public affairs in the developed capitalist countries. In this context, it is believed by conventional wisdom that we are going through a "post"-era, in which all traditional disputes have been "settled." However, this situation does not signify the end of anything, given that nothing really ends in society, politics, ideology and history. The social differentiations which generate conflict and transformation have certainly not come to an end. Neither are we going through the era which, with some embarrassment, has been dubbed post-modern, post-capitalist, post-work-based. We are nevertheless going through an era that favors a way of thinking characterized by global questioning and criticism, a way of thinking, that is, that entails various types of "post-thinking," i. e. of post-theoretical and post-practical reflection on the preconditions of thinking and acting.

The transgression of the limits of dogmatism and of unscrutinized certainties becomes necessary, because, first of all, in our days economy, politics and science are dominated by an objective discrepancy. Critical thinking and progressive politics have suffered obvious and painful defeats. Yet these defeats and setbacks are in contrast with the historical necessity for changes at all levels. They are not due to a transgression of the state of things that had given rise to criticism and questioning in previous decades, but rather to the excessive strengthening of the one-sidedness and violence of those possessing power. Indeed, statistical data concerning "human development" (the indicators of prosperity, education, and manifestation of human liberty) suggest that inequality and oppression dominate all levels of action throughout the world.

However, never before in history have the so-called Western countries been so affluent. This undeniable fact coexists with the rise of some particularly disturbing phenomena. In the USA more than 60 million live in poverty, while the gulf between high- and low-income earners has been steadily widening since the '70s and 1% of the population controls 39% of the total wealth. In Europe there are more than 50 million poor people, with official unemployment levels – unquestionably understated – equal to almost twelve percent of the workforce. On a global scale, the wealth of the 358 richest people exceeds the total annual income of the poorest 45% of the total population (Ramonet 1998).

The institutionalization of social chaos is an ever-present danger, a concomitant of the "desocialization" of economic processes, such that societies nowadays are more and more reminiscent of the violent periods of unregulated capitalism of the nineteenth century and the inter-war period.

According to the conventional wisdom of official thinking, tirelessly reiterated for over a decade and a half, what is involved is a transition period until there is an upturn in investments corresponding to a rise in business profits, whereupon a new virtuous circle of development will get underway, with rising incomes. Yet, despite a clear recovery in profit levels (OECD 1998, Table 25) and the increasing capital income share, both in the EU and in the OECD countries (Table 1), neither investments nor economic growth rates are anywhere near the levels required for recovery in employment, incomes and living standards in the Western societies as a whole. On the contrary, the economic situation of broad social strata is deteriorating. In the name of private interest and the impeccable and flawless workings of the market, social considerations atrophy and collectivities are undermined.

The rule of limitless competition and the ideal of "every man for himself" have caused people to lose all consciousness that "we live together" (Ramonet 1998), stigmatizing all forms of collective and public activity as anachronistic and as such responsible for the present crisis. Within this framework, misfits and the marginalized are perceived as a "burden." The cost of solidarity is regarded as unacceptably high – even by the so-called progressive socialist parties of the West.

TABLE 1   Capital income share in the business sector

	1970-80	1997
EU	33.0	38.4
OECD	33.2	35.3

Source: OECD (1998), Table 24.

The Welfare State is in retreat under the pressures of the perceived need to strengthen national competitiveness, with the result that the attitude of "every man for himself" is transposed to the level of inter-state relations. The disturbing features in this landscape of the "me" society are further amplified by the crisis of political representation, as exemplified by the lack of credibility of political bodies, particularly when it comes to their ability to cope with the violent and abrupt "destructuring" effects of economic activity that have escaped all democratic control. The ideological and political embarrassment and inertia that characterizes the social-democratic parties facilitates the drift towards acceptance of the status quo, which is shaped by private interest and certainly not by the political and social forces that are supposedly sovereign in a parliamentary democracy. Many have noted that we are rapidly and openly heading for a new regime of "oligarchic democracy of the economic elite."

Elite technocrats, orthodox economists, public opinion makers in the media, representatives of financial and economic interest-groups, industrialists, supporters in general of the "pensée unique" and of "political correctness" bombard the community with new myths, disorienting the broad popular masses whose lives have been affected by the "new world order." As the ideal of balanced growth and full employment recedes ever further into the distance, reactionary thinking invents new packaging labels to promote its own socially destructive interests. "Globalization," "flexible labor markets," "deregulation" are the key tenets of the new universal religion behind which there lurks the same aging and reactionary economic elite.

So-called "globalization" chiefly concerns flows of goods and capital but also to some extent labor migration. Despite the fact that all these processes have until now hardly surpassed the levels they had reached at the beginning of the First World War (Bairoch 1997), the scarecrow of capital flight is utilized to legitimate agreements scandalously biased towards the rights of foreign investors and the one-sided obligations of governments (see the provisions of the recently signed "World Investment Agreement," discussed in Albala 1998), wage freezes and the rise of unemployment as a "necessity" resulting from new technologies – not to mention a useful tool for curbing inflationary pressures.

The concept of "flexibility" is pressed into the service of a strategy for handling European labor markets, also accused of being responsible for the high rate of unemployment. "Deregulation" of the labor market is the "magic" word for reorganizing productive relations to the disadvantage of employees, among other things through attacks on institutions tending to favor social cohesion, in particular public education, the health services and insurance. The official justification for cuts in the relevant public expenditures is that they are necessary for the maintenance and the enhancement of national competitiveness, as well as for the proper functioning of the public sector through the introduction of competition and the free market into public sector activities.

Tax cuts, individual accountability and employability, the introduction of criteria of competitiveness and productivity into the public sector of the economy, moral legitimization of the quest for profit by every possible means and in every possible occupation, glorification of the efficiency of a "totally free" market and of self-centered and socially irresponsible behavior in general: these are ideological leitmotifs that typically accompany the neo-liberal onslaught. They aim to persuade that economic and social inequality, marginalization and unemployment are prerequisites for competitiveness, indispensable for the functioning of the world economy.

2. One might well argue that it is peculiar how the international economy in the first post-war decades maintained a high rate of growth, at the same time increasing economic and social equality and building a powerful welfare state, while this isn't possible now.

The answer of a conservative, and perhaps also of an unsuspecting citizen, would be to attribute all present evils to "globalization." By "globalization" is meant, as already mentioned, the vertiginous increase in the international flow of capital and labor and competition from "miracle-working" countries with low labor costs. As revealed by Obstfeld and Taylor (1997) and Taylor (1994, 1996), capital movements now represent

2.3% of world GNP (1989-1994) as compared to 5.3% in the second decade of the 20th century. Even in relation to migration, at the turn of the century the wave of migration from Europe to America came to a million a year, despite the tremendous transport difficulties. Today in Europe only 1-2% of the workforce migrates from one country to another for employment purposes, while on an international scale only 5% of the people in the world live in a country other than that in which they were born (Laindi 1998). As for dangers from the South-East Asian tigers, the "miracle-working" model for economic development until only a few months ago, their economic and social collapse indicates that they did not and even more so do not present a threat to wages and incomes in the advanced countries. Even mainstream economists agree that international trade has not contributed to the worsening economic and social inequality in the Western world (Krugman and Lawrence 1994).

The view is also put forward that the new technologies and the increase in productivity associated with them lead to a diminution in the number of workplaces. But how true can this be when in the countries and regions where there is a high rate of implementation of the new technologies, unemployment tends to be relatively low? Also, despite the truly tremendous potentialities offered by the new technologies, the percentage increase in productivity that has ensued after their introduction is much lower than the equivalent figures for the twenty years from 1960 to 1979, as indicated in the table below. So it is wrong to hold productivity responsible for reductions in the number of job vacancies. So it is wrong to hold productivity responsible for reductions in the number of job vacancies.

TABLE 2   GNP per member of the workforce

	1960-73	1970-79	1980-89	1989-95
EU	4.4	2.3	1.7	0.7
OECD	3.8	1.7	1.4	0.9
USA	2.0	0.2	0.7	0.7

Source: OECD (1997), 53.

Flexibility is deemed necessary for markets to be able to return speedily to the equilibrium of full employment. However, notwithstanding the fact that the markets have been rendered almost fully flexible, even in Europe, unemployment persists, while only in very few of the world's economic centers, and very recently, has something approaching satisfactory levels of economic growth been re-established, albeit at the expense of economic equality (USA).

It is noteworthy that instead of the concept of so-called "dynamic/offensive flexibility," which includes upgrading of technological factors as well as of human resources, discussion centers exclusively on what is called "defensive flexibility," based on downgrading of skills as well as of the position of labor in the productive process, through expedients such as part-time and temporary employment, faηon and informal/black work which usually does not include so-called social contributions such as insurance, health care and a pension.

TABLE 3

	Public expenditure (%GNP*)	Incoming revenue (%GNP*)	Social insurance expenditure (%GNP**)
B	56.7	50.3	24.0
DK	60.3	58.8	20.2
D	49.3	45.6	17.7
F	54.5	50.4	22.6
GR	44.7	37.3	16.0
IRL	36.5	35.6	-
I	43.6	45.9	19.0
L	43.6	45.4	-
AT	53.0	49.1	20.9
FIN	58.3	55.7	22.2
SW	65.4	61.6	22.9
UK	42.1	37.7	-
NL	50.8	48.4	25.9
P	43.7	39.6	-
SP	44.6	40.1	17.3
EU	50.3	46.0	19.0

Sources: * Eurostat & DGII (1996), year 1996.
**OECD (1997). Average 1990-95.

Finally, there are claims that the welfare state, like government intervention through public spending in general, impedes development either by withdrawing resources from the private sector or by adding to the cost of locally-produced commodities on national markets. Typically, the size of the state sector is cited as a particularly detrimental factor from the point of view of a country's performance and prospects on the international markets. As early as 1987 the World Bank took care to argue that the developing countries of South East Asia, with their outward-looking development strategy and minimal state display the highest growth rates. But neither theoretical analysis nor the facts themselves are consistent with the above conclusions.

TABLE 4

	"Openness"*	Trade Balance as % of GDP**
B	72.4	-0.3
DK	32.2	3.7
D	22.9	2.9
F	22.6	0.9
GR	21.8	-14.5
IRL	71.6	18.4
I	25.3	3.7
L	86.9	-11.0
AT	38.9	-3.7
FIN	35.1	7.8
SW	37.1	7.0
UK	29.4	-1.7
NL	50.1	3.7
P	35.1	-10.4
SP	24.2	-3.3
EU	28.7	1.3

Sources: *(Imports + Exports)/2 as % GDP, Pelagidis (1997).
**Balance considered positive, Eurostat & DGII (1996).

Dani Rodrik (1996) has ascertained that in countries open to the international economy, high living standards coincide with a strong presence in the economy of the public sector, reducing the dangers posed by fluctuations in the international economy and protecting national income levels. According to Rodrik, this shows up in all the available statistical material, such as that of UNESCO – where the degree of openness of the economy has a positive impact on educational expenditures – and of the IMF. There is evidence everywhere of a positive correlation between the degree of openness and the level of public spending, this being precisely the factor that renders these economies internationally competitive.

This finding is confirmed by the above tables 3 & 4, where it can be observed that countries such as Belgium, Denmark, Sweden, Finland, Austria, The Netherlands, etc. have high levels of public spending and revenues above the already high European average. Their levels of social expenditure are also high. It is particularly interesting to note that the competitiveness of these countries, as shown up in table 4, recording the performance of their trade balance, is similarly high. Thus, even in the case of the most globalized developed economies, the state sector remains sizable and active, an indispensable factor in the maintenance of international competitiveness. The above findings are also consistent with the view of Stiglitz (1997), that markets and state are complementary players on the international economic scene.

In any case, Persson and Tabellini (1994), Alesina and Rodrik (1994) and Rodrik (1998) all note that a high degree of income inequality depresses the rate of growth of the domestic product and that the inevitable social conflicts – triggered by aggravated economic inequality – have a detrimental effect on productivity and the GNP. Persson and Tabellini (1994) have also concluded that greater equality in income distribution – something observable in countries with developed democratic systems of government – is conducive to investment and growth. Along the same lines, Rodrik (1998) observes that the countries where the downturn in rates of growth was greatest after 1975 are those which present the image of being "divided communities," adding that it has not been empirically verified that growth suffers from high levels of public spending or a high ratio of public debt to export incomes.

Mention might be made finally of the study by Card and Krueger (1994) which indicates clearly that a rise in the minimum income does not lead to a fall in the numbers employed. On the contrary, from this field study, which was carried out in fast food stores in the USA, it emerged that the employment rates rose in parallel with rises in salaries (for the idea that the establishment of a minimum wage promotes employment also see: De Fraja 1996).

It is not exactly news that Europe today faces problems of increasing poverty and unemployment. The democratic polity, a decisive factor in political and social stability, necessary prerequisites for high rates of growth of GNP, (Mauro 1995) is enervated. Decisions concerning crucial matters of European unification are taken over the heads of the citizenry and the democratic deficit grows to the advantage of pressure groups with specific vested interests. Paradoxically, Europe's considerable trade surpluses coincide with both a fall in real salaries and a reduction in the labor income share without any simultaneous reduction in unemployment due to replacement of capital by labor as predicted by neoclassical theory. There is only a minimal increase in investment, clearly lower than in the USA than the rise in profits, despite the fact that interest rates have slumped to low levels.

We thus arrive at the indirect reason for unemployment, poverty and the consequent erosion of democratic institutions and social rights. The restrictive policies of monetary, fiscal and income restraint lock the economy into unacceptably low rates of growth so that the bleakness of prospects for future growth preclude even basic increases in private expenditure.

The above conclusions represent a consensus and are – tacitly, at least – the point of departure for the studies in this collection, which oppose the "pensie unique" of conservatism, i.e. the view that public intervention should be limited to charitable works (job subsidization and pacification of outbreaks of violence attributable to deterioration in living conditions for a large section of the population – Bourdieu 1998) and that democracy is a secondary matter alongside the needs of individual "freedom" and "happiness."

The discrepancy between the real state of things and the lack – or rather the abandonment– of means for its "remedy" renders necessary a way of thinking which will relate the critical assessment of the data regarding social crisis to the elaboration of means of intervening in the latter.

The papers included in this Volume constitute inter-disciplinary contributions to this task. They investigate the "hidden causes" of the present situation in developed capitalist countries and reflect on possible ways out, by analyzing economic developments, social conflicts legal forms and the prevailing directions of economic policy. The reader will perceive that there are two main interpretations of the deeper reasons for the disheartening political and social situation that prevails in the world, as well as for possible strategies for dealing with it.

The first view could be called political-economic and is linked to the projects and the strategies of the post-war period of the welfare state. The present situation is seen as the result of a political choice by the dominant social forces to make a break with a form of social contract that secured relative prosperity for the popular masses of the western world and, by means of state intervention, averted the most extreme instances of the work insecurity that is inherent in capitalism. The exponents of this viewpoint maintain that the creation of an economy of solidarity consistent with the idea of "social Europe" must be based on a "new social contract" of this type. It must therefore include the implementation of policies which not only secure high rates of growth but also strengthen social rights (employment, minimum income guaranteeing dignified living standards for the unemployed and those unable to work, redistribution of income in favor of the underprivileged, establishment of a minimum wage). This would not only strengthen social cohesion, a factor, as mentioned, indispensable for the achievement of high growth rates, but would similarly strengthen demand in low-income households, thus favoring economic recovery.

To this end a break from the established social and economic conservatism would entail a change of economic policies in the direction of full employment. It would also include the injection of the more progressive layers of society with a vision of restoring the collective functioning of the social subject and revitalizing the specific social and cultural characteristics of particular areas, those structures which represent an impediment to the unalloyed logic of the market. Such elements are already to be found in the spontaneous activities of non-governmental organizations (NGOs), both European and non-European, activities which are an important part of public life and already represent a threat to the economic oligarchy in Europe which operates behind the scenes out of the sight of European citizens.

The second viewpoint could be called "structural." It derives from two supplementary findings – Firstly that the social state was the product of class polarization in the context of a balance of forces which no longer exists. Secondly that policies of redistribution, stimulation of demand among the popular strata and strengthening of social citizenship generally, do not represent more authentic democratic and social progress but merely an alternative means for securing the rule of capital in a period which is unfavorable for itself. Thus neither is the mobilization and "conscientization" of the citizenry a sufficient prerequisite for the achievement of a society of peace and "freedom from oppression" nor can policies of a social-democratic type secure a radical and meaningful change from the present day situation.

Implicit in both of these interpretations is a concept of the lack of democracy, of a distortion of democracy, as central to the analysis of "depoliticization" of the economy with its attendant social problems, as well as to the elaboration of strategies for a "future democracy," linked to the welfare state. It is a fact that some elements regarded as constitutive of the concept of democracy – such as the representative way of decision-making itself, or even more the transfer of competencies to the local level or to "European" institutions – result in the narrowing of the democratic horizons, and to "policy vacuums" that impede the emergence of other forms of democracy – which would favor radically different (and politically more fruitful and democratic) decisions through radically new procedures. The obstacles to democratization are compounded, paradoxically, by the very wide and verbally radical use of the term democracy as a universal concept of our political culture. When the "existing democracy" is in obvious incongruence with the meaning that is attributed to it theoretically, the theoretical discourse that legitimizes it constitutes an impediment to democratization, because it conceals the lack of democracy. The *intrusion of reality* into the concept of democracy makes possible a demonstration of its concealed limits, perhaps also pointing the way towards overcoming them.

In this context, the question arises of the relation of democracy to the mechanisms of the economy and the market. Democracy within and against the market; the influence of the market on democracy and the overcoming of the market through democracy; the economic and social policies resulting from democratic decision-making; full employment as a democratic social regulation and right. The investigation of these issues is just another name for the investigation of *the welfare decline, as an obstacle to democratization.*

The Volume is structured in the following five Parts: A. *Globalization and Democracy* (containing the papers of A. Sen, L. Panitch and K. Vergopoulos); B. *Concepts and Limits of Democracy* (containing the papers of R. Wolff, G. Carchedi and J.-P. Garnier); C. *The Market Confronting Welfare and Democratic Policies* (L. Katseli, M. Dunford, T. Pelagidis,); D. *The End of the Welfare State in Europe?* (J. Milios, J. Huffschmid, F. Deppe); E. *Legal and Political Aspects of European Integration: a Democratic Deficit* (D. Dimoulis & D. Christopoulos, K. Sieveking, C. Giannoulis).

References

Albala, N. 1998. *Le Monde Diplomatique*. Mars.

Alesina, A. and Rodrik, D. 1994. "Distributive Politics and Economic Growth." *Quarterly Journal of Economics* 109, May, 1170-88.

Bairoch, P. 1997. "Globalization Myths and Realities." In Boyer, R. and Drache, D. *States Against Markets*. London: Routledge, 173-192.

Bourdieu, P. 1998. *Contre-feux*. Paris: Liber.

Card, D. and Krueger, A. 1994. "Minimum Wages and Employment: A Case Study of the Fast-Food Industry in New Jersey and Pennsylvania." *The American Economic Review*, Vol. 84, No. 4, 772-793.

De Fraja, G. 1996. "Minimum Wage Legislation, Work Conditions and Employment." *CEPR Discussion Paper Series*, No. 1524.

Eurostat and DGII. 1996. *EC Economic Data Pocket Book*. Brussels: EU.

Krugman, P. and Lawrence, R. (1994), "Trade, Jobs and Wages." *Scientific American*, April.

Laindi, J. 1998. *Le Monde Diplomatique*, Avril.

Mauro, P. 1995. "Corruption and Growth." *Quarterly Journal of Economics*, Vol. 85, No. 2, 681-712.

Obstfeld, M. and Taylor, A. (1997), "The Great Depression as a Water-shed: International Capital Mobility over the Long Run", *CEPR Discussion Paper Series*, No.1633.

OECD. 1997. *Historical Statistics 1960-95*. Paris: OECD.

OECD. 1998. *Economic Outlook*, June, Paris: OECD.

Pelagidis, T. 1997. *The European Recession and the Alternative Policy*. Athens: Papazisis (in Greek).

Persson, T. and Tabellini, G. 1994. "Is Inequality Harmful For Growth?" *The American Economic Review*, Vol. 84, No.3, 600-621.

Ramonet, I. 1998. *Le Monde Diplomatique*, Mai.

Rodrik, D. 1996. "Why Do More Open Economies Have Bigger Governments?" *CEPR Discussion Paper Series*, No.1388.

Rodrik, D. 1998. "Where Did all The Growth Go? External Shocks, Social Conflict and Growth Collapses." *CEPR Discussion Paper Series*, No. 1789.

Stiglitz, J. 1987. "An Agenda for Development for the 21st Century." Annual World Bank Conference on Development Economics, Washington D.C., April 30 - May 1.

Taylor, A. 1994. "International Capital Mobility in History: The Saving-Investment Relationship." *NBER Working Paper* 5743.

Taylor, A. 1996. "Domestic Saving and International Capital Flows Reconsidered." *BER Working Paper* 4892.

World Bank. 1987. *World Development Report 1987*. Washington D.C.

PART A
GLOBALIZATION AND DEMOCRACY

2 Fear of Freedom

AMARTYA SEN

Many ideas that have shaped our thoughts (and continue to influence our thinking today), across the world, originated in Athens and in other locations in Greece in the fifth century B.C.

I thought I should take up in this article one such theme - freedom. I take the idea in its broadest form, encompassing the substantive opportunities as well as the procedural arrangements that go with freedom. Freedom in this broad sense includes, on one side, political liberties, civil rights, economic and social opportunities, and on the other, the removal of the basic unfreedoms of hunger, illiteracy, untreated illness, and other absence of social guarantees. Freedom is indeed a very diverse and many-sided concept, and as William Cowper, the English poet, noted:

> Freedom has a thousand charms to show,
> That slaves, however contented, never know.

Lines of Division

Oddly enough, freedom is not only among the most valued ideas in the world, it is also among the most feared of human conditions. With freedom comes both opportunity and responsibility, and while the former may be prized, the latter can be a cause for anxiety and concern. This conflict has engaged many distinguished psychologists. I would nevertheless venture to suggest that in the purely individual context, it is not typically the case that people fear freedom in their *own* lives. Those who are afraid of freedom tend mostly to be afraid of freedom of *others* - the discontented lower classes, the aggrieved rural masses, the disgruntled women grumbling about their assigned "place," the rebellious youth refusing to be compliant and obedient, and the determined dissidents protesting about the existing order. It is other

17

people's freedom that have worried many commentators writing against freedom, who have not, however, offered to give up their own freedom. This applies as much to authoritarian rulers (including military dictators) as to the intellectual commentators (including many leaders of thought) who have championed - what they describe as - "order, discipline and necessary sacrifice" over "freedom, effrontery and license."

The lines dividing the opposing sides have been drawn differently in different debates around this broad, general division. They can be seen in one form in the contrast between, say, Plato and Aristotle in ancient Greece, or between Kautilya and Ashoka in ancient India, and in a very different form in the debates at the height of the European Enlightenment, between, say, Condorcet and Malthus. These divisions continue today across the world, with the guardians of order and authority opposing - and some times penalizing - pro-freedom activists in different countries and continents.

Indeed, while some see freedom as a great ally of progress, others are fearful of individual freedom as a spoiler of development and as a source of adversity. The latter group can entertain disparate beliefs, held by different (and often conflicting) schools of thought, with very different diagnoses of their favourite poison: democratic rights, civil liberties, freedom of market transactions, or basic social opportunities (such as the emancipation involved in women's being schooled). Their common suspicion of freedom leads to the advocacy - and imposition - of unfreedom of one kind or another, in political, economic, or social fields.

Development as Freedom

It is important, I would argue, to counter, in a comprehensive and congruous way, the diverse manifestations of this scepticism about freedom, which can be found plentifully across the contemporary world. In contrast, we can see the reach and power of a freedom-based approach to social progress. I want to see it specifically in the context of development, in the broadest sense, which encompasses the removal of deprivation even in the richer - more "developed" - countries.

The versatile claim that development demands severe curtailment of individual freedoms arises from distrust of cogent human agency in different fields. The distinct suspicions take the form of mistrust of the working, respectively, of democracy, of political and civil rights, of the freedom of economic transactions, or disbelief in the possibility that common people -

women in particular - can make good use of basic education and the associated freedoms. These disparate beliefs, held by different (and often conflicting) schools of thought, have led to the advocacy - and imposition - of unfreedom of one kind or another, in political, economic, or social fields.

In sharp contrast with these views, it can be argued that freedom is both the primary objective and the principal means of development. To consider the ends first, development cannot be divorced from the lives that people can lead and the real freedoms that they enjoy. Development can scarcely be seen merely in terms of enhancement of inanimate objects of use (and their instrumental role), such as a rise in personal incomes, or industrialization, or technological advance, or social modernization. The value of these things depends ultimately on what they do to the lives and freedoms of the people involved.

Freedom to live decent lives depends on a variety of factors of which income per head is only one. To illustrate, in terms of income per head, African Americans as a group, though poorer than white people in America, are many times richer than the population of the third world. And yet in terms of the capability to survive to mature ages, African American men fall far behind those in China, or Sri Lanka, or the state of Kerala in India. Indeed, black men in the American cities of New York, Washington D.C., or San Francisco have significantly lower life expectancies than the average man in India or Pakistan, and marginally less than even in Bangladesh. The capability to live to mature ages is an important freedom and cannot be overlooked on the ground of the high incomes of the short-lived.

However, the importance of individual freedom, broadly defined, goes well beyond this constitutive connection - crucial as it is. Freedoms of different types very often help to sustain each other. Freedom is important also as means, and not just as an end. I have tried to investigate both in my new book, *Development as Freedom* (Knopf and O.U.P., 1999) focusing particularly on the effectiveness of different kinds of freedom in sustaining each other.

What people can positively achieve is influenced by economic opportunities, political liberties, social emancipation, and the enabling conditions of good health, basic education, and the encouragement and cultivation of initiatives. The institutional arrangements for these opportunities are also influenced by the exercise of people's freedoms, through the liberty to participate in social choice and in the making of public decisions, which impel the progress of these opportunities. It is because of these interconnections that free and sustainable agency emerges as a major engine of development.

Democracy and Political and Civil Rights

Take political liberties. It is sometimes asked whether political freedom is "conducive to development." Indeed, a negative answer to this question has often fuelled authoritarian political tendencies in different parts of the world (sometimes supplemented by very odd interpretations of the alleged demands of local culture, such as so-called "Asian values"). It is worth noting in this context, that extensive cross-country comparisons have not provided empirical support to the often-articulated belief that democracy is hostile to economic growth. It appears that growth is helped by the friendliness of the economic climate rather than by the harshness of the political system. But more foundationally, this way of posing the question misses the crucial point that political liberties are among the *constituent components* of development. Their relevance for development does not have to be indirectly established through their contribution to the growth of GNP. Politically unfree citizens - whether rich or poor - are deprived of a basic constituent of good living.

However, after acknowledging this central connection, we also have to examine the role of democracy and of political and civil rights in enhancing freedoms of other kinds, in particular through giving voice to the deprived and the vulnerable. The fact that no major famine has ever occurred in a democratic country with regular polls, opposition parties and a relatively free media (even when the country is very poor and in seriously adverse food situation) merely illustrates the most elementary aspect of the protective power of political liberty. Though Indian democracy has some imperfections in terms of practice, nevertheless the political incentives generated by it has been adequate to eliminate major famines right from the time of independence (the last famine was four years before that, in 1943), unlike China which did have the largest famine in recorded history in 1959-62, with 30 million deaths. Right now, the two countries with the severest famine are also among the most dictatorial, viz. Sudan and North Korea.

The protective power of democracy in providing security is, in fact, much more extensive than famine prevention. The poor in booming South Korea or Indonesia may not have given much thought to democracy when economic fortunes of all seem to go up and up together, but when the economic crises came (and divided they fell), the lack of political freedom was desperately missed by those whose lives were unusually battered. A decline of GNP of 5 or 10 per cent is not really a big calamity seen in the aggregative perspective, when it follows a growth record of 5 to 10 per cent per year for decades. However, if that decline is heaped unequally on the least advantaged sections, they may be in severe jeopardy, requiring social support. Democracy became a central issue in these countries then, as it did elsewhere (such as Thailand). One should not have to wait for an economic crisis to develop to value the protective power of democracy.

Markets and Freedoms

To take a second example, consider the role of markets. Again, the first thing to note is that freedom of exchange and transaction is itself part and parcel of the basic liberties that people have reason to value. In fact, the praise of capitalism by Karl Marx (not a great admirer of capitalism in general), and his characterization (in *The Capital*) of the American civil war as "the one great event of contemporary history," related directly to the importance of the freedom of labour contract as opposed to slavery and the enforced exclusion from the labour market. This is quite a different point from the more discussed efficiency issue of the effectiveness of markets in generating economic prosperity. To be generically against markets will be almost as odd as being generically against conversations between people. The freedom to exchange words, or goods, or gifts does not need defensive justification in terms of their favourable but distant effects; they are part of the way human beings in society live and interact with each other (unless stopped by regulation or fiat).

To point to this often-neglected consideration is not, of course, to deny the importance of judging the market mechanism comprehensively in terms of all its roles and effects, including its proven ability to generate economic growth and prosperity, and under certain circumstances, even economic equity. We must also examine, on the other hand, the down sides of unrestrained market operations (especially with severe inequalities in ownerships and endowments), and the general judgements, including criticisms, that people may have of life styles and values associated with an exclusively market-centred culture. In seeing "development as freedom," the constitutive importance of transactions as well as the direct and indirect effects of markets must be considered together, in terms of interlinkages between freedoms of different kinds.

Social Opportunities and Interdependencies

To take yet another example, consider the role of social opportunities, which the state and the society may facilitate. For example, public education has been an effective means of freeing people from the bondage of illiteracy and ignorance. This freedom is valuable in itself, but it also contributes to economic development (and even to a more shared use of the market mechanism) and to the effective freedoms that result from economic prosperity. That lesson, already implicit in the experience of the West, is spectacularly reinforced by the role of human capability expansion in the fast economic growth of Japan and East Asia.

Contrast India. While the overactivity of the state in Indian industrial policy is often blamed (with considerable justice) for India's comparatively modest growth record, the underactivity of the state in promoting school education (with nearly half the adult population still illiterate) also deserves a sizeable share of the blame. While India may have more than five times as many University-trained people as China, the latter is very much closer than India to universal literacy among the young. Indeed, China's expansion of basic education goes back to the pre-reform period and was driven by a left-wing political commitment, and interestingly enough, the educational expansion in the pre-reform Maoist period proved to be of great help in the effective spread of marketization in the post-reform period. There is no mystery in explaining why the success of Indian industries that are dependent on higher education and training (it is, for example, the second largest producer of computer software in the world, next to the United States) is not matched by widespread production based on school education and basic skill, in which China has excelled.

Development calls for the simultaneous use of many institutions, and as Adam Smith remarked, there are good reasons to take note of the fact that "...for a very small expence the public can facilitate, can encourage, and can even impose upon almost the whole body of the people, the necessity of acquiring those most essential parts of education." Basic education, in particular female education, is also associated with many social changes, in particular the reduction of child mortality, and also a rapid fall in fertility rates.

Population, Fertility and Freedom

This is a good moment to examine briefly an important illustration of the confrontation between pro and anti freedom views in the Condorcet-Malthus disagreement, in the late eighteenth century, on the growth of population. While it was Condorcet whom Malthus quoted for having pointed, first, to the possibility that the size of the population can quite conceivably "surpass their means of subsistence," Condorcet had gone on to argue that this was not likely to occur because of freely chosen declines in fertility rates, resulting from more education and "the progress of reason." Malthus totally rejected Condorcet's faith in freedom and its ability to solve social problems. He insisted that nothing short of compulsion would make people reduce fertility rates.

There is a tendency in modern Malthus scholarship to emphasize the fact that Malthus had changed some of his views over the years, but his basic distrust of the power of reasoning and freedom, as opposed to the force of economic compulsion, in making people choose smaller families, remained largely unmodified. Indeed, in one of his latest works (*A Summary View of the Principle of Population*), published in 1830 (he died in 1834), Malthus insisted on his conclusion that:

> There is no reason whatever to suppose that anything beside the difficulty of procuring in adequate plenty the necessaries of life should either indispose this greater number of persons to marry early, or disable them from rearing in health the largest families.

This particular example of the debate about the consequences of freedom is not hard to settle empirically. Not only have fertility rates come down over time (and it is hard to deny the role of "the progress of reason" in explaining the new norm of smaller families), but also cross-section comparisons across countries show that the decline of fertility rates relates closely to the empowerment of young women whose lives are most battered by over-frequent bearing and rearing of children. This lesson also emerges clearly from cross-section comparisons across the hundreds of districts that comprise India. Not surprisingly, women's education and "gainful" employment, which increases women's voice in family decisions, emerge as the two biggest influences in reducing fertility rates.

There was a lot of discussion recently in newspapers on the belief, based on rather rudimentary arithmetic, that India's population reached one billion on or just around its independence day, 15th August 2000. It would have been an interesting coincidence, if true (in fact, the Registrar General of Censuses in India insists that this would occur only in May 2000), but there is no question that in general the size of the Indian population is a matter for serious social concern. While the total fertility rate for India as a whole - despite a drop from 6 to just above 3 children per couple - is still substantially higher than the replacement level of 2 per couple, it is also the case that many districts in India have substantially lower fertility rates than the USA (2.1), the UK (1.7) and France (1.7), and also China (1.9). The fertility declines in the states of Kerala, Tamil Nadu or Himachal Pradesh in India can be closely linked to the rapid enhancement of female education and other sources of empowerment of young women.

China is often taken as an example on the other side, as positive evidence of the good effects of coercion in family planning (like the "one child" policy). Indeed, fertility decline has been sharp in China, but a roughly similar decline would have been expected because of China's achievements in female education and employment. The Indian State of Kerala, which has also had very fast expansion of female education - but no compulsory family planning - experienced a similarly fast decline in the fertility rate. In fact, Kerala's expansion of female education is faster than China's, and so is its decline in fertility rate, even over the period since 1979, when the "one child" policy was introduced in China. The Chinese fertility rate fell from 2.8 to 2.0 between 1979 and 1991; Kerala's rate fell in the same period from 3.0 to 1.8. Kerala has continued its lead in fertility decline over China, with a fertility rate below 1.7 now, compared with China's 1.9. Also, thanks to the process of fertility decline being freely chosen, rather than coercive, the infant mortality rate has continued to fall in Kerala in a way it has not in China. Indeed, though the infant mortality rates in China and Kerala were very similar in 1979, they are now about twice as high in China compared with Kerala (even higher than that for girls, in particular). It is hard to resist the conclusion that fertility decline demands more freedom, not less.

Concluding Remarks

To conclude, while the fear of freedom - the freedom of others - continues to be a driving force in the contemporary world, a good alternative approach is to take a many-sided, freedom-centred view of development. Such an approach has several advantages over more conventional views. First, it provides a deeper basis of evaluation of development than can be obtained from concentrating on commodities and things rather than on the lives and liberties of people. Second, it allows us to distinguish between (1) the supportive role of the state in enhancing the effective freedoms of individuals (for example, in providing public education, health care, social safety nets, good macroeconomic policies and industrial competition, and necessary epidemiological and ecological protection), and (2) repressive interventions of the state in stifling liberty, initiative and enterprise and in crippling the working of individual agency and co-operative action. Even Kerala, which I compared earlier rather favourably vis-à-vis China remains far behind China - and indeed behind many states in India itself - in opening up the economic opportunities that the market system offers.

Indeed, by focusing on the interconnections between freedoms of different kinds, this approach takes us well beyond the narrow perspective of seeing each freedom in isolation. There are no ideal economies, no unqualified "models" - rather lots of different lessons from disparate experiences put together by the integrated perspective of freedom (including the recognition of its many-sided demands). We live in a world of many institutions, and we have to see how they can supplement and strengthen each other, rather than getting in each other's way.

Finally, this view captures the constructive role of free human agency as a powerful engine of change. In terms of the medieval distinction between "the agent" and "the patient," this is a distinctly agent-oriented view of development. It differs radically from seeing people as passive beneficiaries of cunning development programmes. We have to resist the fear of freedom - the freedom of others - that is so forceful in the world in which we live. Its manifest demands cut across the traditional boundaries of politics and social movement, even as it incorporates many of the demands from different types of discontent and distinct lines of rebellion. We have to look afresh at the basic issues involved, and at the central and integrative role of individual freedom seen as a social commitment.

3 The State in a Changing World: Social-Democratizing Global Capitalism?

LEO PANITCH

Introduction

There are two central developments that define our era. One of these is the historic failure of the socialist project of the mass working class parties, both Communist and Social Democratic. The other is, of course, what has commonly come to known as the "globalization" of capitalism. These two developments are certainly related to one another, but they cannot be reduced to one another. Each also has its own specific dynamics which need to be analyzed separately.

The failure of the Communism was not only due to the strength of global capitalism - what apologists for the USSR used to call "encirclement". It was also due to the Communist parties and regimes lack of understanding that democratic rights alone provide socialism with the political air it needs to breath. Under a dictatorship, without multiple parties, freedom of the press, speech and association, workers could never learn how to become a ruling class, as Rosa Luxemburg chastised Lenin immediately after his dissolution of the constituent assembly; in the absence of political freedom there is no way to generate "the thousand solutions" that need to be discovered in face of "the thousand problems" that revolutionary change inevitably entails.

Social Democracy reveals to us the opposite failure. Too much respect for the inherited institutional forms of liberal democracy produced a form of "parliamentary socialism" which lost the capacity to mobilise for social change in the course of learning how to get elected. It was able, for a certain period, to manage a reformed capitalism; but unable to transform society, it

26

soon lost its vision, and eventually even its socialist rhetoric. The new right's successful association of social democracy with state bureaucracy towards the end of the 20th century proved that Max Weber had been correct to discern, at the beginning of the century, that "in the long run....it is not Social Democracy that captures the town or the state; it is the state which conquers the party".

The loss of mobilizing capacity and vision in social democracy are today epitomized by the "buzz-word", *modernization*. This is a term which amounts to little more than keeping up with capitalist globalization, when what is needed on the left is precisely to try to develop the capacity to issue a political challenge to globalization. But this can only be done on the basis of systematic analyses of the historical trends that globalization refers to and the structural resistances that develop as a result of it.

The Meaning of Globalization

What is globalization? It is a fashionable word, but what does it actually mean? There are many myths and misunderstandings associated with the term, arising from simplistic extrapolations of particular trends and unwarranted generalizations from specific developments. Yet there are, I believe, five dimensions of what is commonly termed globalization today that really are very significant. Three of these are conjunctural; two are structural. In terms of its more contingent, conjunctural dimensions, globalization properly refers to:

(i) the spatial extension of capitalism directly associated with the collapse of the USSR and the Communist regimes of Eastern Europe, as well as with the turn to capitalism in China and Vietnam under the aegis of Communist party elites laying the grounds for transforming themselves into new bourgeoisies.

(ii) the ideological and cultural sweep of capitalist ideas and values that defines our neo-liberal era, whereby the bourgeoisie "makes the world in its own image" with an impunity almost unparalleled since Marx wrote these words 150 years ago.

(iii) the process of international class formation in recent years, especially transnational integration among the capitalist classes; this is a process which is, however, by no means yet very far advanced as is evidenced by the national locus of the owners and boards of directors of the leading MNCs.

Globalization in the stronger sense, i.e. in terms of its more determining, structural dimensions, is best understood as referring to:

(iv) the new stage of capital accumulation on a world scale, developing out of the contradictions of the post-war Keynesian/Bretton Woods order, which is characterized by a vast increase in the size, flow and speed of foreign direct investment and trade, and accompanied by an even more vast creation of international credit, currency flows, speculation, futures markets, and private and public debt.

(v) the internationalization of the state, which, properly speaking, must be understood not in terms of transnational capital escaping the nation-state, but rather in terms of states becoming more and more attuned to fostering and/or accommodating to capital accumulation on a world scale.

Each of these dimensions of globalization deserves very close analysis. This is, of course, especially true of the fourth dimension which far from merely reflecting the strength of capitalism in its new stage, actually grows out the class conflict, inflation and falling rates of profit that ended the previous "golden age", and is itself *beset by recurrent economic crises even in its most dynamic centres of investment and trade as well as by mass underemployment and active impoverishment of large populations and regions of the globe.* It is necessary to stress this in order to understand the nature of the role of the state.

Because the process of globalization has initially taken place under the ideological aegis of the new right, operating with the conceptual optics of neo-classical economics, it has presented itself in terms of reducing the role of the state in relation to both domestic and international markets. Obscured from view has been the active role of states in setting the new rules of the game as well as in shifting the balance of class forces as part of the process of globalization. In what sense is this so? First of all, since states themselves are fields of class relations, the internationalization of capital means that foreign capital becomes interiorized not only within a given territory but becomes a player on the field of the state. Second, states continue to establish the essential infrastructural and juridical conditions of markets, private property and contract within their territorial domain. Third, states are the actual authors of globalization in so far as it is through the changes they made in the rules governing capital movements, investment, currency exchange and trade that permitted a new stage of global accumulation to come about. Fourth, in the process of doing this, states don't withdraw from the economy but restructure their relationship to it, reordering their apparatuses and the role each plays in representing and regulating social actors and markets. Finally, fifth, it is through inter-state relations, as these are formalized in international agreements, treaties, and the rules governing international agencies, that the necessary international juridical and infrastructural conditions for global capital accumulation are established and maintained.

None of this should be understood as functionally automatic; far from it, all this takes place through trial and error, negotiation and compromise, tension and contradiction. These tensions and contradictions, and the class struggles that attend them, may be displaced from one terrain of the state, only to reappear in another, where they reemerge in new forms. Thus we see today a marked increase in corruption and the buying of political favours, as individual capitalists, faced with the insecurities and rigours of global competition, are tempted to secure from particular politicians what industrial subsidies, banking monopolies and tariff protections used to provide to whole sectors of capital.

The contradictions of globalization are such today that the political and ideological leadership of the neo-liberal right is increasingly vulnerable to challenge, as is evidenced in the fact that in 13 of the 15 European Union countries, social democrats now occupy governmental office. But as already seen in the path President Clinton had tread despite his defeat of Bush and Dole, this does not mean that European social democratic parties (which no longer have, for the most part, a distinctive policy stance from that of the American Democratic Party in any case) will not accommodate to neo-liberalism, let alone continue to underwrite globalization in all its dimensions. It has proved convenient for politicians without the deep ideological conviction of someone like Mrs. Thatcher, but also without the inclination either to confront the power of capital or take responsibility for the costs of globalization, to have recourse to the argument that "our hands are tied" by international financial markets and bond traders.

This argument, as *The Economist* noted in an important editorial on October 7th, 1995, entitled "The Myth of the Powerless State", actually obscures the fact that "global integration has left governments with about as many economic powers as they ever had". To *The Economist* there is a "frightening" prospect that "the barriers governments have lowered can be raised again... given the will, governments could do it. Call it their sovereign right". To prevent the "trend to global integration [being] halted and reversed", *The Economist* called on politicians to openly proclaim the state's responsibility for sponsoring capitalist globalization, and to stop using "bad arguments ('our hands are tied') in a good cause (lowering the barriers to international trade and finance)".

The World Bank and the Social Democratization of Globalization

Given the contradictions of globalization, a change in the nature of state sponsorship of it, both ideological and material, is in fact on the agenda. Neo-liberalism has reached its limits, even if globalization has not. This is precisely the message of the World Bank's remarkable World Development Report for 1997, *The State in a Changing World*, released in June 1997 at the Bank's "Global Knowledge" conference in Toronto. This is a momentous intervention by the Bank, a bid to do no less than displace the Trilateral Commission's famous 1976 report with a new strategic perspective designed to carry globalization into the 21st century. In explicit contrast with the "overloaded government" thesis that governed the former report, and in place of the advocacy of a "minimalist state" (which the Report suggests led many countries to "overshoot the mark"), the World Bank now advocates a large role for the state *in protecting and correcting markets*. This perspective, of course, only echoes arguments that have been current in social democratic intellectual circles for the better part of a decade. One might even call this the social democratization of globalization.

The World Bank's central message is that "globalization begins at home" [p. 12]. Not only does it see the state as a necessary "partner, catalyst, facilitator", it goes further in recognising that "markets cannot develop without effective property rights" [p. 41]. The failures of "state-dominated development", the World Bank insists, must not obscure the fact that "development without an effective state is impossible". This means recognizing the positive role played by:

> states working in partnership with markets to correct their failures, [while] not replacing them... The state's unique strengths are its powers to tax, to prohibit, to punish, and to require participation. The state's power to tax enables it to finance the provision of public goods. Its power to prohibit and punish enables it to protect personal safety and property rights. And its power to require participation enables it to minimize free riding...[p. 25]

The World Bank's goal is to shift "attention from the sterile debate of state and market to the more fundamental crisis of state effectiveness" [p. 25]. Effectiveness is defined primarily in terms of developing the kind of public rules and institutions that "allow markets to flourish" [p.1], but this is understood to include taking seriously the legitimation functions of the state. Thus while very much in favour of the removal of restrictions on the trade and cross-border movements of capital, this is seen as only one precondition among many for active global integration, rather than marginalization, for most countries. The report points out that "despite spreading trade liberalization, the share of trade in GDP fell in forty-four of ninety-three developing countries between the mid-1980s and mid-1990s" [p.134], and it especially points to the tragedy of south-Saharan Africa, which it sees in terms of the problem of "states collapsing from within."

Even as regards the advanced capitalist states of Western Europe, the report cites opinion polls which that show a clear majority across all 15 EU states believe that governments should maintain current social benefits and protection levels as opposed to only 12% who think they should be cut to enhance competitiveness in world markets. It cites similar positive orientations in Latin America and Asia, and in contrasting these with anti-egalitarian and anti-welfare state opinion in the United States, it makes the latter look like the exceptional case [p.111].

Such a perspective, especially as it is articulated by the World Bank, will doubtless generate considerable enthusiasm on the part of many people who have for so long been troubled by the nostrums of neo-liberalism. But critics of globalization would do well to temper their enthusiasm. There is no shortage of passages in the Report that insist that states must bring themselves closer to the people, make themselves more accountable to civil society, and reflect "the full panoply of a society's interests". But states are warned against biting off more than they can chew and are advised to constrain themselves to match their role to their capacities. Above all, when it comes to advancing specific reforms, the report carefully ties these to what it calls the "fundamentals", insisting that "maintaining *liberal trade, capital markets and investment regimes* is essential for economic growth" [p. 48, emphasis in text].

What this means is that the Report largely restricts itself to "safe" reforms, that is, to the development of those state capacities which facilitate rather than hinder integration into capitalist globalization. It rationalises the regressive shift in taxation from corporate and personal income taxes, and trade taxes, towards consumption-based taxes like VAT as an inevitable consequence of the global integration it advocates. It endorses the discipline in the area of fiscal deficits that financial markets impose on "open economies exposed to external risk", but it also wants to reinforce this with "the need to comply with the rules and conventions of international treaties [as] another spur to good behaviour" [p. 48].

The report's "recipe for good policies", and its definition of "bad" ones, are, in fact, more than a little familiar. Bad policies "channel benefits to politically influential groups"; examples are macroeconomic policies which are "covert ways of levying unexpected taxes on the private sector or of redistributing economic benefits"; and microeconomic policies which impose "restrictions on the operation of markets", including "import restrictions" and "local monopoly privileges." Good policies, on the other hand, accord priority to restraining inflation and the Bank advocates "locking" this in through central bank independence and "choosing a conservative central bank governor, one who is more opposed to inflation than society in general". The vital ingredients to "rolling back overextended states" are "commitment to competitive markets and an accompanying willingness to eliminate obstacles to their operation" [p. 51].

Even in the areas of urban hospitals, clinics, universities, and transport, where governments concentrate their spending on infrastructure and social services, the Report takes the view that markets and private spending can meet most needs, except for those of the very poorest minority of the population. "Most curative health care is a (nearly) pure private good - if government does not foot the bill, all but the poorest will find ways to take care of themselves." [p. 53] The Bank's concern with the social dimension of globalization is further tempered by its resignation to the fact that developing countries cannot afford western social programs as well as by its claims that greater social security can be achieved at lower costs by relying on communities and households to take up the slack.

What then really distinguishes this cookbook from the neo-liberal one? It is that the goal of market liberalization is now linked by the World Bank to the development of effective regulatory state capacity to sustain private markets. In the crucial case of the financial sector, this is presented in terms of moving from "control to prudential regulation": The Report therefore endorses:

> the near-universal... move away from controls over financial markets and their allocation of finance... Yet liberalization is not the same as deregulation. The case for the regulation of banking is as compelling as ever. Only the purpose has changed, from channelling credit in preferred directions to safeguarding the heath of the financial system [p. 65].

Regulatory reform must also accompany privatization. Since it is opposed to public sector monopolies as well as private sector ones, the Report is in favour of privatization in general and especially the "hiving off" of utilities and social insurance to the private sector. But "successful" privatization depends on "winning the acquiescence of employees" through generous severance pay; winning the acquiescence of citizens through share vouchers or public offerings of shares at "attractive prices"; and developing "a regulatory system that credibly restrains the abuse of power in non-competitive markets" [p.64].

A major concern of the Report - arguably *the* major concern - is the endemic corruption that attends the state-capital interface in so much of the world. For this report, the Bank undertook a survey of 3,685 firms in 69 countries in an attempt to measure the extent of such corruption and their perception of the harm that it does to investment; and it found that "high and unpredictable corruption" especially had this effect [p. 103]. Strengthening mechanisms for juridical monitoring and punishment, making rules more transparent, reducing the scope for official discretion, introducing competitive bidding processes into government - all these are advanced as administrative reforms that would help to contain the problem, albeit always in conjunction with "policies that lower controls on foreign trade, remove entry barriers for private industry, and privatize state firms in a way that ensures competition" [p. 8].

One of the factors the Report is able to identify as most highly correlated with corruption is the erosion of civil servants wages relative to average manufacturing wages. The remedy it advances, notably, is the decompression of public sector salary structures, paying senior officials more while still constraining the overall total public sector wage bill through layoffs and wage restraint at the lower levels. Those at the top are to be given the material compensation to stop them lining their pockets. When it comes the lower levels, the Report looks to securing "worker dedication and commitment" by stressing "the importance of non-monetary rewards – recognition, appreciation, prestige, and awards – in motivating staff, over and above the adequacy of pay and meritocratic recruitment and promotion" [p. 96].

Globalization, indeed, "begins at home". The reforms the World Bank advocates for more effective states depend on the institutional restructuring of state apparatuses, and the reordering of responsibilities among them, beginning "with a few critical enclaves [that] typically include the ministry of finance, the central bank, and the tax collection agency". Restructuring of these apparatuses – "which can mostly be achieved through executive order" - are designed to effect drastic budget cuts, tax reform, price liberalization, deregulation, and some privatization, and above all to "establish effective macroeconomic management by an insulated technocratic elite". But a fully effective state will avoid limiting itself to these "first generation reforms" and will eventually move to restructure the executive itself as well as the legislature and judiciary, the civil service, unions, political parties, media, state and local government and even the private sector - all to the end of "upgrading regulatory capacity", which the Report sees as an "institutional development highly dependent on middle management in the public sector"[p. 152].

All this means that the international institutions that sponsor globalization must not see themselves as by-passing or displacing the state, but rather as operating to guarantee a certain type of state restructuring. While "external support can achieve little where the domestic will to reform is lacking", the World Bank Report repeatedly stresses that the role of international agencies, in addition to providing expert advice and financial assistance, is to provide "a mechanism for countries to make external commitments, making it more difficult to back-track on reforms" [p. 15]. Among these are international commercial or currency treaties through which the state commits to "self-restricting rules, which precisely specify the content of policy and lock it into mechanisms that are costly to reverse" [p. 6].

Conclusions

Jacques Delors, in a relatively recent visit to Athens, posed the challenge to social democracy as that of figuring out how to make accommodating to globalization consistent with progressive social values. The lesson of the World Bank Report, as well as the fate of Delors own "Social Charter" in Europe amidst the effects of the move to the common currency, is that this is the wrong challenge for the left to pose for itself. Attaching side agreements on labour or environmental rights to international treaties will at best reinforce the type of second order state reforms advanced by the World Bank. The overarching priority will remain that of fostering the penetration of capitalist values into every dimension of state-society relations as well as every corner of the globe and every facet of human life.

The World Bank's understanding that this does NOT mean a minimal state, but rather an efficient capitalist state is, increasingly, what social democracy itself stands for today. It has adopted global competition as a goal, which the state must foster, rather than regarding it as a constraint which must eventually be overcome. Social democracy still recognizes the importance of liberal democratic institutions, but it has lost that broader democratic vision that originally impelled socialists to try to use those institutions as building blocks for organizing societies on cooperative rather than competitive principles.

So extensive is this accommodation to globalization that social democracy (incorporating as it does now most former Communists in Eastern Europe) is largely reduced, even in the face of continuing mass unemployment in Western Europe, to accommodating itself to undercutting social benefits in order to advance labour-market flexibility while still advancing the new "cargo-cult" of training. ("If you train them the jobs will come.") It is as though, seeing a man on the street, hungry and homeless, you approach his problem only through the optic of his not being motivated enough, entrepreneurial enough, skilled enough to get a job, rather than through the optic of there being something fundamentally wrong with the capitalist system. There is nothing much socialist in a value system that does not begin, morally, from the latter optic.

Nor can much be said for social democratic economic strategies that increasingly rely on export competitiveness for "success". This ignores not only the ethical dilemmas this inevitably entails in terms of the more successful exporting their unemployment to the countries that are less successful, but also the crisis-ridden nature of globalization, both in terms of the overproduction that must attend a system where everyone is trying to increase their exports and limit their imports, and in terms of the financial instability that attends capital movements attuned to free exchange rates in such a system.

In response to neo-liberal calls for a minimal state, social democratic intellectuals over the last decade have often had recourse to the example of East Asian states which have allegedly proven that efficient markets require active state involvement in the economy. The class-ridden nature of those systems, let alone the "crony capitalism" that characterizes their state-market interface, usually got swept under the carpet. The World Bank Report also adopted the East Asian states as its model for "successful" integration in globalization. The fact that it did so even as the storm clouds of a vast financial crisis were gathering over the region makes the Report look rather bad. Yet the central message of the Report – that regulation is necessary for liberalization – will be now be heard more and more in relation to international finance.

At the launch of the World Bank Report in Toronto last June, a video was shown of women engaged in embroidery production through an NGO in India, one of whose leaders articulated the desire for "a situation where women are not only the producers but are the owners and managers". No one really took these words seriously at the launch, for good reason. This age-old inspiration for genuine democracy cannot possibly be advanced by the World Bank's Report. It will only be met when, in light of the contradictions of globalization, there emerge new socialist forces to challenge the power of capital as it is embedded in the contemporary state.

Out of the inevitable conflicts that globalization is generating and will continue to generate, it is not unlikely that new parties and movements will emerge which will make this their aim. As such forces do emerge they may even want to take a few pages out of the book of the World Bank, at least to the extent of recognizing that building alternatives to globalization also must begin at home. Of course, there will need to be extensive international cooperation among such forces. While located on the terrain of each state, such movements and parties will have to inspire one another across state borders; and such successes as they may have within each of their states will be certainly still be conditional on other states also being transformed by similar movements and parties, allowing for that cooperation among states that will be necessary to make possible effective controls over the mobility of capital. It may also be worth paying attention to the praise the Bank heaps on those "farsighted" political leaders "who played such a large role in bringing about capitalist globalization", and who "have transformed the options for their people... because they spelled out a longer term vision for their society, allowing people to see beyond the immediate pain of adjustment" [p. 14]. As against the Bank's concern to ensure there will be more capitalist political leaders "with a clear vision of the way things could be and a contagious determination to turn that vision into reality" [p 144], it will be necessary to develop a new generation of socialist political leadership in the twenty-first century that has precisely these qualities and capacities, but uses them to the end of advancing very different kinds of structural reforms to that of the World Bank, above all, so as to transform states into creative agencies of decommodification and democratization rather than efficient agencies for capitalist globalization.

4 Globalization and Post Democracy

KOSTAS VERGOPOULOS

Democracy as a Political System

Unlike in antiquity, when the political system of Democracy constituted a polity entailing specific public obligations of the citizen to the state, in its present-day variant it has come to denote - exclusively and one-sidedly - a system of individual rights and access of citizens to the exercise of political power. In this way the demand for democracy, which in antiquity constituted a compulsory civil directive (cogens) from above, in the modern age acquired the character of a petitioner's demand from below. In the ancient model the heart of the democratic polity was the Citizens' Assembly and its public procedures for opinion formation throughout the polity. By contrast modern democracy focuses on the power-holders' problem of gaining ratification for their decisions by means of a "popular mandate" of some kind. But naturally in neither case does Democracy compensate for or "correct" economic or social inequalities between citizens, nor is it dependent on them. It simply brings into existence a special field - the political - on which citizens act as formal equals, even if they remain exceptionally unequal on the other planes of social life. The question is, what is the specific value of this political field and in exactly what relation does it stand to the other areas of social life?

In the ancient model the democratic polity was a value in itself whose purposes and criteria were political. In modern times Democracy has been seen as subsidiary - and supplementary - to economic and social gains, as an extension of the concept of "popular sovereignty." Ancient Democracy was purely political, whereas present-day democracy, though likewise political, has from the outset been stamped with an indelible social element. Modern Democracy has thus from the outset been tied to the vicissitudes of the contemporary social and economic problem, and to the politics that seeks to deal with it.

The political radicalism of the 18th century, with Jean-Jacques Rousseau as its celebrated exponent, had insisted that the political equalization of individuals is not only unavoidable but also feasible, even if social and economic inequalities are maintained. The French Revolution, above all in its Jacobin expression, confirmed the political egalitarianism of Rousseau, irrespective of the social determinants and economic inequalities between citizens. Rousseau put forward the idea that the concept of "the people" does not exist as such but so as to come into being must be given political form. The democratic political system is the necessary mechanism by which the citizens constitute the political concept of "the people."[1] In the same way, the political legitimation which flows from the concept of "popular sovereignty" is itself based in its turn on the idea of "general will." Political Democracy, finally, is defined by Rousseau without reference to the problem of society and the economy. But modern political thought has not followed the same course. According to Rousseau, the political equalization of citizens is feasible irrespective of their economic and social situation: it is a value in itself and its own justification, exactly as in antiquity. However, modern political theory and practice has rejected the political voluntarism of Rousseau and made politics and the democratic polity contingent on economic and social determinants.

The tradition of the European Left after Marx and in contrast to Rousseau ascertained in turn that politics cannot and must not come into contradiction with the other planes of social life but by its nature is and must be in profound harmony with them. As a result, the democratic egalitarianism of the present day was founded not on the conception of politics as a value in itself as Rousseau conceived of it, nor on the idea of it which had prevailed in antiquity, but on the subordination of politics to the social realm, on the proposition that politics as an ideological superstructure is not independent of its economic and social base. Given this, premature establishment of political Democracy in Europe was inconceivable in the absence of a state politics aimed at reducing social inequalities, i.e. more concern for the socially weaker and prompter support for those on lower incomes. The generalization of political Democracy, though arousing distrust among individual bourgeois, was nevertheless perceived by political thinkers as serving the deeper needs of the bourgeois order of things and remaining in inextricable correspondence with it. Although political Democracy does not necessarily improve the economic condition of the workers and of the people, it has nevertheless been imposed as a popular gain for the consolidation of freedom of expression and of criticism. However, from this safeguarding of freedom of expression there arises a parallel need for an economic policy to reduce social inequalities.

Be that as it may, Democracy by virtue of its own generalization offers the bourgeois system a privileged space for preserving cohesion between citizens by means of politics, even if the social and economic fabric remains deeply fractured. In discussions on the purposefulness, advantageousness and feasibility or otherwise of political Democracy, the criterion in the modern era always remained social. While in antiquity the criterion for the legitimation and functionality of the democratic polity was always not social but almost exclusively political: Democracy had been adopted as a value in itself and its own justification. By contrast the contemporary democratic political system had been promoted historically as the object of social negotiation and invariably imposed with explicit or implied references to its being socially beneficial or conducive to greater economic productivity.

In antiquity the political order was separated from the economy and constituted a public polity that was an end in itself. In the contemporary world, notwithstanding the oaths of allegiance to political Democracy and the democratic political theories of the eighteenth and nineteenth centuries, the European political systems remained tax qualification systems and until the beginning of the twentieth century were oligarchic in character. The linking of the right to vote with the size of one's personal fortune constituted a patent case of subordinating politics to the economy. This was the historic innovation of modern times, as confirmed in the course of the 20th century through the further extension of political Democracy hand in hand with the development of the welfare state.

Essentially it was only in the postwar period, after WW2, that European political systems made their wholehearted opening to the generalized democratic model, in combination and in harmony with the corresponding incorporative trend of the economic and social policies. The political incorporation of working people in no way counteracted but on the contrary supplemented their social and economic incorporation. Obviously in modern times the concept of political Democracy has always tended to complement those of "society" and "economy" - it has never been acknowledged as an end in itself. Neither Karl Marx nor Friedrich Hayek would dispute that point.

The Crisis of Democracy in the Era of Globalization

Today, at the end of the 20th century, with the ideological elevation of the arena of globalization, references to the political model of Democracy are greeted with overwhelming condescension. But what is scorned today is not so much the pure model of Democracy in its ancient form as the contemporary political system with its pretensions to social relevance, in fact precisely because of the discredit into which these social pretensions have fallen. The trajectory of today's ideological retreat is a very straightforward one: along with the current idea of the decline of the Nation-State on account of globalization, a supplementary ideology of decline of concepts such as "society" and "national economy" is also put forward. The political model of Democracy is also shaken to its foundations today as regards its presuppositions, insofar as present-day politics has been linked in an uncomplicated linear fashion to the economic and social plane.

Erudite scholars today terrorize public opinion, underlining the "exorbitant" economic running costs of democratic institutions. On the other hand there is also emphasis on the "substantial" political cost of the supposedly "necessary and unpopular" economic decisions. While Democracy could develop into a bastion of political resistance to present-day economic options of the social elites, democratic institutions and procedures are denounced today as "old-fashioned" and "out-of-date" things compared to the prescribed "imperative" of accelerating descent into disintegration and decomposition. In the present-day collapse of the social factor, the political is dragged down with it - to the extent that the political has been defined in the modern era as a simple extension and sub-department of the social. If in our day politics had been defined as in the ancient world, i.e. as an end in itself, then there would be no reason for the present crisis of the social factor to drag down with it the political as well.

A significant sector of the present-day European left legitimates, at the very least passively, the current devaluation of the democratic polity through its attachment to the seemingly Marxist view that politics cannot be a value in itself, as implied in the "extremist" stance of Rousseau and 18th century political theory, but is always overdetermined by developments in the economic and social base.

Again, both the present-day undermining and devaluation of democratic institutions and the prior adoption of them in the past were always put forward in conjunction with social and economic-type arguments, never with arguments derivable from the drawing up of a functional proposal on the political plane.

The most recent exponent of the concept of the "decay" of democracy was the American Allan Bloom, of the University of Chicago, whose analyses became world-wide best-sellers at the end of the 80s.[2] With references to the ancient model and to the elitism of Plato, Bloom charged modern Democracy with being mediocre and cliched, of second-rate quality and decadent. With commonplace references to the social "good" and the aesthetically "beautiful," Bloom criticized present-day democratic political principles for pandering to the socially insignificant and the aesthetically trivial. He himself condemned present-day Democracy not with political arguments but with social and aesthetic "cases in point." From his analyses there emerged on one hand a current of nostalgia with aristocratic overtones and drawn towards some distant past, on the other hand another current which accepts and takes over the social insignificance, henceforth promising a future of eternal ennui and boredom with humanity, within a low-profile democratic system devoid of the slightest social and economic risk-taking. Bloom's student, similarly an American, Francis Fukuyama, sporting Marxo-Hegelian titles, announced not only the end of history and of humanity but also the necessary demise of politics and the ineluctable and irreversible discrediting of the democratic polity.[3] From now one, he announced, politics and democracy are marginalized because socio-economically nothing is any longer "at stake," given that the course of modern society is now mapped out in advance. It is a one-way street, and where it leads is prescribed forcibly by the development of technology.

With the global character of information technology and the globalization of the economy, the prerequisites for a national political scene, for society, economy and thus politics and Democracy - are swept away. Today's political system has come to a dead end because of the lack of conviction that anything is at stake socially, but apart from that there are no longer any alternative political options, according to this student of Bloom. It was essentially he himself who secured acceptance for the current notion of the one-way street and of one-track thinking. Since there is no longer a range of alternative choices and the road to the future is given and is the only one on offer, discussion has become superfluous, devoid of social and economic content, while the demand for dialogue turns out to be equally old-fashioned and out-of-date. Fukuyama locked the political system of Democracy into a state of decline, offering no alternative solution, but in defence of this verdict appealing to the "evidence" of the economic one-way street, not to political arguments.

With the ideological wind from "the West" in their sails, political greenhorns, reactionaries and repentant former Leftists, who had never had any time for the democratic political system or for public life in general, today return to the fray, glamorising self-interested aspirations and models, wielding "economic" arguments to consummate the work of undermining and disintegrating the social and political institutions of democracy, using as their pretexts the phenomenon of globalization and the drive for competitiveness. Modern Democracy is undermined today with economistic arguments, just as its advent in former times was similarly ushered in with a comparable economistic logic and presumptions. Present-day Democracy is proving exceptionally vulnerable, and it was always vulnerable from the time of its first institution on account of the economistic thinking in which it was grounded. In our days the so-called Chicago School is particularly keen to emphasize the "crippling" economic costs of non-economic variables. Concepts such as "tradition," "identity," "nation," "country," "democracy," if they are assessed in terms of micro-economic cost/benefit analysis, run the risk of looking like very bad investments, in fact as liabilities. This is even truer of the key concept of "freedom": there is no more absurd and anti-economic aspiration than this, in the name of which nations and people revolt demanding their freedom and independence and making immense human and material sacrifices for it without hope of repayment. The supposedly modern dynamic of globalization renders "old-fashioned" and "behind the times" all these movements of cultural separation, individual identity and difference.

Today's prevailing philosophy of neo-liberalism demands the triumph of the individual, individualism which does not accept subjection to any determinant other than the economic. Every non-economic bond which ties the individual down for ideological reasons or by virtue of friendship or family ties, is stigmatized from an economic viewpoint, since it inevitably and irrevocably entails a diminution in his economic productivity. With the victory of neo-liberalism today the full implications of the anthropological model of the so-called Homo Oeconomicus are now on display. This is the individual who remains cut off from every social determination and free from every limitation of an extra-economic type. According to today's economic neo-fundamentalism, anything extra-economic must perforce be characterized as "old-fashioned and behind the times." Under the cover of the triumph of the individual, today what triumphs is essentially the opposite of this: hyper-simplistic economism, uncontrolled despotism of the markets and of money.[4]

Just as Fukuyama appeared on the scene as a by-product of the analyses of Bloom, so there also subsequently appeared the by-product of the by-product: the American political writer Hans-Hermann Hoppe, of the University of Nevada in Las Vegas, with his inflammatory essay "Down with Democracy."[5] It is essential, opines Hoppe, that we do not surrender to the principle of "one person one vote": if this rule were observed, world government would be transferred to somewhere in the Himalayas, between China and India. With Sino-Indian world government, the consequences are predictable: the West would be considered excessively affluent, and the East excessively poor. Inevitably the world would be prevailed upon to transfer resources from West to East. Each individual and his personal fortune would be exposed to public abuse from those without any such fortune, as well as to their aggressive looting. Given that the rich by definition are always a minority, it follows that they will suffer in conditions of Democracy, which as is well-known glorify the will of the majority. The tone of Hoppe's observations is uncommonly reactionary and their content cliched, but for all that he is expressing what is par excellence the present-day social reaction against the democratic political system, in conditions of supposed globalization and above all on the pretext of such conditions. It is characteristic that his anti-democratic argumentation is based exclusively on observations to do with social inequality, from which he extrapolates his conclusions concerning the weakness of the political system of Democracy.

The American economist Joseph Stiglitz of Stanford University recently issued an unanswerable condemnation of present-day American political leaders, depicting them as people "lacking democratic culture" insofar as they assess democratic political values with criteria of economic efficiency and so subordinate Democracy and the political plane to the economy, to international competitiveness and to globalization.[6] The same writer notes that to this day the International Monetary Fund refuses to apply the elementary democratic rule of "one country one vote." Once again it is confirmed that historically the economistic outlook of Western democracy has decisively shaped its overall character, which remains particularly vulnerable to economic fluctuations.

Present-day US foreign policy is crucially afflicted by this contradiction. Following the crisis and then the collapse of the Asian economies after 1997, the US announced the following approach to the question of Democracy: while the Asian economies were demanding emergency assistance in order to secure a breathing space, the Americans put forward a "dogma" on the basis of which they justified their inertia. Under the terms of the present American dogma the essential aid which is being requested for the rescue of the economies of the Third World is not being donated while ever the countries in question fail to implement the required democratic reforms in the direction of freeing and deregulating their markets. This American veto has also been issued to Russia: first reforms and then the assistance. America thus appears as the champion of the new global democracy which denounces and isolates every variety of family rule, nepotism and crony capitalism. But apart from that, once again not only is the basic distinction ignored between the democratic political system and the economy, but also - entirely arbitrarily and anti-historically, political democracy is equated with so-called "transparency" and the democracy of the marketplace. America, while projecting itself as the champion of global democracy, in reality merely functions as the promoter of its own economic system throughout the world: it promises economic benefits to whichever countries adopt some semblance of the American economic system without being interested in how democratically representative are the local political systems. While altogether intransigent in its demands for market transparency, it remains notably lenient on the question of respect for democratic representation in politics.[7] Its belated interest in individual rights and freedoms does not in any way extend to the question of democratic political systems. Democracy continues to be confused with economic expedience, while the aim of Democracy should be to remain independent of all extra-political considerations.

Paradoxically, liberalism's anthropological model coincides with that of economistic Marxism, insofar as both schools focus on the individual totally cut off from every non-economic determination. Keynes once aptly remarked that insofar as Communism was based, as in its British and Soviet variants, on nationalizations and centralized economic planning by the state, it was really nothing more than the reductio ad absurdum of capitalism: a hyper-rationalistic totalitarian capitalism without internal contradictions, all anarchic elements having been removed from the production process. Yet Communism as "hyper-rationalistic" capitalism, i.e. without competition and an internal market, proved Utopian in its

Soviet manifestation. Instead of that, liberals now demand globalization for the model of a new "hyper-rationalistic and totalitarian individualism": but why should this model of "hyper-rationality" have better chances of success than the preceding one? Hyper-rationalistic totalitarianism, whether as capitalism or as communism, is always at a dramatic disadvantage in comparison to reality, which is always much more complex and not economistic. The value of political Democracy remains, irrespective of the projects of totalitarian expediency either of communism or of unfettered individualism.

Questioning Globalism

With the recent events in Seattle, in Washington and in London, a new philosophical stance came to light which will quite possibly put its stamp on the 21st century. Resistance to the liberal economism of our age is evolving at last on the basis of non-economic criteria. Human beings and the world they live in are not commodities, are not subordinated to the laws of the market, irrespective of whether this overturns the economic teachings of the Chicago School. After three thousand years, the thinking minorities of today are rediscovering truths with which the ancients were already quite familiar. According to Aristotle the polity uses commodities for its needs but is not itself a commodity. Trade, as a social practice, is assigned to the province of the metics, who do not enjoy rights of citizenship. He who chases commercial gain is not authorized to give lessons in politics and democracy, nor of course may he be permitted in any way to influence the outcome of public affairs. The democratic polity is not natural situation that can be relied on to occur spontaneously; it is the result of painstaking and complex effort on the part of the citizens, essentially a sacrifice for which moreover they are to be compensated by the polity.

In our times, modern Democracy, which was never conceived of as a political obligation and a duty of the citizen, is now questioned even as an individual right, on the basis of economistic and sociological arguments. It is undoubtedly the case that economic and social developments exert an influence on what happens in a democratic polity, but they do not do through a simple reflective process but rather through the medium of politics and ideology. In our age the number of unemployed, the homeless and the destitute is rising in an unprecedented fashion. And the system of labor relations is also being undermined and destabilized through liberals' insistence on imposing individual work contracts. With the collapse of state arbitration and collective bargaining in relations between labor and capital, the social and economic space in which politics can find expression undergoes a similar collapse. The unemployed, the homeless, the destitute, even more than the problem of survival face the political problem of social exclusion. At the same time, the promise of the new digital economy to thrust the business world and society in general into a new stage of human development does not include a commitment to social reconstruction but merely aggravates the present-day social and political crisis.

Political reformation of modern Democracy could constitute a basis not only for resistance to the disintegrative consequences of globalization so evident today but also for reconstruction of communities with respect for the their specific anthropological characteristics. Because it places priority on the human factor, the democratic community checks the tendencies to social dissolution that are inherent in markets, stock exchange speculation and uncontrolled movements of capital. By contrast the total and unchecked domination of markets, of speculation and of "abstract" money establish an economic totalitarianism, not Democracy. The democratic polity finds its legitimation not so much through economic criteria as through political. To the economic authoritarianism of today it counterposes the democratic political system with its human values situated outside the market.

Some people imagine that the democratic deficit of our times can be managed by the promotion of democratic procedures within the big business organizations. But this is an entirely different problem: democracy inside companies is an idea with its origins in Anglo-Saxon corporatism and has to do with the internal life of the corporations, whereas political Democracy concerns the whole of society, citizens' relations to each other and the problem of exercising political power.

Refounding Democracy

In the modern age only Amartya Sen was able to get onto the same wavelength as the recent movements in Seattle and Washington, insofar as he again, after so many years, designated democracy the desired goal "irrespective of any economic value."[8] Democracy is indispensable and non-negotiable, at any cost and any price, like freedom, to the extent that both of them safeguard "the capacity for fulfillment in human life." However, Amartya Sen goes even further: not only are democracy and freedom independent of economic values - they constitute political criteria by means of which a distinction may be drawn between positive and negative economic values. There is nothing positive about development as such except insofar as it is subordinated to serving the human need for freedom and democracy. Finally, there is such a thing as a "good" and a "bad" economy, and the criterion for the distinction remains political.

Recently the New York Times tried to prove that Democracy is justifiable even in our age because of its contribution to economic development.[9] But it came to the conclusion that for economists this was hard to prove. Nevertheless it is equally difficult for economists to prove the opposite: that Democracy is harmful for economic development. At the very least, the American newspaper concludes, let us accept that dictatorships and authoritarian regimes do not necessarily promote development. But the historical experience of the Asian countries of the Far East indicates that authoritarian and dictatorial political regimes can for many decades quite satisfactorily promote economic efficiency and competitiveness. The American newspaper nevertheless passes over the evidence from the Asian experience and in its own way introduces the question of the need in our age for Democracy to acquire extra-economic underpinnings. But it fails to make explicit the specific object of Democracy: the New York newspaper maintains that the revolution in information technology brings back the human being and Democracy into the heart of the social dynamic, which is why Democracy today is preferable to authoritarian systems. Along with information technology, creativity and dynamism from below also flourish, in the form of the advancement of new ideas which replace natural capital.

However, all this American problematic, despite its undeniable interest, cannot get it clear that Democracy does not have to do with human beings in general but specifically with citizens, and not with freedom in general but with the safeguarding of concrete public institutions that make it possible for democratic processes to function. When politics is recognized not as a derivative of the economy but as a special field in itself with a priority status independent of other fields of social relations (or at the very least with "relative autonomy"),[10] then Democracy will emerge as less problematic, certainly less vulnerable to the fluctuations of the economic conjuncture and also less exposed to such ideological totalitarianisms as may be temporarily in fashion.

Notes

1. See J.-J.ROUSSEAU, "Du contrat social," GF-Flammarion 1992, book I, chapter V and VI, pp. 37-40.
2. See Allan BLOOM, "Closing of the American Mind," 1988, The Republic of Plato, 1991.
3. See F. FUKUYAMA, "The End of History And The Last Man," 1992.
4. See V. FORESTER, "Une étrange dictature," Fayard Editions, Paris 2000.
5. See H.-H. HOPPE, "Down With Democracy," in "Enterprise and Education," Summer 1995.
6. See J. STIGLITZ, "The Insider', in "The New Republic," 17 April 2000.
7. See Tina ROSENBERG, "America Finds Democracy Difficult To Export," The New York Times, 25 October 1999.
8. See A. SEN, "Development As Freedom," 1999.
9. See Jeff MADRICK, "Democracy Has The Edge When It Comes To Advancing Growth," New York Times, April 13 2000.
10. For the concept of relative autonomy see N. POULANTZAS, L'Etat, le pouvoir, le socialisme, PUF 1979.

PART B
CONCEPTS AND LIMITS
OF DEMOCRACY

5 Marxian Theory as a Critique of Democracy

RICHARD D. WOLFF

Marxism and Democracy

The relationship between democracy and Marxism reveals a sequence of reversals. Sometimes Marxism has projected itself as the full completion of democracy, at other times as one of its harsher critics. Sometimes Marxists dispute one another's credentials as such based on their commitments to democracy (or lack thereof). At other times Marxists attack democrats as enemies of transitions to socialism or communism (often by attaching adjectives like bourgeois or petty-bourgeois to the democracy they advocate). While there have always been some proponents of all these positions, they oscillate in terms of which has prevailed among Marxists. In the recent words of one Marx scholar, "The world-wide controversy over Marx's legacy today turns largely on its ambiguous relation to democracy..." (Meister 1990, 99).

Marx punctuated his personal passage from radical democrat to communist by strong critiques of the politics of those he often called democrats (Riazanov 1973, 88ff). Later Marxists have differed in their attitudes toward democracy and democrats. Some have embraced democracy theoretically and democrats as political allies. Other Marxists have rejected democracy and democrats as elements of a movement that basically deflects workers from class revolutionary projects. Where Marx changed his position (mostly in one direction) across his lifetime, among Marxists ever since the movement has been more an oscillation between opposing positions as variants of one or the other gain sway over the majority. Most recently, the collapse of Eastern European socialism accelerated the post-1945 shift of Marxists more toward enthusiastic embrace of democracy and democrats – expressed, for example, in the view that insufficient democracy caused that collapse (Kotz 1997).

The particular Marxist position I want to advance here aims to break out of these oscillations on the grounds that both polar positions are inadequate.[1] I thus do not argue for yet another reversal, for Marxists to distance themselves from democracy and democrats as they have done in the past. Rather, Marxists should draw clear lines of demarcation between the kind of democracy they affirm and the very different kinds typically affirmed by most democrats today (as in the past). Such lines entail issues of urgent importance for Marxism's future, theoretical and practical.

Marxism's distinctive approach (and, hence, contribution) to democracy focuses on the objects of democratic decision-making: the "what" of democracy's concerns. This alone distinguishes it from many other approaches to democracy. Many of the latter stress, for example, the "how" of democracy: for example, can it be indirect and representative or must it be direct and immediate? The "how" democrats debate such alternatives and sometimes denounce each other as not genuine democrats because of their positions on them. Other democrats debate the "who" of democracy: must it include all or can only some members of the community participate in a democracy? If it is the latter, debate focuses on what will determine eligibilities: age, gender, race, property, education, and so on. While Marxists have engaged these debates, Marxism's distinctive contribution to democracy as a concept and as a social movement does not, in my view, lie in propositions regarding the "how" and "who" of democracy.

Marxism focuses primarily on what is to be decided democratically. However, before describing Marxism's distinctive view on the "what," I need to acknowledge that Marxism is, of course, not the only approach to democracy concerned with the "what." Implicitly or explicitly, *all* approaches take a position on what is to be decided democratically within any community. The reason for this lies in the inescapable limits of human communities confronting the complexity of their own social organizations.

The potential objects of decision-making in any community comprise an infinite list: spatial location, population growth, kinship systems, what to produce, how to distribute products, how to organize political life, class structures, cultural expressions, and so on. Any decision-making system, whether democratic or not (by any definition), always selects from the infinity of potential objects those few that become its actual objects across any particular historical epoch. Marxism's distinctive contribution to its epochs' debates over democracy concerns what should be included among the actual objects of democratic decision-making and why.

Democracy and Class

At all times, while some potential objects become actual objects of decision-making in any society, others remain merely potential. For example, contemporary feminists who are also democrats stress that their contribution (and commitment) to democracy prioritizes gender relations as an object of democratic decision. Anti-racists who are also democrats likewise focus on making race relations into actual objects of democratic decision-making. Such feminists and anti-racists link their commitments to democracy (whatever their particular views on the how and who) inextricably to the what of democratic decision making. They refuse to continue to allow gender and race relations to remain potential but not actualized objects of such decision making.

The Marxist position I am arguing for takes a parallel position toward democracy, but its focus is on class. The point is to make class and class change into actual objects of democratic decision making. What Marxism contributes to the debates over democracy is, first and foremost, the demand and argument for placing class structures as such on the list of objects to be decided by democratic decision making. Marxist democrats refuse to embrace democratic movements that keep class structures off that list.

To say that Marxism's contribution to democracy inserts class on its agenda of objects for decision requires that the meaning of class be specified. This is because Marxism has a long, contentious history of coexisting multiple, different, and often incompatible concepts of class in its theory and its practice. Having documented these in detail elsewhere, so I will be brief here (Resnick and Wolff 1986, 1987). The concept of class I mean here is one *not* defined by reference to property ownership, nor to the distribution of power in society, nor to the consciousness of particular groups of people. It is rather defined in terms of surplus labor: more specifically in terms of the three social processes of (i) producing, (ii) appropriating, and (iii) distributing surplus labor or its products.

Property concepts of class define it as persons in any society grouped according to how much wealth each group owns vis-a-vis the wealth of other groups. Rich confront poor, propertied the propertyless, and so on. In contrast, power concepts of class group members of society according to how much authority or power they wield vis-a-vis other groups: powerful vs. powerless, ruling versus ruled, and so on. Consciousness concepts stress that classes arise only if and when a sub-group within a society (e.g. a "class in itself") becomes conscious of itself as such a distinct sub-group (e.g., a "class for itself"). These different concepts need not be compatible, nor do they reduce to one another. Which class concept an analyst uses to think about society will shape what conclusions he/she reaches. People with wealth may not have power nor consciousness; people wielding power may not have wealth; people with consciousness may lack wealth or power, and so on.[2]

Class by one definition is not so by another. Moreover, the property, power, and consciousness concepts of class (and the social analyses and political programs based upon them) long predate Marx. For thousands of years in many parts of the world, people have made sense of their social circumstances in terms of class defined as property, power, and/or consciousness. They developed programs for social change focused on altering the distributions of property and/or power and/or changing consciousness. While Marx clearly knew of, sympathized with, and made use of many of those analyses and programs, he also offered a new and different concept of class and a correspondingly unique social analysis and project for class transformation.

Class and Surplus Labor

Marx's distinctive contribution focused attention on a set of three social processes others had overlooked, namely the production, appropriation, and distribution of surplus labor.[3]

He argued that all societies display a sub-group of their populations engaged in transforming nature by their labor. Part of the produce of this labor is consumed by these laborers: this is the "necessary product" produced by the portion of their labor that is likewise "necessary." However, in all societies these laborers also produce more than the necessary product (they do more than the necessary labor). This Marxist "more" has come to be known, in its English translation, as "surplus".[4]

Thus all societies display the production of some quantity of surplus product, the fruit of surplus labor. Moreover, all societies also display a process of appropriating that surplus product, some mechanism sanctioned by society whereby some members receive the surplus as it is produced.

Lastly, all societies display a particular distribution of the surplus product from its appropriators to others in the society, some socially sanctioned apportionment of the surplus. The combination of the three class processes – production, appropriation, and distribution of the surplus – Marx called a class structure.

Marx's analysis – developed across the three volumes of *Capital* – argued that any society's history depended in significant ways on the class structures interacting within it. Capitalism, he showed, was but one particular way to organize a class structure (feudal, communist, slave, and ancient are among the other kinds of class structures he discussed). Since capitalism was, in his mind, the prevalent (but hardly the only) class structure in modern European society, he aimed to show his contemporaries that the social injustices of Europe were products in part of the particularly capitalist class structure (the capitalist organization of surplus labor) prevalent there. In other words, his work aimed to overcome the failure of other analysts – and especially of the social critics and radicals he saw as his allies – to understand the three class processes and to *include their explicit transformation on their agendas for social change.*

From this perspective, it follows that what Marxists want within a democratic movement now is a commitment to include the class structures of society – in the surplus labor sense – among the actual objects of the democratic decision making which is that movement's goal. This means that when a proposed democracy's goals are limited to the distribution of social wealth and/or the distribution of political power and/or the organization of popular consciousness, that does *not* accommodate the Marxist goal specified above.[5] For example, democratic movements which commit to making state versus private ownership of productive assets an object of democratic decision making do not thereby become Marxist or include Marxism, since they make no reference to the way in which surplus labor is to be organized. Neither do movements committed to making the social distribution of political power (e.g., suffrage) or the cultural formations of consciousness (e.g., education) into such actual objects. Only insofar as a democratic movement commits to including the class structures of a society – the particular ways in which surplus labor is organized – among the actual objects of democratic decision making does it accept what is here called the distinctive Marxist contribution to the democratic project.

Contradictions

Like feminists and anti-racists, Marxists face the following possible contradiction. A particular democratic movement may focus on the hows and whos of democracy and only upon actual objects of democratic decision-making *other than* what feminists, anti-racists, and Marxists prioritize as such objects. What then is to be done? If the society in which this democratic movement arises is sexist and racist, it will be understood that feminists and anti-racists will voice strong criticisms of the democracy proposed by such a movement! They may plausibly claim that such a democratic movement secures and even strengthens sexism and racism by deflecting its activists' thought and action away from those injustices. They may declare such a movement to be among their enemies politically. Yet this would hardly amount to any blanket, totalizing opposition to democracy as an ideal or to its concretization in particular systems of how democracy is organized (direct versus indirect) or who shares democratic activity (all or some) and so on. It would an opposition over the what of democracy, an opposition over what are included versus excluded among the infinite potential objects of democratic decision making.

The Marxist position advanced here is parallel. When Marx denounced petty-bourgeois democratic movements, I think he meant to specify not their notions of direct or inclusive democratic decision making, but rather their complicity in keeping the object of class in its surplus labor sense off the popular agenda for social change (Marx 1933, 45-47). Such movements' foci on suffrage, empowerment, direct elections, recalls and referenda struck him as crucially inadequate precisely because they colluded in the efforts of exploiting classes to repress alternative organizations of surplus labor as an issue for debate and action for social change. When Marxists focus on class to undo that repression, they face a serious contradiction when confronted by a movement for democracy that is complicit – intentionally or not, knowingly or not – with that repression.

Under those circumstances, Marxists may do what feminists and anti-racists have done. Marxists too may criticize such democratic movements and their definitions and visions of democracy even to the point of declaring them to be political enemies.

Marx did that in his time. I think it is appropriate again, adjusted for changed circumstances, in our time.

The USSR, in the early years after 1917, involved masses of people in democratic decision making who had previously been excluded from it.

The Bolsheviks altered the how and who of democracy in radical ways stunningly exemplary for their time and ours. They also altered the what of their democratized decision making: property distribution, power distribution, cultural expression and much else were made actual objects of democratic decision making for a while. Moreover, the tragic history of how that democracy was soon narrowed, curtailed, and largely abolished – associated with the name of Stalin – is too well known to need repetition here. But a distinctively Marxist critical history of Soviet democracy constructs a different narrative.

Neither in the immediate aftermath of the 1917 revolution nor later under Stalin (or Khrushchev or Gorbachev or anybody else) did the Soviet leadership make the actual organization of surplus labor in industry into an explicit object of decision making, democratic or otherwise (Resnick and Wolff 1994). A communist class structure would have entailed that the industrial laborers who produce the surplus collectively appropriate and distribute their own surplus. As Marx argued, that would be the end of exploitation, defined as the organization of surplus labor such that those who produce it do not themselves appropriate it.

Especially given the Marxist thinking and commitments of the Soviet leadership and many of its activists, it might have been expected that among the explicit objects of democratic decision making after the revolution there would appear the questions of whether and how to move beyond the capitalist class structures of the industries inherited from Russia.

In surplus labor terms, that would have meant debating and deciding on whether to reorganize factories such that the laborers within them would collectively appropriate and distribute their own surpluses. That was not done. Nor was it done later after Stalin had undermined many of the earlier experiments in democracy. The class issue was never on the democrats' nor anyone else's agendas for industrial change in the USSR.[6]

Instead, it was declared that changing industrial property from private to state ownership, subordinating free markets to state economic planning, subordinating state power to a workers' political party, universalizing access to medical care, education, and housing, developing workers' culture and consciousness, etc. were all themselves "class changes." Where Lenin (1961, 696) had had the courage to call the early USSR "state capitalism," his successors repressed the issue of class in terms of surplus labor by simply declaring that capitalism (and exploitative class relations) had been vanquished and replaced by socialism. That achievement and the progress toward communism were grounds for declaring that discussion or action on the social organization of surplus labor inside the USSR was unnecessary, irrelevant, or evidence of hostility to the USSR. Communism came increasingly to be characterized as the goal of the USSR and defined in terms of production according to ability and distribution according to need. This formulation, too, served further to obscure the issue of the social organization of surplus labor.

Marxism, Class, and Democracy

For class to become an actual object of democratic decision making would mean that the range of alternative social organizations of surplus labor would have to be discussed, debated, and chosen among. The strengths and weaknesses of past and present historical experiences with all of them would have to become matters of historical and theoretical research, public education, popular debate, and practical experimentation. The complex social effects of exploitative versus non-exploitative class structures would have to be exhaustively explored.

To the extent that class becomes an object of democratic decision making, derivative questions would likewise become such objects. Class is not only a matter of what kind or kinds of organization of surplus labor should be decided upon for any society: communist, capitalist, feudal, and so on. Derivative questions to be decided by democratic decision making would include, among others, the following:

- will the society wish to allow different class structures to coexist; if so, in what proportions and which class structures will be allowed in which industries, regions, and so on?
- which individuals or groups will occupy the positions, respectively, of producers, appropriators and receivers of distributions of the surplus in the allowed class structures and will they rotate periodically through different positions or occupy the same ones during their lifetimes?
- in communist class structures, how would the people who are not producers of surplus – and therefore not its appropriators or distributors either – nonetheless participate in such distributions since their lives are affected by them?
- what mechanisms would need to be established to enable the question of changing a society's class structures to be raised for democratic

decision making whenever people wish such change?

• at the moment when class is finally placed on the agenda for decision making, how will account be taken of each society's prior history of celebrating some class structures and demonizing others?

The contribution to democracy and to movements for democracy that Marxism can offer is lost when Marxists simply add their voices to support democracy in some general, abstract way. A democracy whose selection of objects to be decided democratically excludes class structures represents simply one more way that existing class structures – and especially the predominant capitalist class structures – can repress opposition to those class structures. Marxists have the right and the obligation to criticize such kinds of democracy and the movements that advocate them. A Marxist critique of democracy on that basis can contain as well its own vision of what kinds of democracy are consistent with Marxist class objectives (communism).

Notes

1. I use the word "particular" here to acknowledge that Marxism includes many different positions. I support one such position. I do not wish to engage in debates – rarely fruitful – as to what might constitute a "genuine" Marxism. Marxism, like beauty, lies largely in the eyes of the beholder.
2. To say, as so many Marxists and others have, that class "is a group of people who all relate to the labor process in a similar way" (Roemer 1988, 5) resolves nothing. People "relate" to the labor process in one way as owners, in another as wielders of various powers, in still another in terms of their consciousnesses, in still another in terms of surplus labor, and so on. Phrases such as Roemer's avoid the difficult task of specifying class – taking a position within the debate over what class, class analysis, and class politics mean – by collapsing all the different terms into one composite definition as if all the terms cohere in a non-contradictory amalgam.
3. Marx did, however, acknowledge his intellectual debts to forerunners who had glimpsed but not developed adequately notions of surplus different from his own. Those debts and the difference between those glimpses and his own theory are developed in detail in Marx's multivolumed *Theories of Surplus Value*.
4. In Marx's German, he used the word "mehr" which means "more," but the much more troublesome term (in the sense of multiple, ambiguous meanings) – "surplus" – has become the better known term, so it is used here.
5. Of course, Marxists can support these objects, but that is secondary for them while it is primary for the others. In turn, what is primary for Marxists is secondary for the others. A democratic movement that explicitly allies different elements with different primary and secondary objectives would accommodate Marxists in the sense intended by this text.

6. As argued in detail in a forthcoming book on the USSR's class history by Resnick and Wolff, the collectivization of Soviet agriculture after 1929 did entail the establishment of collective farms in which communist class processes prevailed. Thus the irony of Soviet history: the communist class processes presumed to arrive first in industry actually materialized there first in agriculture. Moreover, the Soviet state's relentless demands for distributions of surplus from the collective farms crippled their communist class structures, focused collective farmers instead on their individual plots, and so precluded any spread of the communist class structures from agriculture to industry.

References

Kotz, David and Weir, Fred. 1997. *Revolution from Above: The Demise of the Soviet System.* New York: Routledge.

Lenin, V.I. 1961. *Selected Works, Vol 3.* Moscow: Foreign Languages Publishing House.

Marx, Karl. 1933. *Critique of the Gotha Programme.* New York: International Publishers.

Meister, Robert. 1990. *Political Identity: Thinking Through Marx.* Oxford: Basil Blackwell.

Resnick, Stephen and Wolff, Richard. 1986. "What Are Class Analyses?" In Paul Zarembka, Ed., *Research in Political Economy, Vol 9.* Greewich and London: JAI Press, pp. 1-32.

_____. 1987. *Knowledge and Class: A Marxian Critique of Political Economy.* Chicago: University of Chicago Press.

_____. 1994. "Between State and Private Capitalism: What was Soviet 'Socialism'?" *Rethinking Marxism* 7:1, pp. 9-30.

Riazanov, David. 1973. *Karl Marx and Friedrich Engels: An Introduction to their Lives and Work.* Trans. by Joshua Kunitz. New York: Monthly Review.

Roemer, John. 1988. *Free to Lose: An Introduction to Marxist Political Philosophy.* Cambridge: Cambridge University Press.

6 Democracy, the Market, and Egalitarianism

GUGLIELMO CARCHEDI

Privatization and Rationality

While medical science has failed to discover the miraculous potion which can cure all diseases, economists have succeeded in finding an extraordinary medicine against all economic illnesses: the market and privatization. Notwithstanding the theoretical emptiness of the arguments claiming (higher) efficiency for the market and market prices as an allocational mechanism, there is hardly any public figure nowadays in the Western countries who does not accept the myth of the rationality and efficiency of the market (and thus of classic capitalism). The East too follows the lead of the West not only in massively privatizing public enterprises but also in arguing that this process is justified by the fact that private enterprises are more efficient than public ones.[1]

In their drive towards privatization and the reintroduction of the market, neo-liberalism does not fail to argue that capitalism is more efficient than central planning. But it can be shown that (a) this comparison is not between capitalism and socialism but between two types of capitalism, which could be called classic and spurious or state or centrally planned capitalism,[2] (b) the comparison is in terms of capitalist efficiency, (c) spurious capitalism is less efficient than market capitalism not because "communism" is contrary to human nature and other nonsensical reasons but because of social, objective, restraints and (d) in terms of satisfaction of human needs both centrally planned and market capitalism score abysmally low. In any case, it should not be forgotten that, when the two systems are compared, it is both the First and the Third World which should be contrasted to the Second World, since the possibility to satisfy certain human needs (up to a certain degree) in the

First World is specularly related to the impossibility to satisfy those same needs in the Third World.

Moreover, it is precisely the constant increase of this kind of efficiency that, paradoxically, causes economic crises. It can be shown (Carchedi, 1991, ch. 5. Carchedi 1997) that the ultimate cause of capitalist crises is the increasing production of use values and at the same time the decreasing production of value and surplus value. This contradictory movement is the result of increased productivity, (i.e. to that quality the "communist" countries were so envious of) within capitalist production relations. The states of the developed capitalist economies cannot re-pay the debts which they contract in pursuing anti-crises economic policies. As all insolvent debtors, they must eventually sell (actually, undersell) part of their property, i.e. privatize. And it might be fitting to recall that what is now being privatized is what has been nationalized decades ago, when the same system of private property failed and the state had to jump in and salvage many enterprises by nationalizing them. This, the repayment of state debts, and not the higher efficiency of the market, is then the main reason for privatizing in classic capitalism.

But there are also other reasons. T. Clarke mentions two important ones. One is "introducing people to some of the mechanics of capitalism with which they were unacquainted, while giving them a very small financial stake in the dismemberment of the public sector, and an interest in electing future Conservative governments." The other is "concealing the enormous transfer of assets from the public sector to large financial, multinational, and overseas corporations under the camouflage of 'popular capitalism'" (Clarke 1990, 502). To these, at least two more reasons can be added. First, privatization breaks those state-owned monopolies where higher profits can be made thus providing new channels of profitable investments for privately owned capitals.[3] Secondly, there is the "belief that a private company would be better able to control the trade unions" (Dixon, 1991b). Clearly, these four reasons as well are related to the need the revitalize a deeply troubled economy. The optical illusion arises that the market, and thus classic capitalism is the best and most rational economic system.

The Eastern countries too are in the midst of a deep economic crisis. The causes, however, are different. The reason must be sought in the different nature of these systems. Very schematically, before the recent radical changes, they were imitations of the Soviet Union[4] which, in its turn, was a spurious system whose movement towards socialism had been halted long ago and which was fatally attracted to classic capitalism. Those countries had to rid themselves of all juridical, economic, ideological, political, etc.

constraints in order to become fully capitalist. In particular, it became necessary to introduce the market as the determinant allocational system and private property. In these countries, then, privatization is the necessary step towards a fully capitalist economy. Here too privatization makes possible the reduction of budget deficits.[5] But this aspect is secondary compared to the introduction of fully capitalist social relations. The optical illusion arises that the market is the best allocational system also for "socialist" countries.[6] However, "market failures" in the West are hard to conceal and plan failures in the East are equally obvious. This explains the attraction some feel for a supposedly "third way," market-socialism.

The centrally planned economies of spurious capitalism had already tried a mixture of "socialist" production and capitalist, i.e. market-based, distribution. As M. Ellman points out, according to the supporters of market-socialism, "the market should be seen not as the negation of planning but as an instrument that could be used to achieve efficiently some of the goals of the plan" (1989, 53-4). These notions rest on a mythical view of capitalist distribution, i.e. of prices. The interplay of demand and supply is far from being unrestrained and prices, even under conditions of perfect competition, (a) are not determined by this interplay (b) indicate profitability rather than the satisfaction of needs (c) inasmuch as they satisfy needs, they satisfy manipulated human needs only for a minority of society and (d) do not clear the markets, they solve the crisis of realization only cyclically, i.e. only after massive destruction of capitalist production relations, unemployment, and physical destruction of goods. Moreover, these prices implicitly treat nature as just another, and thus reproducible, resource instead of as an irreplaceable source of life in all its multifarious forms. The market- socialist "reformers" might be the last people on earth who still believe that micro-economics textbooks depict, and thus are useful for the understanding of, the real capitalist world.

Market-Socialism and Democracy

But the market-socialism thesis has gained ground also among those, in the countries of classic capitalism, who while being dissatisfied with capitalism, want to retain the "rationality" of capitalist distribution (and possibly the "rationality" of capitalist production as well). It has just been said that the supposed rationality of capitalist distribution, i.e. of the market and thus of the price system, is based on a myth and that there is nothing rational in capitalist distribution except that it is the type of distribution which makes possible the continuation of capitalist production. We must now inquire into the reasons why this system of distribution cannot be functional for a social system based on solidarity, egalitarianism, and self-management.[7]

To begin with, an egalitarian distribution requires egalitarian prices. These cannot be money prices. In fact, money is the form of manifestation of value and value, in its turn, in its necessary money form, is the form of manifestation of the contradictory and exploitative content of the capitalist ownership relations (and more generally of the capitalist production relations), i.e. of the power the owners of the means of production have on the non-owners. In short, money has a social content, the exploitative character of the capitalist production relations.[8] Any attempt to change these relations while retaining money cannot but be doomed to failure. This is why it is absurd to try to conjugate an egalitarian production system with the market and its money prices on grounds of the latter's supposed higher distributional efficiency. An egalitarian system too needs a price system but, here, prices have a quite different nature: *egalitarian prices should indicate, and reward the producers according to the new labor contained in the products.* Only in this way can they correspond to the principle "to each according to their labor." Let us dwell on this point a little longer. Consider capitalism.

If we start from the fact that each commodity has cost a share of society's labor, and if in a capitalist economy labor manifests itself as money (so that each unit of money represents a fraction of society's labor), prices measure how much of society's labor the commodity owners receive for their commodities, i.e. for the (share of society's) labor contained in those commodities. Now, it can be shown that the labor contained in commodities deviates systematically from the labor appropriated through the sale of those commodities because basically of two reasons. First, capitals constantly chase more profitable investments thus moving from one sector of the economy to another. This generates a tendency towards an equalization of the rates of profit into an average and thus a tendential appropriation of value from those sectors with low organic composition to those with high organic composition. Second, within sectors, innovative capitals appropriate value from technologically backward capitals thanks to the former's higher efficiency.[9]

Consequently, the value produced and contained in the commodities gets redistributed in such a way that (1) tendentially all capitals with average productivity in their sector realize a share of societal labor corresponding to the average rate of profit and (2) above and below capitals realize more and less than that average (share of societal labor), proportionally to productivity differentials. This is the tendential movement. The forces of demand and supply cause the real movement (market prices) to oscillate around these tendential prices. There is thus no equality between value produced and value realized. Discrepancies between demand and supply can and do cause fluctuations around the tendential prices so that the value (labor) appropriated by each capital can either move in the direction of, or diverge even more from, the value produced by it. But only by chance does a commodity give its owner the same quantity of society's labor (through its price) as that contained in it.

Consider now a system in which society indicates which goods are desirable on the basis of existing and foreseen needs (no matter how this decision is taken). This would be one element of solidaristic production (but by no means the only one). Each product would have a tag with the hours of new labor which have been needed to produce it. These products could be distributed through coupons (they could also be electronic cards storing the necessary data) which each economic agent would get for his or her labor performed. Egalitarian logic mandates that each economic agent receives a coupon which gives right to a certain quantity of consumption goods equal to the relation between the total product of consumption goods divided by the total hours of new labor performed multiplied by the hours of labor carried out by that agent. A simple example will clarify this point.

Given an initial endowment (it could correspond to the first year after the transition to an egalitarian economy) of:

I $100MP + 100L(=200h) = 150MP$
II $150MP + 300L(=300h) = 300MC$

where L indicates the number of laborers, h the number of labor hours worked, and MP and MC indicate the means of production and of consumption. This means that laborers in sector I work twice as long or as intensively as laborers in II. Each laborer in I should then get double MC as each laborer in II. Each hour of labor gives right to $300MC/500h = 0.6MC$. This is the labor price of one MC. Each laborer in I gets a coupon for $2h=1.2MC$ (for a total of 120MC) and each laborer in II gets a coupon giving right to $1h=0.6MC$ (for a total of 180MC). Notice that while each MC has cost one hour of new labor, each hour of labor gives right not to one MC but to 0.6MC (given that also the laborers producing MP have a claim on the MC). Or, each hour of new labor worked gives right to a proportion of the hours of new labor incorporated in the MC.[10]

The MP too would have a similar price tag but with a key difference. Their allocation to the different production units would have to be determined according to a plan drawn up in the first instance for the production of the desired consumer goods and more generally for the satisfaction of society's needs. This means that there would be no reason to compute the past labor embodied in the MP.[11] As for the new labor embodied in them, this might be an important factor in determining for example how much of the new total labor available in the next period would have to go into their production, given the relation between the production of the desired MC and the MP needed to produce them. The production of the MP to produce MP would have to follow the same criterion. But the new labor embodied in the MP would be only of secondary importance in determining their allocation to the different production units.

Suppose now that, instead of the coupon system just sketched, prices are determined by demand and supply, i.e. by the market. Those submitting this scheme argue that solidarity at the level of production would be conjugated with the market's efficiency at the level of distribution. But, in this case, prices would not correspond any longer to the new labor contents and, given that the producers would earn their income through the sale of those commodities on the market, there would be no correspondence between new labor performed (incorporated in certain goods) and labor received (through the sale of those goods). It becomes then impossible to know whether one really gets a number of labor hours, in the form of goods, proportionate to the number s/he has worked, as written upon that coupon.[12] It follows that *egalitarian prices should not be subject to fluctuations determined by demand and supply* because such fluctuations are inherently contradictory to the principle "to each according to their labor."

In an egalitarian economy, goods should be valued in terms of their labor costs to society, i.e. in terms of the new labor hours actually contained in them, and prices should be nothing more than an expression of these quantities, tags with numbers of labor hours on them. It is on this basis that incomes should be determined. These would correspond to hours of new labor after the reduction of more intensive to less intensive hours of labor has been performed (but one hour of skilled labor would not count as a multiple of one hour of unskilled labor). In the determination of these prices, demand and supply should play no role because goods which are not wanted are not produced and, contrary to the Soviet type of planning which did not rest upon a really democratic decision making, goods which would be produced would be wanted.[13] Only in this case does the principle "to each according to his or her work" make sense. Planning mistakes or changes in tastes could also result into unwanted goods. But then this would be society's fault, not that of the producers whose task has been that of making those goods. The disadvantages would have to be distributed equally throughout society.

More generally, egalitarian prices should not be subjected to fluctuations determined by discrepancies between *demand and supply* because such *fluctuations generate injustice, inequality and waste*. One of the most startling features of capitalism is that those commodities which do not meet the needs or the taste of the buyers remain unsold (so that labor and natural resources are wasted) while the skewed distribution of wealth and concomitant accumulation (both within nations and internationally) result in this system's inability to provide even the minimum necessities of life for the greatest part of the world population. While these features cannot be brought back exclusively to the role played by demand and supply in (market) price determination, demand and supply not only contribute to them but also are the manifestation and necessary corollary of a system based on inequality and waste.

This is of enormous significance for the reproduction of a system in transition towards an egalitarian one. First, the reward for producers based on demand and supply *a posteriori* dispenses with the need for a planning system and thus with the possibility for everybody to participate democratically in the planning of production, distribution, and consumption. Second, those producers meeting the (manipulated) taste of the consumers would be able to sell their goods at a higher price and thus to accumulate wealth at the expense of other, less able or fortunate, producers. Solidarity among producers would be substituted by egoism and competition. At the same time, individual laborers, or groups of laborers, would be made to pay for the discrepancies between supply and demand. A skewed distribution of wealth would emerge and this could not but corrode the initial socialist egalitarian principle "to each according to their labor."[14] Third, whenever goods were not to be sold, the labor gone into their production would be wasted. Waste would become an inherent feature of an egalitarian system, even in the absence of production for profit. Fourth, even if endowments were initially the same, a skewed income distribution would facilitate accumulation of wealth, power relations based on these differences, and ultimately the re-appearance of capitalist relations.

Egalitarianism, then, requires a planned economic system. This is certainly a startling statement, after what has happened in 1989. But the planned economy referred to in this work is the opposite of the so-called socialist economies of the Soviet type. At this point, one meets the often heard question: if production is planned beforehand, would consumer freedom disappear? Of course not. The point is that there can be no generalized consumer freedom if the producers themselves are not free. In other words, the question is whether a system is based on some form of planned and egalitarian production or retains the anarchy of production. In the former case, there would be not only the production of the needed quantity of goods, given that production would be based on previously surveyed needs, but also consumer freedom, given that the consumers would have indicated beforehand what they wish to consume in the coming period. This is not socially irresponsible freedom, freedom to consume irrespective of other people's needs and at the expense of other, less wealthy, consumers (given that production is geared to the needs of those who have sufficient purchasing power, it is production for these latter's consumption and not for those who cannot afford those goods), but socially responsible freedom, freedom to consume goods whose production has been socially approved through democratic planning and taking into consideration each other's needs. Moreover, this freedom would be paired to consumer satisfaction. In fact, under solidaristic economic relations, producers would identify themselves with consumers and, because of this, production units would turn out the best feasible quality goods. But this presupposes a self-managed socio-economic system.

Only an egalitarian price system can be a condition for the supersession of capitalism and of all its dehumanizing aspects. A mimicking of the capitalist distribution system (market, money prices) implanted in a "market-socialist" context cannot but reproduce inequality, waste, egoism, injustice and all those features upon which capitalism thrives. The most informed and candid supporters of market-socialism do recognize that "the regulation of production and consumption by markets can lead to major injustices, economic irrationality, and ecological damage" (Sayer and Walker, 1992, 232) but seem to accept these negative features simply because:

> The chief advantage of markets over other modes is their ability to facilitate allocational efficiency while minimizing the information costs of microeconomic coordination. Markets allow decentralized coordination of individual consumers' and producers' actions, and the price mechanism makes the allocation of resources responsive to relative scarcities and consumer demand, insofar as that demand is backed by purchasing power (ibid.).

The simple truth is that for the great (and growing) majority of the world's population demand is *not* backed by (sufficient) purchasing power. Therefore, the allocation of resources might be responsive to relative scarcities backed by sufficient purchasing power but is totally indifferent to those needs whose satisfaction cannot be backed by sufficient purchasing power. Another way to put this is by asking the question: how do we measure allocational efficiency? If efficiency is measured in terms of profit maximization, then indeed the markets' and market prices' "ability to facilitate allocational efficiency" cannot be disputed. If, on the other hand, efficiency is measured in terms of obliteration of "major injustices, economic irrationality, and ecological damage," then the answer cannot but be different. It all comes down to what one thinks a better society should be. If one means a less unequal production, distribution, and consumption system but still a capitalist system, then prices might be introduced together with various forms of safety nets for the less fortunate. If one means a different socio-economic system based upon solidarity, equality and real freedom, then the capitalist (money) price system should go.

It follows that socialism is not only a different socio-economic system. It also requires a different type of mentality, an altruistic, cooperative, egalitarian mentality. *This*, the creation of such a mentality is the real challenge ahead for socialism. But the market and market prices are functional for the constant reproduction of the opposite type of mentality, egoistic and individualistic. Thus, if one accepts the former one has to accept the latter. The standard critique of a system based on planning on the other hand, is based on the supposed impossibility to wholly coordinate planning, production and consumption of "millions of goods" and submits that this task is easily performed by demand and supply *a posteriori*:

> At the limit, suppliers and buyers need know little or nothing of each others' situations and motives, for feed-back in terms of exchange value –or more particularly price– can prompt appropriate responses without expensive surveys, endless committee meetings or cumbersome political agreements, which can never produce more than approximate and inflexible assessments of relative scarcity and demands (Sayer and Walker 1992, 232).

However, first, we are not told in terms of which rationality (profit maximization versus the satisfaction of needs) the appropriateness of the responses should be judged. Second, "expensive surveys, endless committee meetings or cumbersome political agreements" are features of both spurious capitalism and classic capitalism (think of how much time and labor goes into the negotiation of international prices) and therefore would be an element of market-socialism as well. Third, in terms of waste and lack of utilization of human possibilities, human labor, and natural endowments, the capitalist system is unsurpassed (think of economic crises, unemployment, poverty, the production of weapons and wars, the conscious destruction of commodities or the conscious restriction of production in the middle of huge unsatisfied needs, etc.). Fourth, scarcity is partly artificially created (think of the new needs created by sales efforts). It is because of these and other reasons as well, the statement that ex-post assessment of needs (through the market) is to be preferred to the ex-ante assessment (through the plan) is gratuitous. But, aside from all this, the crucial point is that these advocates of market-socialism clearly (and consistently) reject the need to develop an egalitarian mentality, i.e. the "suppliers and buyers need know little or nothing of each others' situations and motives." As Sayer and Walker put it:

> Why should individuals have to get involved in decisions regarding production or consumption of specific products about which they know nothing and could never know enough, however much time they devoted to the task? If we want the benefits of division of labor...then we have to accept much of what goes with it, including the division of knowledge and the anonymity and functionality of social relations between producers and consumers (Sayer and Walker 1992, 250).

Here another standard argument against egalitarianism emerges, the impossibility to conjugate solidarity and egalitarianism with efficiency. However, the question is not whether some type of technical division of labor should be retained or not. Rather, the question is *what kind* of division of labor should replace the capitalist one. Aside from the fact that a technically feasible egalitarian division of labor is possible (see below), the above passage rests on a widespread misunderstanding. An egalitarian division of labor does not imply that we know about, and even less that we carry out, all the tasks necessary to participate to all of society's labor processes. What it does imply is (a) a restructuring of tasks into clusters (positions) such that each position offers equal possibilities for balanced human development and (b) maximum mobility between these balanced positions both within and among labor processes for maximum human development. This implies a type of planning which does provide sufficient information to all producers and consumers for them to know which consequences their planned production and consumption have for the rest of society. Technical knowledge of nuclear reactors is not needed to decide whether this way to produce energy is desirable or not. There is thus no purely technical reason to retain the anonymity and thus the egoism of the capitalist social relations.

There is a qualitative difference between producing and consuming goods while being aware of the effects these economic acts have on other producers and consumers and a system which disregards such considerations. This latter system is precisely the one which is based on the market. The market "communicates nothing social or personal to producers any more than [does] to consumers-only prices and quantities" (M. Albert and R. Hahnel, 1981, 35. See also 1991a and 1991b). In other words, the market is impersonal, the very antithesis of a human-centered economic system. Moreover, market and prices are competitive and cannot but generate a competitive ethic, which is inherently at odds with a solidaristic ethic. Prices indicate what one consumer can purchase in competition with, and thus at the cost of, other consumers and what one producer can appropriate in competition with, and thus at the cost of the consumer.[15]

Many commentators either to fail to see or dispute this point. For example, A. Sayer and R. Walker (1992) claim that "markets are modes of integration which can co-exist with several different kinds of social relations of production." However, egalitarian production relations require egalitarian distribution relations which are inconsistent with markets as sites of price formation. The only type of "market" which is consistent with egalitarian relations is the place at which people pick up the goods they need by turning in labor vouchers indicating the number of hours worked and thus giving right to a certain proportion of the hours of new labor contained in those goods. But this is neither the usual meaning of, nor the meaning attached to, the notion of market by the advocates of market-socialism. Once the capitalist market is accepted, the rest of the capitalist society must follow. This is most clearly portrayed by D. Elson's model of a socialized market.

Essentially, a socialized market is one in which prices are set by public bodies. The principal role is given to a Price and Wage Commission which, among other thing, "should guide the formation of prices and wages" (1995, 33). The Price and Wage Commission would generate (set) price and wage norms. However, buyers and sellers can, if they so wished, depart from the norm (op. cit., 33). Moreover, frequent departures from the norm might suggest the need for these norms to be revised. Finally, this commission as well as other "public market makers need to be complements by publicly organized networks of buyers and sellers" which "would form the basis of a decentralized social planning process" (op. cit., 34). Elson's examples of what she means clearly indicate that she thinks of a type of indicative planning. As she says, "Japanese and French strategic planning are perhaps the nearest to what I have in mind" (op. cit., 34). One cannot but be puzzled by this grotesque notion of socialism, until when the other features of Elson's model are appraised.

In Elson's view, worker-managed enterprises would seek to maximize profits (calculated on the basis of these centrally regulated prices) while at the same time producing those goods which have been indicated as desirable by a democratic decision making process. It does not take much to see that this proposal transforms the workers into capitalists collectively aiming at the maximization of profit for *their own* enterprise. The egoistic features inherent in market-based distribution are introduced at the level of production as well. This is because the relations of production have not been truly socialized. Rather, their ownership has been enlarged to all members of the enterprise, instead of being restricted to only some of them. In this blueprint, conflicts of interest are systemic and can only be held in check by, and mediated through, central bodies. The implicit assumption behind this conception seems to be that individuals (or individual enterprises) can promote the welfare of the collectivity only by pursuing their own egoistic interests. The invisible hand is elevated to the common feature of all economic systems rather then being seen as the theorization and rationalization of a socially specific exploitative economic system.

Moreover, once profit maximization becomes the driving force of the economy, the capitalist concept of economic rationality is bound to introduce the division between mental and material labor, the alienating (capitalist) technical division of labor, the emergence of a layer of experts concentrating knowledge and thus power, and all other features of the capitalist organization of production. Enterprises might be legally worker-managed but, inasmuch as they aim at the maximization of profits, they are based on production relations which necessarily lead to the re-emergence of a class of capitalists (perhaps in a different form, as in the case of spurious capitalism). They, in the end, will have to become also the legal owners of the means of production. The objection that "worker-owners need not use their profits to employ wage laborers and hence become capitalists" (Sayer and Walker, 1992, 266) ignores that these worker-owners are already capitalists exploiting themselves and that, if their enterprise must survive through competition, they will have to hire other laborers. If they will not do it, others will and they will face bankruptcy.

In short, the notion of socialism inherent in this type of proposals is basically an improved version of capitalism which, oddly enough, seems to have found its ideal model in the "relations of reciprocity, good will and persuasion, as happens in Japanese economic coordination" (Elson 1995, 42). Neither the eternalization of the invisible hand nor the belief in the possibility of a radical improvement of the capitalist system are very new. The only new element in Elson's proposal seems to be the status ascribed to the Japanese model of economic coordination as a socialist ideal.

Capitalist Rationality Versus Egalitarian Rationality[16]

Against capitalist rationality, a different rationality should be set. This is that of a society based on *co-operation*, on *self-management* (the free association of producers who decide what to produce, for whom, why and how), and on *egalitarianism*, in short a *socialist society*. The notion of human nature subscribed to in this view is diametrically opposed to the neo-liberal one and which has been smuggled into the several notions of market-socialism. This notion pushes "specialization" to its extreme and makes of people caricatures of themselves. The alternative, egalitarian, notion stands for the largest possible development of the individual, for the unfolding of all the facets of the individual's personality. This must hold for everybody and thus must imply egalitarianism, which implies co-operation, which in its turn implies self-management. Neo-liberalism claims that it aims at the free development of the individual, but at the same time it hides the narrowest notion of human beings. The contradiction inherent in the neo-liberalist approach is that the individual reaches maximum freedom through the performance of only one task, i.e. through the development of only one aspect of an individual's personality. This thesis has been challenged on a variety of grounds. Here I shall briefly mention only four of them.[17]

First, there is the question of the presumed impossibility to achieve a different, egalitarian, division of labor. This objection rests either on the notion of a supposedly "egoistic," a-historical, human nature[18] or on a carefully cultivated and endlessly repeated misunderstanding: the impossibility, it is said, for everybody to be able to do everything. But the realistic question is not the abolition of any form of technical division of labor. Rather, the question is how to restructure the division of labor in such a way that all positions (jobs) are "balanced" in the specific sense that they all, while requiring different tasks, offer roughly the same possibility for self-realization (including a balanced "mix" between material and mental labor). This new structure of positions should be complemented by their flexible nature (the internal composition of positions should be changed whenever the exigencies of the individuals so require) and by the possibility for individuals to move from one position to another (again, whenever the exigencies of the individuals so require). *Maximum feasible balancing within positions,*

*flexibility of positions, and rotation among positions should be the three
basic principles of an egalitarian technical division of labor.* This implies
constant re-qualification of labor.

Second, it is argued that if "specialization" enhances "productivity," less
specialization also implies less production and productivity. The question
then would become one of a trade-off between production, productivity and
specialization on the one hand and human self-realization on the other. It
should be clear by now that what is referred to in this critique is capitalist
specialization and productivity. Put in these terms, the critics' argument
becomes irrelevant and the question meaningless. To begin with, the aim of
an egalitarian society should not be the maximum production and
productivity of use values (this latter being the maximum amount of goods
per unit of capital invested). Rather, its aim should be *to achieve the
maximum development for each and for all.* This *should be the yardstick with
which to measure productivity.* The production of use values should be
subsumed to this basic principle. Also, it can be argued that even in terms of
use values produced, productivity might be greater if laborers will really be
in charge of their own lives than if they have to be either forced or convinced
to do unrewarding and alienating jobs. Moreover, even if one were to
concede (for the sake of argument) that a socialist system would be less
"productive" than a capitalist one, the transformation of the organization of
production and thus the abolition of the waste inherent in advertisement and
in the production of weapons, of economic crises, of the public and private
institutions of repression, etc. would liberate sufficient labor power and time
for the production of a quantity of use values adequate for all to satisfy their
socially determined needs, i.e. to afford the luxury of being less
"productive."[19]

Third, de-skilling has been denounced as a negative feature of the
capitalist technical division of labor. But, the critics ask, would not there be
de-skilling also in a socialist society based on an egalitarian division of
labor? For example, should everybody have to write their own computer
program before being able to use it? Would the use of pre-written programs
(rather than the actual writing of those programs by the users) not imply a
process of de-skilling?

This question has actually already been answered above, through the
concept of balanced positions. If one loses the abilities inherent in being able
to write a computer program, he or she should be put in a position to develop
other skill (perhaps through the use of that program) which offer equivalent
chances for human development. Or, the use of pre-written programs might
increase free time. In this case, if the task of an egalitarian society is the

fostering of human self-realization for everybody as fully as possible (given biological, technical and social constraints), the question is whether these possibilities for maximum development are created in the time set free thanks to the use of pre-written computer programs. Under capitalism the incorporation of knowledge in machines (e.g. software) is time saving but, aside from counter-tendencies, this extra free time is used neither to reduce the working day[20] nor to increase the possibilities for self-realization of those operating those machines. Through de-skilling people are robbed of their freedom to develop themselves. This is why de-skilling should be resisted.

In an egalitarian society, on the other hand, given that human self-realization should be a continuous and changing process requiring, among other things, not only constant cultivation of the same skills but also continuous a acquisition of new skills and an abandonment of already acquired skills (if not needed any more), the incorporation of a skill in the machine should be both justified and compensated by the possibility to learn and use other, more desired, skills. Within this context, the notion of de-skilling loses its meaning and it is theoretically confusing to retain this notion in a different social setting. Taylor, the father of "scientific management," in trying to pre-empt the above critique, makes the following clumsy move:

> The frontiersman had to be not only a surgeon, but also an architect, house-builder, lumberman, farmer, soldier, and doctor, and he had to settle his law cases with a gun. You would hardly say that the life of the modern surgeon is any more narrowing, or that he is more of a wooden man than the frontiersman. The many problems to be met and solved by the surgeon are just as intricate and difficult and as developing and broadening in their way as those of the frontiersman (Taylor 1985, 125-6).

In this example, the task of the surgeon has indeed replaced all other activities but at the same time it has been greatly expanded, not narrowed. The Tayloristic division of labor, on the other hand, implies that the surgeon would be reduced to, say, manning a machine which has incorporated the surgeon's qualities so that the surgeon would have been reduced to an unskilled laborer performing a de-qualified, repetitive, etc., task. Moreover, there is absolutely no reason why in an egalitarian society the surgeon could not perform also (some of) these other duties, with the exclusion of course of settling his law cases with a gun.

Fourth, ask the critics, could not a capitalist technical division of labor, for example the Tayloristic one, be used in an egalitarian society, for example on a rotation basis, if everybody so desired? Of course, it will be the exclusive right of those who will be confronted by this alternative, and who will bear the consequences of this choice, to opt for any kind of division of labor they might want, right or wrong. However, on the basis of what said above, it is possible to argue that this choice would be mistaken. There is no difference between, on the one hand, some people forcing some other people to engage in alienating work and, on the other, everybody agreeing to engage in alienating work, either in turns or all together. The de-humanizing aspects of work do not disappear just because that decision has been "freely" taken. One thing is to leave people free to make their own choices, right or wrong. Another is to have one's own opinions about what people should do and argue for them. By not choosing sides on such matters one, far from showing a tolerant and democratic attitude, simply ducks the question.

Moreover, the argument just criticized does not adequately assess the dangers inherent in the adoption of a capitalist organization of production. If, whenever possible,[21] no sustained and vigorous effort is made to abolish undesired activities exactly in that realm in which people must engage (given that the reproduction of society and of humans is dependent on those activities), the structural possibility that some people will systematically try to dodge those activities and that some other people will be systematically stuck with them is re-created. In this case, the need to force some people to do some types of work might re-emerge. This is why, as far as human self-realization is concerned, one of the features of an egalitarian society should have to be the abolition of the separation between labor time and free time, i.e. this is why labor too (just as those activities outside the realm of labor) would have to become a spontaneous and joyful activity making human self-realization possible.

The real alternative is between classical capitalism, spurious capitalism, and market "socialism" on the one hand and, on the other, socialism, which I mean to be a socio-economic system based on cooperation (solidarity), egalitarianism, and self-management in planning, allocation, production, distribution, and consumption in harmony with nature. The specific forms of this radically alternative systems cannot be forecast. They will emerge as a result of each country's specific history, including the history of its struggle to move from a capitalist society to a egalitarian one. However, just as there are general principle of capitalism which apply to all specific capitalist countries, so there are general principles which will apply to all egalitarian countries. But the identification of these principles belongs to a different work.

Notes

1. Tittenbrun (1991) argues cogently that there is no relationship between private ownership and efficiency.
2. There are advantages and disadvantages for each of these (and other) names. Here, they are used interchangeably.
3. The recent wave of privatization of public telephone companies is a case in point. "An investigation by the Financial Times [disclosed, G.C] that public phone companies around the world were over-charging their customers between $10bn and $20bn a year. International call prices, which are typically two to four times more than costs, are kept high by a series of cartel-like practices" H. Dixon, 1991a.
4. Imitation does not mean carbon copy. The Eastern European countries were imitations of the Soviet economy because of the determinant role the central plan had vis-à-vis the market. But there were large differences among the different countries as far as, for example, the role of the market was concerned.
5. For example, in 1991 Kazakhistan planned to retain the revenues of the sale of state enterprises "to help it plug a Rbs13bn budget deficit" (L. Boulton, 1991).
6. In this case too ideology holds that privatization and the shift to capitalism will increase efficiency and ultimately wealth and prosperity. Again, the paper by Tittenbrum (1991) disposes of this myth. The standard argument is that "in a market model, cost minimization is 'natural,' a consequence of trying to make profits. Markets being imperfect, cost is sometimes not minimized, but the propensity is there, in the model. The "central-directive model depends on the planners doing the minimizing, and if they do not, no one else will" (Nove, 1986, 40). The bitter irony is that this "remedy" –the market– is proposed just when mounting privatization in the West is an indication of how deep the economic crisis is, i.e. of how much human misery (e.g. unemployment and poverty) is increasing, in short of how inefficient the capitalist economy is as a means to satisfy human needs.
7. Given that "socialism" and "communism" have been disqualified and are associated with the exact opposite of what is advocated here, I prefer to refer to cooperative, egalitarian, and self-managed societies. I shall use any of these three terms according to the aspect of these societies singled out for discussion. It will be possible to use the terms socialism or communism again, to indicate an egalitarian, cooperative and just society, only when, and if, the labor movement will have redeemed these terms from their present connotation associated with "actually realized socialism," i.e. spurious capitalism.
8. One way money manifests its social, class, content within a different social system is that it makes possible the accumulation of private wealth and thus the re-introduction of capitalist ownership and production relations.
9. See Carchedi, 1991, chaps. 3 and 7.
10. Two more points are usually mentioned in this connection. First, labors can be of different intensities. These latter can be measured according to physiological criteria, as for example the amount of calories consumed. Hours of more intensive labor can count, then, as a multiple of hours of less intensive labor and be rewarded accordingly. Second, labor can be more or less qualified, according to the education, training, etc. which has been necessary to form the different categories of laborers. This is a significant redistributional variable within a capitalist context but not in an egalitarian one. In this latter type of society, the fact that one has cost more to society to be educated and trained gives him or her no right to a greater proportion of societal wealth. The objection that in this case people might not improve their capabilities overlooks the fact that in an egali-

tarian system people would pursue those activities in which they can realize their inner potentialities at the most. This, rather than income differentials, would be the reason for engaging both in education and in practical training.

11. There is thus no equivalent to the "transformation problem" in its backwards ad infinitum version. This is supposed to impugn the computation of prices, according to the labor theory of value, in a capitalist system but is in fact no problem at all. See Carchedi, 1991, chap. 3.

12. Of course, a part of consumption and production goods has to be set aside into a fund for unforeseen circumstances, etc. These and other considerations are not essential for the present purposes and can be taken on board once the basic differences between capitalist prices and egalitarian prices have been highlighted.

13. For an example of how could take place concretely, see Albert, M. and Hahnel, R. 1991.

14. Of course, any measures aimed at re-distributing the "excess" wealth thus accumulated would only de-motivate production based on these principles.

15. According to J. Robinson (1962, 45), the aim of the price system in a socialist economy is "to make the prices of commodities sold in the shops proportional to their *values*." But under socialism there is no value (labor performed under capitalist production relations) and thus no market, money, and money prices. The importance of this point is not terminological but ideological. Whenever labor embodied is a-critically identified with value, it is the notion of the inevitability of the capitalist system (based on value production) which is surreptitiously, even though unwillingly, propagated.

16. In spite of the fact that the terms "socialism" has been disqualified and is associated with the exact opposite of what is advocated here, I retain this word for lack of a better alternative. I shall refer to socialism as the ensemble of egalitarianism, self-management and cooperation which is referred to. I shall refer to only one of these aspects if emphasis has to be placed on this aspects.

17. Eight partly similar objections have been formulated by J. Elster and convincingly refuted by N. Mobasser (1987).

18. In observing that nearly a decade after the fall of "Communism" no "Western style" capitalism has been created in the former "Communist" countries, A. Greenspan, the Chairman of the FED, recently discovered that "much of what we took for granted in our free market system and assumed to be human nature was not nature at all, but culture" (Hoagland, 1997). What for a first year Sociology student is a plain fact, becomes for the neo-classical economist a revelation.

19. The claim that the principal aim of a socialist system should not be the maximization of production and productivity may sound peculiar, given that Soviet type "socialism" has been characterized as an "economy of scarcity." But the Soviet type societies were not socialist (in the sense highlighted above) and scarcity should and can be explained exactly by the fact that they were not socialist but an incomplete and inefficient form of capitalism.

20. It is important to realize that longer working days and increased intensity of labor can be and have been resisted. But (1) shorter working days and less intensity of labor are not the intention of the capitalists and (2) whenever long periods of time are considered in order to decide whether there has been a shortening of the working day, it is the collective laborer on a global scale (with situations in the Third World reminiscent of the English Industrial Revolution) which should be considered, rather than only that of the developed capitalist countries.

21. Of course, even in an egalitarian society there might be undesired activities. If it will be impossible to "balance" them with other, more desired, activities, only one solution is left:

an equal share of those activities for everybody, exceptions being made for special cases based on special needs.

References

Albert, M. and Hahnel, R. 1981. *Socialism Today and Tomorrow*. Boston: South End Press.
_____. 1991a. *Looking Forward. Participatory Economics for the Twenty First Century*. Boston: South End Press.
_____. 1991b. *The Political Economy of Participatory Economics*. Princeton: Princeton University Press.
Boulton, L. 1991. "Born-again Kazakhstan preaches privatization doctrine." *Financial Times*. October 10.
Carchedi, G. 1991. *Frontiers of Political Economy*. London: Verso.
Carchedi, G. 1997. "The EMU, Monetary Crises and the Single European Currency." *Capital and Class*, No.63, Autumn, 85-114.
Clarke, T. (1990), "Socialized Industry: Social Ownership or Shareholding Democracy?" In S. Clegg (ed.) 1990, 485-513.
Clegg, S. (ed.) 1990. *Organization Theory and Class Analysis. New Approaches and New Issues*. Berlin: De Gruyter.
Dixon, H. 1991a. "Cartel may not yet be broken but it is cracked." *Financial Times*. October 7.
_____. 1991b. "The sleeping giants awaken." *Financial Times*, October 7.
Ellman, M. 1989. *Socialist Planning*. Cambridge: Cambridge University Press.
Elson, D. (ed.) 1995. *Male Bias in the Development Process*. Manchester: Manchester University Press.
Hoagland, J. 1997. "Look who says capitalism needs government." *International Herald Tribune*, August 28.
Mobasser, N. 1987. "Marx and Self-Realization." *New Left Review*, January-February, No.161, 119-128.
Nove, A. 1986. *The Soviet Economic System*. Unwin Hyman.
Robinson, J. 1962. *Economic Philosophy*. Harmondsworth: Penguin Books.
Sayer, A. and Walker, R. 1992. *The New Social Economy*. Oxford: Blackwell.
Taylor, F.W. 1985. *The Principles of Scientific Management*. Hive Publishing Company.
Tittenbrun, J. 1991. "Privatization in Poland: People's Capitalism?," Paper presented at the Conference on *International Privatization: Strategies and Practices*, University of St. Andrews, 12-14 September.

7 Local Democracy Facing with Globalitarianism

JEAN-PIERRE GARNIER

"It is very likely that all the world's
governments will be more or less totalitarian
(...) There is, of course, no reason why these
new totalitarianisms should resemble the old ones."

Aldous Huxley
(*The Best of Worlds*)

Introduction

It has become commonplace to stress the link between capitalist globalization – the universalization of the market, neoliberal deregulation, the abolition of economic controls, domination by commercial firms and transnational conglomerates exercised through supranational institutions – and the growing difficulties which result for nation states seeking to work out coherent and effective economic policies and put them into practice on their national territory, and more generally to maintain their role as cardinal social and cultural reference points in the eyes of their citizens.

Day by day one vital decision after another on investments, employment, health, culture, recreation, information, is transferred from the public sector to the private, whose sole concern is the maximization of profit. Globalitarian logic constrains nation states to implement policies which conform to the world-wide interests of certain financial and industrial groups, as evidenced in the characteristic bias in the edicts handed down by international organizations – towards flexibility, salary cuts, reduction of public expenditure, the elimination of "rigidities" in social protection. It

80

"subordinates the social rights of citizens to the rationale of competition" (Ramonet 1997). By allowing "markets" – that is to say, the social forces linked to their expansion – to set the guidelines for all activity in the societies they dominate, they are in the process of subjecting the entire world to a new type of totalitarianism: globalitarianism.

Inside each country, economic integration into the world-wide market is accompanied by social disintegration. Globalization, in reality, is not all-embracing. Its networks to not encompass the entirety of social space but only certain fragments. From the economic viewpoint, it will include such-and-such a sector, branch, enterprise, type of industry or service, at the same time brushing aside every activity thought unlikely to be of sufficient profitability. From the geographical viewpoint, globalization will include such-and-such a continent, country, region, agglomeration, urban or rural zone, leaving to their own devices such areas as are deemed "uninteresting." From the sociological viewpoint, it will penetrate such-and-such a social stratum in the population – employing diverse criteria – condemning a mass of individuals judged of little use or useless, at best to a precarious existence, at worst to pauperization and marginalization.

Escaping the control of states, which must – by contrast – abide by its "laws," globalization does not entail only the exacerbation of inequalities and, for poorer social layers, a continual downgrading in their conditions of existence. This veritable dictatorship of the economic over the political also empties democracy of its content. For if statesmen (and stateswomen) henceforth confine themselves to managing what "the markets" decide, what remains of the sovereignty which the people is said to exercise, albeit through the mediation of representatives?

Two phenomena result from this which, as they perpetuate themselves and intensify, may in the long term threaten the very reproduction of capitalist productive relations: the weakening of social cohesion and the exhaustion of democratic modes of thought and behavior. Behind these "politically correct" but scientifically inept terms there lurk two very real dangers for the dominant classes.

On the one hand the supposed unity of a society more divided than ever sees itself undermined not by traditional class antagonisms, with the risks of "explosion" so long associated with them, but with an insidious process of social disintegration whose contours seem closer to those of implosion. Collective confrontations where the adversaries are defined and the objectives clearly marked out seem, in effect, to belong to a bygone era. Cleavages of a novel type have appeared where the ever more marked inequalities separating individuals and groups seem to create between them a sort of no-man's-land, isolating them in universes that are not only distinct but also very remote from each other. The interdependence and complementarity, albeit conflictual, which formerly prevailed between people belonging in the last resort to the same "society of equals" has given way to a generalized dissociation and segmentation – some speak of "desocialization."

Exacerbated by the "economic war," the struggle of each against all and "every man for himself" have not only broken up the solidarities engendered in the workplace. One by one, every institution which had been the vehicle for a collective consciousness sees itself caught up in the cataclysm: public services, the social security system, school, churches, parties, trade unions. Unlike open confrontation between social forces with a sharply defined profile and clearly delimited goals, this slow decomposition, whose sporadic explosions of atomized and anomic "urban violence" represent little more than spectacular reaffirmations of the problem, does contain the seeds of serious social dislocation, which could involve local breakdowns of the capitalist system implanted in that society.

On the other hand, but related to the preceding, the endless rotation in and out of office of political parties and leaderships offering no social alternatives robs representative democracy of its credibility in the eyes of citizens. Many lose confidence in those that govern them, whoever they are, and so lose interest in public affairs. The victims of capitalist globalization take refuge for the most part in a stance of disillusioned withdrawal or spiteful resentment. At election time, the former don't vote and the latter vote "incorrectly," that is to say, for the extreme right. But the exhaustion and passivity prevalent up until now among the socially oppressed should not be misread.

It is conceivable that discouragement and resignation could once more give way to rage and revolt. But in the absence of alternative programs, projects and ideals, these could well take on aberrant forms, the danger of which is illustrated both by history and by the events of the most recent past. Among young people, the impression of vegetating inside a society as profoundly unjust as it is unreformable is frequently translated into a hate and rage which, precisely because they are unfocussed, can vent themselves on anything, or anyone. Deprived, seemingly forever, of all hope of seeing an improvement in their situation, some of these ill-fated souls may be led in the long term to express their refusal in apolitical or "subpolitical" forms which are nevertheless profoundly destabilizing for the social order (civic defection, right-wing extremism, religious fundamentalism, delinquency, civil disturbance, terrorism) calling forth a repressive response whose inefficacy grows increasingly apparent.

Faced by these two dangers, certain strategists in French ruling circles, following the advice of a host of social engineering experts, are counting on the resurrection of "local democracy" to enable them to kill two birds with one stone. This at any rate is the picture one gets of the "major project" which, if one is to believe a researcher who has published a summary presentation of it, is henceforth to inspire all thinking and action in relation to urban development in France. "To achieve, thanks to the reconstructed local community, a new social integration with an ongoing democratic order, implying the conscious mobilization of social actors" (Gaudin 1994). Throughout this "learned" formulation in which, as has become customary in urban studies in France, scientific pretension goes happily hand in hand with apologetic designs, a dual objective can be discerned.

On the one hand compensation for disengagement or weakening of the welfare state at the center through decentralized management of the marginalized mass (at the level of the region, the urban area, the borough, the neighborhood), in this way counteracting the tendency to social fragmentation through the reintegration of the excluded into a local collectivity. On the other hand "local self-management," that is to say the franchising-out of domination on a territorial basis to the dominant fraction of the subaltern classes (the municipal or regional political elite or techno-bureaucracy, for the most part of petty-bourgeois intellectual extraction) so as to provide the illusion – with the help of procedures of "participation" and co-operation with residents – of a re-appropriation by the citizenry of the affairs of the *polis*.

This "localization" of democracy as a remedy for social delinkage and civic desertion is more than a little perplexing. One can always dream of reconstructing locally what the global blueprint relentlessly destroys at the national level, namely solidarity and citizenship, among other things. But this comes down to imagining oneself able to extract a particular social space from the grip of globalism without needing to go through a showdown with it.

Towards a Local Democracy?

If one is to take literally the political trademarks utilized to characterize the parties in power in Europe at this particular *fin de siecle*, one could get the impression that social-democracy is once again enjoying palmy days. Taking heart from the recent electoral victories of moderate left-wing parties first in Italy, then in Great Britain and France and, more recently, in Germany, certain optimistic commentators have made their prognosis and have already drawn the conclusion that: "Everywhere in Europe the neo-liberal capitalism which triumphed in the seventies is under pressure" (Mitzman 1997). No doubt it is this pressure that sent share prices skyrocketing at all the world's stock exchanges after each of the victories of the institutional left!

It seems evident to us that the coming to power of "responsible," "reasonable" and "respectable" left-wing coalitions is not a phenomenon which is about to menace the reign of neo-liberalism. Quite the contrary! It will consolidate it, putting the finishing touches on a process which has been under way since the beginning of the seventies, namely the conversion of social democracy to local democracy, a metamorphosis which, all things considered, is the real element of novelty in this *fin de siecle* liberalism.

There is nothing all that new about the grand principles that have been evoked to legitimate its return to power: they are nothing more than a renewal of that secular creed that puts its faith in the glory of the self-regulating free market. The neo-liberal vision consists in essentially nothing more than an "actualization," that is to say an adaptation to the present phase in the development of capitalism, of economic rationalizations drawn from an ideological miscellany including some of the most classical assumptions of conservative thought. Globalization represents nothing more or less than a deterritorialization of the dynamic of competition which, having embraced the entire planet, no longer operates within a politically or socially defined space.

On the other hand, this in no way applies to the management of the social consequences of this economic change. More than ever this management calls for social and political definition of a particular space. But more and more it is the *local* which is being called on to take over from the central state as a framework of reference and a field of action. And that this is so is due, as we shall see, to the fact that "the social" itself is no longer what it was. For, to keep in step with this new social dimension, social democracy must itself undergo renewal. Hence its progressive (or regressive) transformation into a *neo-social-democracy*. Closely bound up with the reign, once again uncontested, of liberalism, it is perhaps this element more than any other which justifies the attachment of the "neo" prefix to the latter also.

As for the reign of the welfare state, which one was in the habit of associating with the preponderance of social democracy on the political scene, it seems already to be largely a thing of the past. Until the mid-seventies, the presence at the summit of the state, in Western countries, of political formations classified as "left-wing" had done much to transform the liberal state into a social state. The rise in living standards, the extension of rights and guarantees, the proliferation of safeguards and protective regulation, the new opportunities for professional advancement...: the popular strata, and particularly the working class, seemed caught up in an irresistible upward movement. But elevation is not emancipation.

The "integration" of the proletarians went hand in hand with the maintenance of their dependence. The disappearance of the particular historical circumstances (the workers' combativeness, the weight of the USSR, economic crisis and world wars, lack of market openings for business...) favoring the compromise on which the welfare state was founded was enough to make integration into dependence give way to dependence without integration (re-christened as "exclusion"). The compromise between capital and labor was in fact only acceptable for the dominant classes to the extent that it promoted a linkage between production and mass consumption within each country. With globalization, capital's strategy for accumulation was gradually freed from its national fetters.

The day is past when the welfare state could be the instrument for partial redistribution of the "fruits of growth" – gains in productivity – to the benefit of workers and their families. In the never-ending quest for profit in which companies are engaged on the global scale for the "conquest of market sectors" – commonly dubbed "economic warfare" – given that the fragile balance between capital and labor did not entail a dissolution of social antagonisms but merely a provisional regulation of their dynamic – it should not come as a surprise that the bourgeoisie, profiting from the downturn in the workers' movement, should once again take the offensive. In short, no "economic war" between capitalists without a renewal of the social war against the proletariat, this time with the former taking the initiative.

Since the heyday of the welfare state, the more or less extended presence in power of "socialists" or "social-democrats" has not checked the steady contraction of the beneficent role of the state, as evidenced by the abolition of salary scales, the dismantlement of social protection, the provision of incentives for capital concentration, through lockouts, or the opening of nationalized enterprises to private capital... when they are not purely and simply privatized. It is also quite possible under the cover of "modernization" for the Left in power to accelerate the process, with the Right, so as to avoid social unrest, gladly leaving to it the task of doing the dirty work. Thus alternations in office may well take place at the summit of the state without this in any way hindering the pursuit of the politics of "rigor" or austerity, of deregulation, flexibilization, restructuring. This is why, following the example of their overtly "liberal" counterpart, social-democratic or other comparable governments no longer succeed in putting up an effective resistance to unemployment and poverty.

"It is necessary to choose between the confidence of the markets and the confidence of the people. Policies which aim at retaining the confidence of the markets lose the confidence of the people." (Bourdieu 1997). Collaborate or resist, such – in other words – is the most important choice which should have separated the Left from the Right in the face of the veritable "class warfare" conducted on a global scale at the initiative of the bourgeoisie since the seventies in order to claw back the rights won by the working class over the preceding decades (Chomsky 1996). Because, as testified in Europe by the intergovernmental consensus forged around the Maastricht Treaty, the Stability Pact and the establishment of the Euro, the "convergence" is not only of an economic order; it is also political.

It is well, from this viewpoint, to be wary of certain simplistic, even Manichean, interpretations, opposing the State to the market. As in the historical phase of institution of a market economy in the last century, notably in England, "it is always the political authorities who create the conditions for self-regulation by the market by arranging their own eviction from the economic sphere" (Barillon 1996). The only thing that has changed is the scale on which this voluntary resignation takes place. It is governments and not "markets" – for which they are tending to become the proxies, on the planetary level this time – that at the time of the G7 conference at Lille, for example, in April 1996, reached agreement on "conclusions," always oriented towards globalitarian logic: reinforcement of the "essential role" of the private sector; promotion of the entrepreneurial spirit and investment in humans as in capital; pursuit of the liberalization of foreign trade; lowering of social charges in European countries. In the same way, free-exchanges zones such as ALENA, MERCOSUR, APEC,

AFTA and, of course, the European Union, appear as political creations involving several nation states, on the basis of accords which owe nothing to the spontaneity of the markets. "In short, it is not so much that the economy seizes its independence as that the State grants its emancipation to the economy and to the markets" (Barillon 1996).

Thus, in the face of the imperatives of globalization, "social capitalism" is no longer in fashion. But it does not follow that the authorities are no longer interested in social issues, particularly now that these pose themselves anew and with such acuity. Accordingly, both Right and Left have been brought to converge on a second point, complementary to the first; "localizing the social," that is to say *entrusting the local agencies of the state with the mission of handling the local fallout from economic globalization.*

Many authors have emphasized that socio-spatial polarization engendered by globalization greatly increases inequality, to the extent where it threatens society with disintegration. Even if this perspective of fragmentation matters little to most of those who reap profits from capitalist globalization, the same is not true of the most clear-sighted of them and particularly those who are charged with the long-term defense of the established order. The countless dissertations devoted to the maintenance of "social cohesion" bear witness to this. The recourse that is had to this sociological "concept" is not to be explained only by the desire to downplay (in impeccably pseudo-scientific language) the triviality of an imperative more political than secular: to preserve the said order against the divisions, the tensions and conflicts which sap its foundations. Formerly one preferred to speak of guaranteeing social peace or safeguarding national unity. But the specter which will henceforth haunt certain ruling class circles is no longer revolution. A new apparition has taken its place: the specter of decomposition.

The ever-growing contrast between the expansion of new high-income strata and the massive increase in urban pauperization is beginning to alarm political leaders and their advisers, who are convinced that the days of peaceful coexistence of rich and poor are numbered. Doubtless, with the failure of "real socialism," the decline of the workers' movement and the discrediting – perhaps temporary? – of progressive utopias, the possessing classes no longer have to fear a showdown with conscious and organized popular forces embodying a radical spirit of social transformation. In any case, the ruling elite have enough confidence in their apparatus of repression, which is constantly being reinforced and perfected, to tolerate the existence of pockets of poverty to which one can always in the last resort apply the police-state strategy of urban "containment" imported from the United States. It consists in isolating and containing the "new barbarians" inside the catchment zones of the most run-down popular neighborhoods, their "demographic equilibrium" being in any case greatly assisted by malnutrition and the lack of medical care due to downsizing of welfare. Under intensive surveillance, the marginals are then permitted to fight it out between themselves or destroy themselves through the consumption of hard drugs. At the same time the self-isolation of the privileged in super-protected residential enclaves, often enclosed in barbed wire and guarded by private police, has so far sheltered them from this encroaching urban violence, the "return of the repressed" corresponding to the economic and social violence they have sustained from globalizing capitalism.

From this viewpoint, as one commentator aptly put it, "the social question becomes not so much the problem posed by the poor as the preoccupation expressed by the rich" (Commaille 1997). But this is so precisely because the latter, in spite of everything, sense that the proliferation of security measures, both public and private, will not succeed forever in stemming the rise of a diffuse delinquency and criminality, even harder to control insofar as their manifestations are often unpredictable.

When there is nothing more to claim and to negotiate, and when one has lost all hope of seeing an improvement in one's situation, "gratuitous" violence is the sole luxury which the dispossessed can afford. Deprived to the point of being devoid of ideals and political objectives, the powerless henceforth have only one power, that of destabilizing the social order by indulging in destructive, indeed self-destructive, behavior: theft, violence, riots, sabotage, bloodshed... This is why, from the heights of the office towers which symbolize, in urban space, the position they occupy in the social hierarchy, the power elite does not serenely survey the misery of the world stretched out at their feet. Even if they have nothing more to fear from the focused violence of the class struggle, they have everything to fear from the *erratic violence of the declassed.*

In the fierce competition which pits one country or one city against another, to be regarded as a "bad risk" is at all events a handicap for those charged with the administration of a population center. To attract investors, managers, researchers or engineers, the "general climate" is not unimportant. It counts among those factors in competitiveness that are designated "non-cost" factors because they have to do with "intangible" features of culture and human relations whose importance for economic development is said to testify to the relativity of the totalitarian encroachment of the global market, whereas in fact it merely confirms it, as we shall see below. More generally, beyond a certain threshold of desocialization, that is to say atomization and breaking up of the social fabric, the reproduction of the relations of production itself runs the risk of being affected by it. "We should be very careful," one expert warned. "A significant proportion of our productivity is bound up with social capital, for which we are the heirs to a number of forms and conventions, of social accords patiently elaborated over the years. Too much exclusion can progressively undermine this social capital" (Brender 1997).

But how can this "social capital" be preserved when economic capital, that is to say globalized capitalism, is putting in question the forms of social regulation inherited from the preceding period? Has one not for nearly two decades now been subjected to a barrage of criticisms of the inefficiency, the rigidity and the wastage of the welfare state? And do its defenders, for their part, not deplore the way that it has contracted and ultimately crumbled? This is to leave out of account the radical change that the forms of the state have undergone in most European countries, and particularly in France. It consists in delegating the management of social issues to local areas. For, contrary to what is often claimed, *it is the decentralization of the social state that one is currently witnessing, not its abolition.*

The process got under way in the 70s. Globalization served merely to make it more urgent. More than ever, the social state is called on to pick up the bill for the damage, i.e. repair or avert the damage caused by capitalist accumulation to the quality of life and living standards of the popular masses. But with the green light given by governments of all political shades to "restructuration" and flexibilization, the damage for which the bill must be picked up is not only more extensive. The fragments of the damaged society are more and more difficult to stick back together!

The increase in the numbers of those left on the shelf, left to their own devices, exposed to risk, disaffiliated or otherwise excluded – has got to the point where is causing a hypertrophy of the social sector, that is to say an overdevelopment of those institutions, measures, procedures and professions bound up with the control of populations which are debilitated and marginalized or threatened with becoming so. The central agencies of the State are no longer in a position to assume this mission on their own. This is even more so the case insofar as they are being subjected simultaneously to the pressures of the new reality which is weighing down on them and weakening the nation-state, namely globalization. Under threat of being submerged, absorbed, engulfed by the management of a civil society in a state of radical upheaval, the central government is forced to unload onto its periphery, that is to say onto its regional sub-agencies or external services (local collectivities), a great part of the work of social assistance, direction, rehabilitation or repression of the strata of the population that have fallen victim to globalization. To put it differently, the central state, overburdened with social tasks, must jettison all of its functions that can be accomplished at lower cost and with greater efficacity at lower levels. The orientation and general thrust of social policy will nonetheless remain within its exclusive jurisdiction. In France researchers have invented a new "scientific" label to facilitate the ideological promotion of this new form of state domination: "the animating state." In other words, instead of trying to regulate everything – i.e. the totality of the "social" – through direct bureaucratic management of its every detail, the central state will be henceforth in a position to exercise overall control without needing to have control over all (Bihr and Heinrich 1980).

With all the variations proper to the socio-historic particularities of each country, the social-liberal policies of some and the liberal social policies of others have thus led to the institutionalization of a form of decentralized regulation of the contradictions born of the destructuring and restructuring of capitalist social relations on the global plane. In this respect the municipalities and the regions administered by the elected representatives of "progressive" parties, whether socialist, social-democrat or communist, have played a pioneering role, facilitated, it is true, by a long tradition of municipal socialism or communism. Governing from the Left in the local level so as to be better able to govern from the Right nationally: such seems, in effect, to be the implicit principle which has guided the new apportionment of tasks between central and local government, if you can really describe as "Left" the *therapeutic territorializing of mass marginalization*. For this therapy does not aim at cure.

Certainly the effects of the diminished redistributive capacities of the social State at the center have been to some extent alleviated by the transfer of resources to the local level. But this transfer could not really operate in accordance with the principle of communicating vessels, because the strict austerity policies implemented from the beginning of the seventies applied to the state as a whole. In any case, the role of local collectivities in reducing what in France today is called the "social fracture" is not limited to distributing benefits and assistance to the needy. Nor is it restricted to providing welfare housing and collectively owned goods. In some towns affected by de-industrialization, public and quasi-public employment (in municipal administration, health, education, socio-cultural activities etc.) plays an important economic role. It is not at all uncommon, for example, in a typical urban agglomeration affected by factory closures as a result of bankruptcy or emigration of capital, for the largest remaining employer to be the municipal administration, along with, often, the hospital. This tendency has been accentuated by a proliferation of collective goods and services, and, more recently, the spread of "neighborhood employment" designed to provide assistance to – and above all, as we shall see, to police – the poor. In the France of the 80s and 90s, economic stagnation and the contraction of the number of available jobs in the private sector has thus been very partially compensated for by a movement towards provision of employment in the local public sector, particularly as a consequence of decentralization, which has given a real shot in the arm to personnel recruitment.

Having said this, it is worth going back to what was mentioned in passing above, namely that in the era of globalization the "social question" is dealt with in such a way as to *regulate the non-solution* of the problem of unemployment, poverty and low quality of life, but not solve it. One reason for this is that in the course of the same evolution the meaning of the concept of the "social" has itself undergone a change.

It is no longer a question, as in the three decades of the post-war "golden age" of compensating for the lack of earning power which then afflicted certain social strata characterized as "underprivileged." They were called this because they benefited little, or less, from the social progress which for the majority of the population resulted from economic development. By contrast, with the rise of globalism economic growth is in no way incompatible with social regression. One could even argue that growth nowadays implies regression, as has been recognized by the heads of the World Economic Forum themselves: "in the past higher profits meant more work security and better salaries. But the way in which transnational companies are forced to operate in the global economy means that it is now routine for companies simultaneously to announce a new increase in profits and a new wave of sackings" (World Economic Forum 1996). In these circumstances there is nothing surprising about the fact that when a fall in unemployment figures is announced, the Dow Jones index also falls!

One after another, Left governments have rallied willy-nilly to the virtues of capitalism restructured along the lines of the Anglo-Saxon model, i.e. recentered on the financial markets with their first priority the satisfaction of shareholders. It is therefore only to be expected that the social consequences will become ever more catastrophic in future: increasing unemployment and under-employment, salary cuts – except for senior executives and managers – growing insecurity in professional life, the consignment of millions of individuals to living standards below the poverty level, including numerous underpaid employees (the working poor). It is evident that in these conditions changes in standards will entail corresponding changes in the nature of "the social," with the latter largely explicable by the former.

In every country where it has come to power, social democracy is less and less likely to steer the socio-economic system in a direction favorable to workers. Lacking the ability to establish or maintain a social capitalism securing as it once did the well-being of the popular strata, it too comes to revise downward its criteria for "the social." Instead of presiding over recovery, the new social criteria will have the function of presiding over regression. *The "social project" of which the Left still claims at time to be the vehicle is no longer that of a different society but simply that of a different style of management.*

"Localizing the social" does not henceforth amount to working at the grass roots for an impossible reintegration of the rejects of globalization into society as a whole. On the contrary, assuming at the outset the impossibility of this (elevated to the status of fatal inevitability) one strives to "administer" non-employment or pseudo-employment, as with the TUCs[2] and CES[3] (city job schemes, youth job schemes, etc.) that is to say to *regulate on site the social turbulence* that this situation quite naturally engenders. Day after day local authorities bend over backwards in the name of "urban social development" to promote, sustain or encourage in the relegation zones innumerable "activities" thought to be conducive to the "re-creation of social bonding." One fashionable formulation among many others which we should not allow to mislead us.

On the plea of favoring the acquisition of solidarity and civility among people who have nothing more in common than their shared social exclusion, what has been got under way, in short, is a new strategy for keeping poor people in their place. It "invites them to live together peacefully so that the affluent can live in the exclusiveness of their own comfort without feeling the menace from without of these populations without resources in the heart of the cities or on their periphery" (Donzelot and Jaillet 1997). Such an interpretation may perhaps seem extreme. It is taken from a report submitted to the Committee on Challenges to Modern Society set up by ... NATO!

Corresponding to the "new social question" there is thus a new treatment which, as we argued above, does not aim at curing the patient – which would mean opposing capitalist globalization – but at putting him on drip-feed. This treatment assumes a number of different guises, which it would take an entire essay to describe.[4] Let us confine ourselves to enumerating them: the economic treatment (make - work jobs, the neo-domesticity of "neighborhood employment," "youth job schemes" including "mediation" (i.e. social control where the controlled become controllers, etc.); social treatment (charitable and assistance-oriented); cultural treatment (artistic and sporting or games-oriented); media treatment (a mixture of propaganda and advertising); repressive shock treatment (the courts, the police, the military) as the ultimate recourse when the others fail.

In all cases, including in matters of security, it is in the first instance up to the local authority to assume the role of protecting the weak, even though – as will be seen below – what has to be protected, preserved or safeguarded is not so much a fragile, vulnerable or endangered population as a society whose functioning could be seriously upset by a rebellion of the rejected. As one expert already quoted has put it: "when social solidarity is assumed in a clear-headed manner, it is a central factor in competitiveness" (Brender 1997). In other words, when capital has, whatever people say, largely reverted to its primeval savagery, it is up to its local agencies to "social-democratize" themselves, if one may put it thus, in order to give the resulting barbarity a veneer of civilization. But this is not their only mission.

On the political level, the decline of the welfare state has only served to add to the constraints imposed by globalized market forces to further bring into question the relevance of national territory as an arena for democracy. Given the skepticism which even today surrounds the idea of an emergent European citizenship, in spite of the energies expended in selling it to the public through ideological exhortation and other forms of mass media promotion, it is on the sub-national plane, at the level of towns and regions, that the interested parties have been obliged to transfer an equal measure of their hope for a renaissance and a renewal of the civic spirit. This hope runs a great risk of being disappointed.

Governance Versus Democracy

In the face of the prevailing political disenchantment, these superfluous perorations on "local citizenship" truly have about them an air of exorcism. If one were to believe the sociologists, the political scientists or the anthropologists charged with providing a scientific pedigree for them, the mere fact of living in the same place is enough to forge links between people, who from that time on can unite together in the quest for the "common good" to achieve the tasks which are too big for them as individuals. This nevertheless means abstracting from the socio-historic conditions which prevent citizenship, in the case of most people, from being anything more than an....abstraction.

The situation at the national level is mirrored at the level of individual cities and regions. For a growing part of the population, the pretended universality of civil law smacks of intellectual charlatanry. "For more and more people, respect for accepted values would presuppose enjoying some rights, and respect for the obligations of the citizens the *material* possibility of being a citizen" (Commaille 1997). The capitulation of the public authorities before the diktats of the globalitarian order renders them incapable of assuring *all* the inhabitants of *any* community that they will enjoy living conditions and a social position commensurate with the capacity to act effectively as a citizen. The civic spirit which is so celebrated in France in our day, and even demanded by certain individuals who see nothing wrong in refusing to treat as full citizens those who either fail to vote or vote for the National Front, is a mere abstraction devoid of any concrete referent for individuals who have been put at the mercy of the "iron laws" of the market. "How can one speak of citizenship, or civic obligations, or of recognizing fundamental human values to an individual who has been stripped of every characteristic which might serve to sustain him *socially?*" (Commaille 1997). What can citizenship, local or otherwise, possibly mean, for example, for the young inhabitant of a suburb ravaged by "restructuring" and "delocalization," the member of a family broken up by unemployment and poverty, having grown up like some kind of rank weed among policemen, drug dealers and educational consultants, without any prospects beyond those of performing some abysmally paid small-time job funded by a public authority? Who does not perceive the absolute incompatibility between social marginalization and effective participation in a political community?

It is true that the majority of individuals designated as economically and socially integrated hardly give evidence of any more real involvement in the "affairs of the city," including in the true sense of the term, where it denotes a present-day urban agglomeration. Like national citizenship, local citizenship for most inhabitants is confined to participating in voting in council elections – or in some referendum or other organized at the initiative of local authorities – and to being physically associated with a territorial entity, the municipality. Less than ever is a citizen seen as an active member of some collectivity capable of self-government.

Without harping on a question which goes beyond the framework of this analysis, it might be worth mentioning here one of the vices of representative democracy as it is currently practiced. The combined powers of technocrats, bureaucrats and ever more professionalized elected representatives discourage the ordinary individual from any attempt to involve himself in decision-making processes which have a major influence on his day-to-day existence. His only powers of opposition and proposition are mediated through associations, committees and other groupings of discontented individuals. And it is no secret how well office-holders in local government know how to instrumentalize these "counter-powers," notably through institutionalizing their functioning, blackmailing them through the offering and withholding of financial assistance and dignification of their leaders, many of whom in any case end up becoming absorbed into the ranks of local councilors.

Presented as a master-key opening the door to "the democracy of everyday life," the spatial proximity factor does not in any way alter the basic parameters of the problem posed by the persistent gulf between rulers and ruled. At most, it displaces it in the geographic sense of the term. In the framework of the competencies over which they dispose, the local political elites monopolize the strategic decisions – those which truly decide the future orientation of a city or of a region – without the majority of the population really having a voice in the matter. At most they are "informed" as part of the routine of municipal public relations policies oscillating for the most part between propaganda and advertising.

Surrounded by counselors and specialists, often – like themselves – coming from the higher education field, the only partners with whom these local elites will agree to discuss anything, or to negotiate, collaborate or in any way associate – in other words in the most general sense co-operate – are the representatives of various ministries or public and quasi-public institutions, personalities from the world of science and culture and, needless to say, the "vital forces of the economy" (heads of enterprises, company directors, managers..) As for local or regional associations, militants and/or people of goodwill, their services are merely solicited when there is a need for intermediaries for the accomplishment of *certain tasks of organization, control or indoctrination*, tasks which are best delegated down so that interventions can be more accurately targeted, i.e. so that "flexible modes of administration can be put into effect, adjusted to the particularities of individual situations" (Commaille 1997). A "flexibility" which comes to bear on anything and everything related to the preservation of "social bonding": social and educative action, welfare assistance, cultural mobilization, prevention of delinquency, etc. In return, the choice of *tasks and goals* to which these social support programs are to be subordinated is left more than ever in the hands of the competent authorities, that is to say the institutions of local government.

One would therefore be wrong to interpret the upgrading of local as opposed to centralized authority as at once harbinger and mentor of a genuine democratization of public life. In particular, "the mobilization of citizens themselves to confront the social question," to take up one official slogan in current circulation, does not aim in any way at bringing these citizens out of their subordinate state in order to help them assert themselves as political subjects. It is part of the new strategy currently being set in motion by authorities confronted with rampant social warfare engendered by the state of permanent "economic warfare" into which globalized capitalism has plunged the world.

The "involvement of each person as a citizen" is supposed firstly, as already emphasized, to relieve both the central state authority and its municipal agencies from a whole complex of pressures, burdens and duties linked to their engagement in welfare state politics. On a more specifically political plane, this "assumption of responsibility by citizens for matters which concern them" is evidently not aimed at revitalizing democracy, as many in high places like to reiterate. Emanating from the proponents of given freedoms and possibilities within a given institutional framework, the "initiatives," "experiments" and "innovations" whose rank and file provenance is so conscientiously celebrated by the elite are not the work of free and autonomous subjects. The space, social as well as physical, within which these model citizens move is narrowly circumscribed. It is precisely here that the element of ideological subterfuge in "everyday democracy" is to be located: in making these newcomers to the local scene believe that they can become fully-fledged political actors, all the better to convert them, unbeknown to themselves, into the zealous protagonists of ends that have been prescribed by the State.

There is thus more than a little demagogy in this relentless invitation to all and sundry, including the most deprived, to conduct themselves as "organizers," as "entrepreneurs" as "bearers of projects." On the pretext of inducing them to transform themselves into public-spirited citizens, an attempt is in fact made to inculcate concern for what is called "the general interest" but is in fact represents nothing more than the pre-occupations of various levels of the machinery of State. In short, it is less a matter of "reactivating civil society" than of endeavoring to establish a *civic* society where executive power, transmitted to the "grass roots" by elected politicians in the different localities, will succeed, after a fashion, in filling in for those who carry it out.

If "local democracy" exists at all, its effective exercise remains confined within a very narrow framework, to the framework, precisely of "cadres" more at home in technocratic exchanges between "movers and shakers," administrators and "those in the know" than in democratic debate with the uninitiated. Contrary to hopes or promises, the "rapprochement" which decentralization was supposed to favor between the authorities and the citizen has not, for most of the latter, been anything more than geographic in nature. Social distance, for its part, has not diminished. The result has been a reappearance of the gulf between the people and their representatives at the very place that one believed oneself safeguarded from it by virtue of spatial proximity. A "civic fracture," as it were, which merely serves to reinforce the "social fracture" and which also explains the contradiction city administrations find themselves facing.

To judge from the assertions of the ideologues charged with promoting this concept in France, it serves to designate a form of city government at once renovated and reinforced which no longer has anything at all to do with politics "defined in terms of legal and rational domination" (Bagnasco and Gales 1997). All that is involved is the elaboration of "collective projects" and strategies that enable a city to assert itself "as against other cities, the State, Europe and the forces of the market" (Bagnasco and Gales 1997). Nevertheless, among the "interests," "social groups" and institutions combined in a coalition and mobilized to this end, one searches in vain for some trace of the dominated classes. In their capacity as *subjects* of politics, they are purely and simply excluded from the game. Whether workers, white-collar employees or unemployed, these citizens remain above all "administered," a bureaucratic term confirming their status as *objects* of policy, which must be assisted and/or controlled. Certainly, resident "participation" is an idea frequently evoked, but only in terms of their status as electors or members of associations playing the role at once of democratic alibi, suggestions box and subaltern staging post for municipal action.

Due to the dictates of its component parts (local elites, chambers of commerce, groupings of employers, promoters, high functionaries in the public services of the State, executive cadre in public or private corporations) the first instincts of the collective agency called a "city" would be to privilege "glocalization," i.e. the insertion of local economic development into the dynamic of globalization, taking care to factor in the "needs" and the "constraints" of the market. But for the reasons indicated above, the political elites at the municipal or regional level are obliged at the same time to concern themselves with the "social," that is to say with the *desocialization* brought about by this same dynamic. Which comes down to trying to place a direct check at the local level on what you contribute to favoring indirectly at the international level. Moreover, the priority accorded to the development of infrastructures, facilities and accouterments, often costly (administrative centers, conference halls, teleports, technology points, opera houses, museums, etc.) designed to charm and attract the representatives of globalized capitalism can only be carried out at the expense of the needs of the mass of the population, whether it be for cheap housing, collective goods and services in deprived neighborhoods or social assistance and other benefits for the most disadvantaged.

Economic growth and/or solidarity, modernization and/or social cohesion, efficiency and/or equity:[5] these are objectives which are to say the least difficult to reconcile and which in turn necessitate a linking up of local collectivities because the welfare state, having contracted as a result of reductions in public expenditure following the fall in the rate of employment and in consumption by wage-earners, has decided to opt out of the contest. A dilemma which one French journalist has summarized as follows: "Between the IMF and the Social Minimum Wage."[6]

This is nevertheless a misleading way of presenting the contradiction which local collectivities find themselves up against nowadays. The Social Minimum Wage, like any other measure adopted in the "war against marginalization," would in reality have no reason for existence if the IMF, one of the key symbols of the globalitarian order, did not set the terms of the debate. Taking into account the evolution in the balance of forces between bourgeois and proletariat, at the global level as well as at the national, no "urban authority," however autonomous and voluntaristic, is capable of counterbalancing the powerful pressures towards globalization. In short, faced with the weight of the market, "local democracy" is not comparable as a counterweight.

The view has been put forward by a number of specialists who have set out to study the repercussions of current economic change on geographic and spatial parameters that the globalization of markets will have the paradoxical effect of favoring a certain "return to the local." While the world-wide scale of production and exchange, the strategy of transnational firms and the telecommunications revolution, by removing the significance of national frontiers, gradually make states irrelevant as producers of norms and regulators of economic activity, these same processes will offer a chance to cities, or at least to some cities: urban enclaves, "global cities," technopoles – to regain autonomy, power and allure, similar to that which was enjoyed centuries ago by the city-states of the Middle Ages and the Renaissance. But this analogy is really only of value as a mobilizing image suited for pandering to the megalomania of neo-petit-bourgeois elites who are rather too quick to forget, it seems, that this redistribution of roles between the national and the local or, if one prefers, between the State and the City, is being carried out under the aegis of capital.

Certainly cities – or at least the more important of them – have ceased to be integrated into a national economic space. The "urban poles" between which the transactions of the globalized economy are conducted today have many more dealings with each other, often across national borders, than they do with their respective hinterlands, thus contributing to a contraction of the initiating or corrective role of national political authority in this respect, as testified by the decline in state planning policies.

Nevertheless the cities, immersed henceforth in an international open economy, can have no pretensions to independent, self-determined development on their territory. Doubtless the great metropoles have in fact once again become privileged sites for capital accumulation, but only in their capacity as territorialized linkages in an ever-shifting network whose logic is subordinated to the designs of an autonomous, frontierless economic order. Points of anchorage in the planetary web woven by industrial firms, financial groups and specialized service industries around the needs of enterprises, great international public sector, scientific and technological projects, and naturally the infrastructures of communication and exchange, whether material or "non-material," they nevertheless cannot, as many imagine, elevate themselves into a front-ranking collective agency, political as much as social. Even if the governing coalitions placed at their head knew how to organize themselves in such a way as to make most profitable use of the opportunity that is thus given to them, they are not mistresses of the game. Which, as it happens, is the game of competition. Even if they do have the status of players, the management of the game still remains in the hands of capital.

The cities are for sale, if one is to judge from the rapid, indeed kaleidoscopic development of urban marketing. Everything which might constitute the specificity of each of them has now been stamped with the imprint of exchange value. "Local identity and urban territory, as places where the successive strata of the natural and cultural heritage have been deposited, do not have value for what they are in themselves, but for what they become through the process of valorization" (Dematteis 1997). In the interurban competition which pits the cities against each other as they vie for positions of relative advantage in the global system, countryside, architecture, usages and customs, the art of living, is reduced to a degraded status – also downgrading, as we see it, its "competitive advantages." From this utilitarian perspective, none of the efforts made by municipal councilors to improve the appearance of their towns and liven them up give any priority to the welfare of the larger part of the population which is already resident there. They participate first of all in a "politics of images constructed for the eye of the outsider, turned towards the supposed desires of the world economy, subject to the whims of the extraneous and the nomadic" (Gaudin 1989). The first priority is to create an environment favorable to enterprise and a type of life that will appeal to the most highly qualified salaried employees (directors, engineers, executives, technicians, researchers) and their wives. In other terms "the most urgent need seems to be in the first instance to tie down wandering capital and secure vagabond jobs" (Gaudin 1989).

It would be as well, then, not to be under any misconception concerning the significance of the "partnership" which links the public agencies on the local level and the private on the "global." When the power of the State over the company is called into question, as has become the norm in societies caught up in the current of neo-liberalism, *it is the cities that depend on the companies* for the creation of jobs and wealth, and not vice versa. Faced with the spectrum of business opportunities offered by local promotional bodies – conglomerations of public authorities and private interest groups – each of which is canvassing for its own region among potential foreign investors and the new middle classes, companies have an embarrassment of choice. Which explains the raising of stakes for the latter with the offer of every kind of advantage and the blackmailing of the former over what is being demanded. Even if this is only one aspect among others of the new mode of domination which it institutes, globalitarianism does – precisely – enable an insurance company, a banking group, a commercial consortium, an industrial firm or a media conglomerate to pit different "sites" against each other in the confident expectation of being able to open its branch where it gets the best deal.

In other words the so-called "revenge of the cities against the State" for which certain people are congratulating themselves today is sheer humbug. City politics may well be acquiring a certain independence vis-à-vis the central power of the weakened nation state, but in the last resort it is the power of capital which emerges victorious from this pseudo-confrontation. The "rise of local power is nothing more than the corollary of the pressure of the markets and the incapacity of the central governments of nation states to withstand its disintegrative effects through coherent and effective economic policies.

According to one theory in vogue among the "contemporary urban renaissance" enthusiasts, the key feature of the modern European city from the economic viewpoint is its "particular capacity to mobilize, in the very heart of the market economy," resources generally considered extra-economic – shared cultures, networks of diversity, co-operative experiments – with a potential to moderate the most brutal and impersonal manifestations of pure market logic (Veltz 1997). In other words, in the globalitarian age, capitalism with a urban face will also be capitalism with a human face! Some would even go so far as to conceive of the possibility of this "localist politico-cultural energy (...) acquiring leverage over economic forces which greatly transcend the local sphere, and even gaining the power to control and direct them" (Veltz 1997).

This is a slightly paradoxical way of presenting the submission of local agencies to the imperatives of "performance" and "excellence" the local elites are required to subscribe to if they want to see their territory included in the archipelago of the globalized economy. One could quite well demonstrate that that far from controlling and guiding the economic forces which are remodeling the planet, non-market social elements such as the spirit of co-operation, the confidence born of people knowing each other personally, the ability to work together in elaborating common projects, are more and more being *placed at the service* of the new "masters of the world." If there is "reinforcement of the role of non-market interaction" this is permitted precisely to the extent that these factors are, in turn, conscripted into the service of the mercantile logic, as factors in competitiveness. Far from being moderated, i.e. restrained, the market channels the politico-cultural energy of the local elites to its own advantage.

The way that the Anglo-Saxon concept of "governance" has been imported into France and applied to the administration of cities is moreover extremely revealing. It in effect encourages the establishment of a semantic link between what the term designates in its original field, business, and the meaning it acquires on the urban terrain into which it is now seeking to transfer itself. To translate "corporate governance" into French as "gouvernement d'entreprise," as has become the custom, is misleading, because this neologism "elevates private pension funds and corporate financial investment funds to the status of industrial groupings." The name of the game, in other words, is competition (Chesnais 1996). This penetration imposes the positions of "the markets" on the company, thus confirming the ever greater domination of global capitalist accumulation by finance capital. At the same time in the heart of the cities we are witnesses to the constitution, more or less institutionalized, of coalitions founded on a "partnership" which permits private interests to play a more and more active role in "city government." From this viewpoint, the recently fashionable talk of "governance" is explicable in terms of a desire to legitimate this evolution, namely the obligation imposed on public administration to integrate into its policies for urban development the globalitarian logic of which the above-mentioned private interests are the vehicle.

When all is said and done, the rise in the power of "local democracy" has more of the aspect of a political surrogate and ideological compensation for the growing impotence of public power at the national level in the face of transnational private interests. It cannot put up any resistance to the globalitarian tyranny because it is itself an integral part of it. Doubtless this is implicitly acknowledged in the increasingly frequent substitution of the themes of "governance" for those of "local democracy" in discussion of questions of public administration at the sub-national level.

Perhaps the term could be equally well appropriated to take into account another development related to local, and more specifically city, administration. It is a disturbing development which is nevertheless not unrelated to that previously mentioned since it has to do with the same infeudation within the realm of the global market. But on this occasion it goes clearly contrary to the logic of democracy.

One often hears talk of a "new world order" established by a directory of heads of state representing the common interest of capital. But much less is said about a *new local order* gradually taking shape which aims to place some restraints on the disorder engendered by the former. However as setbacks accumulate and the misery spreads, city politics – to limit ourselves to the French example – reveals its ultimate raison d'etre, the policing of the city.

Redeployment of the gendarmerie and the R.G.[7] in "problem" suburbs; extension of the Vigipirate plan which, on the pretext of combating terrorism, authorizes systematic military-police control in public places of the populations "at risk"; the large-scale recruitment of "security assistants" by the Ministry of the Interior to "cover sensitive neighborhoods" in the framework of "new careers" for unemployed youth; a proliferation of symposia, seminars and other official gatherings dealing with the subject of "urban security", and so on.

In this security-centered mobilization, the central State authority does not stand alone. Here too elected local politicians are resolutely engaged in carrying out a mission which, for all that, traditionally has closer affinity to the quasi-monarchic prerogatives of the State: the maintenance of the "republican" order. To be specific, for certain town-councilors, to the evocation of law and order the better to overstep the limits of their powers, as for example with the decrees forbidding beggars to lie on the footpath in tourist precincts. It was the "socialist" mayor of a Paris suburban district Epinay-sur-Seine, who, in an official report commissioned by the Ministry of the Interior, proposed a massive increase in police numbers and their equally massive deployment as patrolmen in poor neighborhoods, under cover of bringing "security" closer to the citizen. It is also a "progressive" mayor who is preparing to place the totality of public space in Vaulx-en-Velin under the inquisitorial eye of video-surveillance cameras. And if this "blockwatch" becomes generalized, if municipal police forces proliferate, it is still the mayors who are to be thanked for this, whatever their party-political allegiance. At the local level the welfare state seems to be on pretty much the same downhill grade as it is nationally: from welfare to warfare.

The transmutation of social-democracy into local-democracy is in no way unrelated to this regression. If the Left in government rivals the Right in matters of security, this is not purely for electoral reasons. No longer having anything consistent to propose to workers and the unemployed that might improve their condition, security demagogy has taken the place formerly occupied on the Left by "social" promises. Now that the hour of globalization has come, the struggle against "big capital" is no longer in fashion. It therefore gives way to the "struggle against petty delinquency"![8]

It is as if in the final analysis, instead of renewing the torn fibers of "social fabric" one should merely polish the armor of repression to prevent dislocation. Incessantly tightening the legislative meshes and the networks which bury alive the victims of capitalist globalization on the pretext of "integrating" them, the elected local politicians more or less authoritarian but always infatuated with security are well on the way to establishing a new variety of totalitarianism in which local democracy is transformed into its opposite. To identify this system and highlight the elements of innovation entailed in it, one might coin a neologism: *localitarianism*. Although if one chooses to emphasise the complementarity of the latter with globalitarianism, another neologism might seem appropriate: *glocalitarianism*.

And so it is that at the conclusion of my paper I reach the point where I wonder whether I should not perhaps have changed the title. A renovated Social-democracy, even "local-democratized" is effectively not an *opponent of* but a *collaborator with* globalitarianism. Because if globalization signifies growth in the mobility of capital and the opportunity for capitalists to some extent to emancipate themselves from the constraints of physical space, paradoxically this emancipation goes hand in hand, as we saw in the case of the globalized cities, with a heightened sense of territory as a site for strategic command, for organization and for investment. To put it differently, however deterritorialized it might be, capitalism nevertheless has a predilection for certain locations. Starting with the precincts of the stock exchange and other "central business areas" where the inward and outward financial flow is determined. These are sacred sites as it were of this religion of profit whose reign is henceforth uncontested, if one is to judge by the universal reverence or fear evoked today by the "reaction" of the "markets": "anxiety" or "relief," "hostility" or "satisfaction," "defiance" or "confidence," "depression" or "euphoria." And as for its possible "sanctions," they are dreaded like the wrath of God.

I will close by quoting the words of Robert Reich, a distinguished American academic who served as Minister of Labor during the first term of office of his friend Bill Clinton. "Never in the history of humanity have the sentiments expressed by a single street – Wall Street – had so much power. The Ancients were solicitous of the humor of the heavens, the mountains, the seas and the forests. We seek to propitiate a roadway" (Reich 1977).

Notes

1. It would be wrong to speak of "dualization" in this connection. The neologism "trialization" is more accurate in the sense that the population tends to fall into three great categories: the economically active, occupying stable and well-paid positions demanding a high level of qualification; those who are assigned to jobs that require fewer qualifications and are frequently precarious and badly paid but are nonetheless indispensable to the functioning of globalized cities; and a third group comprising "unemployable" people, whose survival is assured only by what remains of the welfare state or, increasingly, by the informal economy.
2. Travaux d'utilite collective (works of collective utility).
3. Contrats emploi-solidarite (employment solidarity contracts).
4. For a detailed analysis one might consult two among our works: *Les barabres dans la Cité,* (Barbarians in the City). Paris: Flammarion, 1996; *La Bourse ou la ville,* (The Stock-Exchange or the City). Paris: Éditions Méditerranée, 1997.
5. Even if equality still figures among the official principles of the Republic, it has been replaced de facto by equity as an acknowledged social value. This enables ideologues of the established order to shift the emphasis to inequalities and the impossibility of eliminating them.
6. Fonds Monetaire International. R.M.I.: Revenu Minimum d'Insertion
7. Renseignements Generaux. The political police of the French state.
8. The Labor politician Tony Blair like the Socialist mayor of Montpellier Georges Freche or the Social-Democrat mayor of Hamburg, Henning Vorscherau. to cite just three recent examples, made it one of their "priorities" in the course of their respective electoral campaigns.

References

Bagnasco, A. and Le Galès. P. 1997. "Les villes européennes comme société et comme acteur." In Bagnasco. A. and Le Galès. P. (eds.) *Villes en Europe.* Paris: La Découverte.

Barillon, Michel. 1996. "L'homme et la nature dans la fabrique du diable." *Agone,* no. 6.

Bihr, Alain and Heinrich, Jean-Marie. 1980. *La néo-social démocratie ou le capitalisme autogéré.* Paris: Le Sycomore.

Bourdieu, Pierre. 1997. "L'architecte de l'euro passe aux aveux." *Le Monde diplomatique,* septembre.

Brender, Anton. 1997. Interview in *Le Monde,* 6 mai.

Chesnais, F. 1996. "Mondialization du capital et régime d' accumulation à dominante financière." *Agone,* n° 16, 1996.

Chomsky, Noam. 1996. *Class warfare.* Monroe: Common Courage Press.

Commaille, Jacques. 1997. *Les nouveaux enjeux de la question sociale.* Paris: Hachette.

Dematteis, D. 1997. "Représentations spatiales de l'urbanization européenne." In Bagnasco. A. and Le Galès. P. (eds.) *Villes en Europe.* Paris: La Découverte.

Donzelot, Jacques and Jaillet, Marie-Christine. 1997. "Europe. États-Unis, convergences et divergences des politiques d'insertion." *Esprit.* mai.

Gaudin, Jean-Pierre. 1989. *Technopolis.* Paris: PUF.

_____. 1994. "Le gouvernement urbain." In *La Ville*, Le Courrier du CNRS.

Mitzman, Arthur. "Principes économiques et sociaux d'une nouvelle économie européenne." *Recherches*, n° 9 , 1er semestre.

Ramonet, Ignacio. 1997. "Régimes globalitaires." *Le Monde Diplomatique*, janvier.

Reich, Robert. 1997. "A warning to Blair : It's foolish to drift to the right." *The Guardian*, 2 April.

Veltz, Pierre. 1997. "Les villes européennes dans l'économie mondiale." In Bagnasco. A. and Le Galès, P. (eds.) *Villes en Europe*. Paris: La Découverte.

World Economic Forum. 1996. *The global Competitiveness Report*. Genève.

PART C
THE MARKET CONFRONTING WELFARE AND DEMOCRATIC POLICIES

8 European Integration and the Need for Democratic Reconsolidation

LOUKA T. KATSELI
(Assisted by D. E. Papaefstratiou)

Introduction

Few years before monetary integration and the institution of a common currency, there are repeated references to the "democratic deficit" of modern day Europe. In fact one of the principal stated objectives of the Intergovernmental Conference (IGC) was to make the Union more democratic, efficient and transparent.

The call for the democratization of the Union has been interpreted in many different ways, namely, as a call for:

a) the rebalancing of power among its key institutions, most notably the Parliament, the Council, the Court of Justice and the Commission,
b) the modification of procedures or the introduction of new authorization to ensure larger involvement of the European Parliament in decision-making,
c) greater involvement of national parliaments into the Union's institutional networks,
d) the recognition of civil society as such and for its inclusion as a third partner alongside employers and trade unions,
e) the extension of the powers of the Court of Justice and the safeguarding of the rights of European citizens to have access to the Courts. Finally,

f) as a call for a more citizen-friendly Europe or as the Irish Presidency stressed in the introduction to the draft Treaty, for a "Union which responds to the concerns of its citizens."

None of these interpretations of the "democratic deficit," however, links systematically the appearance of a democratic deficit to the dynamics of the integration process, the policy choices that shaped it and the policy outcomes that are produced.

It is the central hypothesis of this paper that the quality and the speed of the democratization process in present-day Europe is intimately tied to the exigencies of economic integration, as pursued so far by governments and political leaders.

Furthermore, that dissatisfaction with the present arrangements has to do more with what are perceived to be negative policy outcomes and the deprivation of basic economic and social rights, rather than with institutional processes.

The deprivation of economic and social rights limits, in turn, the exercise of citizens' claims on the state and as David Held perceptibly noted in his book on *Models of Democracy*, "without state rights new forms of inequality of power, wealth and status could systematically disrupt the implementation of social and economic liberties" (Held, 1987, 285).

In the case of the European Union, where competencies between national and European institutions continue to be in a state of flux, what are State and what are Community Rights and obligations, remains unclear; hence, the implementation of social and economic liberties and the full exercise of political democracy is severely hindered.

In summary, it is argued that economic integration as pursued so far, has introduced systematic policy biases and produced policy outcomes that, in turn, have eroded the democratic functioning of the political process. Democratic re-consolidation can only be achieved if there is a re-equilibration of the policy process and of the respective competencies between national and community institutions.

The Characteristics of European Integration

Already by 1962, economic and monetary integration was high on the political agenda of the European Communities.

As early as 1960, in his pioneering work on *Gold and the Dollar Crisis*, Triffin spoke of the need for a European Reserve Union and a common currency to contribute to international liquidity and to minimize risks from the use of the dollar as the principle reserve currency. The aim at that time was "to turn the EEC into one of the three economic blocs in the world, the other two being the dollar and the sterling areas" (Tsoukalis, 1977, 53). Similarly, the Commission's Action Program for the Second Stage, in 1962, put great emphasis on economic planning at the Community level and on the need for a common monetary policy. It considered fixed exchange rates as the very essence of monetary union and envisaged the creation of a European reserve currency arguing that "this would facilitate international monetary cooperation and a reform of the present system." (EECE, 1962, 63 f.).

More than thirty five years later, a common currency, EURO, is about to be introduced in an enlarged Union of fifteen members and to be used as a reserve currency, managed by a European Central Bank.

If the formation of a Customs Union, the smooth functioning of the Common Agricultural Policy (CAP) and the quest for a sustainable fixed exchange rate system were the driving forces of European integration in the 1960s and 1970s, the creation of a competitive internal market, and the introduction of a common currency system became the cornerstones of policy in the 1980s and 1990s.

The process of integration has been characterized since its beginnings, by the transfer of competencies from the national governments of the member states to the central institutions of the European Communities.

These competencies were mostly exclusive in nature and pertained to the economic aspects of the Communities established. Given the differences in opinion and interest among member states over such highly politicized issues as foreign policy or defense, it was taken for granted that only "issues of welfare" could be dealt with at the supranational level.

For some proponents of what came to be known as the "neo-functionalist school of thought," entrusting welfare issues –which were assumed to be inherently non-controversial — to international technical agencies and politicized bureaucrats would create its own momentum and have spill-over effects to other more highly political issues. The supranational institution was seen as an honest broker, which take an active pro-European stance, striking package deals across different issues, mobilizing an increasing number of experts and relying on a number of technocrats and committees for policy making and conflict resolution (Tsoukalis, 1977, 22 ff.).

Even for some of the key proponents of the "power politic school," for whom Grosspolitik was taken for granted, the transfer of competencies on economic and welfare issues transferred to international agencies was not only acceptable but desirable as well.

Thus, under the assumption that economics and politics were discontinuous, important economic decisions, such as the management of exchange rates, was removed from the domestic policy agenda and assigned to technocratic inter-governmental committees such as the Board of Governors of Central Banks and the Monetary Committee of the Union. This was facilitated by the highly technical nature of exchange rate management and the fact that monetary policy was never under tight parliamentary control to begin with.

This fundamental assumption was not seriously challenged, as long as Community competencies focused essentially on monetary and exchange rate coordination, in a period of great turbulence in exchange rate markets and the Community behaved as an intergovernmental organization as opposed to a truly supranational one.

One of the implications of this early Europeanization of the financial and monetary policy domain was that financial and monetary authorities were able, already in the 1980s, to reap strategic, early-entry, advantages over economic policy decision making at the Community level. Furthermore, the creation of a system of decision making, where by the interests of financial capital and monetary authorities were overpresented influenced the perceptions about the causes of economic problems and the choice of policy instruments for policy adjustment, in a way that was consistent with these groups' preferences over targets and instruments (Katseli 1989a, 37, Ibid., 1989b, 4).

Thus, till the mid 1980s, the rise of unemployment in Europe, was attributed to limited labor market flexibility, to real-wage rigidities and to an unfriendly business environment, identified in both academic and non-academic circles as "Eurosclerosis." The pursuit of appropriate adjustment policies was perceived to be the responsibility of national and regional authorities (*European Economy*, Annual Economic Report 1986, 34) which were responsible for "pruning the public sector deficits that were threatening the consolidation of the convergence towards monetary stability (Katseli 1989b, 30).

The preoccupation with monetary stability coupled with a strictly classical view of macroeconomic adjustment espoused by most monetary authorities, led to macroeconomic inactivism even in the face of lagging demand and rising unemployment. This was seemingly justified on economic grounds: since labor markets in Europe were characterized by real wage rigidity, there was no room for either unilateral or coordinated expansion. Even though, already by from the mid 1980s, real unit labor costs declined considerably in all major European countries and many studies have demonstrated that Europe has been suffering from a substantial Keynesian output gap (Gordon, 1987, Solow 1991), this position remains prevalent even today and provides the analytical underpinnings of the Maastricht Treaty.

Policy inactivism at the European level was challenged in the 1980s, largely as a response to the loss of competitiveness and market shares of European enterprises in world markets. Squeezed in domestic markets as a result of falling profitability the low growth environment at prevalent that time and having to face an increasingly more competitive world environment due to technological innovation and globalization, European enterprises and industrial capital interests initiated and supported actively the internal market experiment. In so doing, European enterprises, with the active assistance of the Commission, — sought to reap strategic trade advantages vis-à-vis American and Japanese transnationals in world markets— via the reduction of transaction costs, the exploitation of economies of scale and scope, the rationalization of industrial structures and the harmonization of national tax and procurement policies. Greater cost effectiveness and the facilitation of the relocation of production became principle objectives of policy. (EC, *European Economy*, 1988a).

The initiation of the Internal Market Project signaled a further important step in European integration. Intergovernmental institutions now were called upon not only to simply coordinate monetary and exchange rate policy across member states but to underpin the creation of an internal market through the elimination of all sorts of trade impediments, including subsidies and taxes and the abolition of capital controls, through the harmonization of procurement policies, and the introduction of an active competition policy. Thus, European institutions extended in a very short period of time their effective sphere of competencies over large areas of trade, industrial, credit interest and tax rate policies without any prior institutional restructuring or revision of traditional modes of decision making.

Both the European Court of Justice and the Commission became actively involved in the process of enacting legislation and undertaking initiatives that broadened EC jurisdiction extensively. The separation between economics and politics started becoming tenuous, especially since the four freedoms which are the cornerstones of the single market, namely the freedom of labor, of goods and services, of capital and the freedom of establishment, a closely intertwined with fundamental economic and social rights.

The free movement of goods, services and capital is intimately tied to the structure of the domestic market and the conditions in which competition takes place; the freedom of establishment impinges on environmental and property rights, domestic regional development and social policy, finally, the free movement of labor cannot be divorced from employment and other social rights.

Hence, the basic distinction along issue lines that dominated thinking and theorizing about European integration in the 1960s, 1970s and even 1980s became inoperative with the creation of the Internal Market and the deepening of integration.

The Limits of the "Deregulatory Race to the Bottom" and of Nominal Convergence

Both the European Court of Justice (ECJ) and the Commission despite their activism, proved to be unable to produce a comprehensive set of positive harmonizing measures.

The ECJ, on the one hand, being a judicial body, has contributed to the expansion of the Community's jurisdiction but it has been naturally barred from legislating. Its help towards the European cause was mainly in the form of "negative harmonization," focusing on breaking down barriers to the single market erected by the legislatures of the Member States. Thus, using the conduit of the Article 177 reference procedure, the Court may only strike down national measures which are incompatible with the aims of the Treaty. Any national measure, which may be deemed to have a protectionist or discriminatory effects may come under the Court's scrubing, unless justified by the Treaty or one of the judge-made justifications. Many aspects of the market structure and functions of member states may naturally fulfill these criteria, even though they may initially be thought to be relatively innocuous: the laws forbidding Sunday

Trading in the UK, for example, became a case in point. An assault on the structure of any market could, however, succeed, only if its operation had been remodeled and restructured through positive legislation.

Reaching a decision on a legislative proposal which is under the competence of the Commission, is only the tip of the iceberg. Once such proposals are submitted, then a real struggle begins, since there exist about fifteen different types of legislative procedures, each requiring the participation of different institutional arrangements and voting patterns. Furthermore, the activist pro-European stance of the Commission often runs counter to the politics and interests of Council Ministers.

Thus, whilst the competence of the central institutions has steadily expanded, their ability to pass positively harmonizing legislation has not increased correspondingly, producing, what came to be known, as a "policy deficit" or "policy vacuum."

The persistence of this "policy vacuum" in conjunction with the enforcement of deregulation and market liberalization has had real economic effects.

Already in 1979, in the celebrated *Cassis de Dijon* case, the German government spoke of a European "deregulatory race to the bottom," warning that all member states are forced to the lowest common regulatory denominator, lest traders mooring across borders are faced with "double burdens."

The same can, in fact, be said about the exercise of macro policy. Lest any member state is tempted to impose an inflation tax in order to reduce its debt or to gain a competitive advantage through a devaluation, member states have been increasingly deprived of national policy instruments to manage aggregate demand and to meet internal and external imbalances.

The Maastricht Treaty through the introduction of convergence criteria came to institutionalize this macro-policy inactivism on the part of national governments agreements.

The obligation assumed at Maastrict, to reduce inflation to the lowest rate prevalent in the Community, to preserve the rate of budget deficits to GNP under the 3% limit, and to maintain the exchange rate practically fixed for two years prior to entry into EMU effectively ties government hands vis-à-vis the exercise of macro-economic policy and eliminates the use of important economic policy instruments from the national policy agenda. Taking into account the fact that, in the context of present-day European economic institutions, monetary authorities and financial capital interests are overrepresented, these decisions amount to the institutionalization of deflationary policies throughout the Union and the introduction of a systemic disinflationary bias in Community policies.

This bias has become even more pronounced after the endorsement of the Stability Pact at Amsterdam, where by the fear of excessive budget deficits, prompted decision makers to restrict even further the competence of national governments in the conduct of fiscal policy, to introduce penalties and even to allow a pro-cyclical policy stance, if necessary, to maintain "the sanctity" of the 3% target.

As in the case of the deregulatory race, no positive measures have been initiated to counterbalance the negative effects of the diflationary race on aggregate demand, on incomes and on employment. Once again, economic and social rights have been weakened, challenging further the separation between "welfare issues" and "high politics," as well as the premises upon which competencies have been traditionally divided between the Union and Member States.

The Need for Democratic Reconsolidation in an Enlarged Union

The above analysis of European integration has thus highlighted at least three things:

a) that politics can not be separated from economics since both negative and positive measures influence economic activity and economic and social rights.

b) that, the emergence of a "democratic deficit" in Europe can be explained in the light of the negative real outcomes, that have resulted from the "policy deficit" that is inherent to the way European institutional arrangements have been built and allowed to function and

c) that the continuation of the erosion of member states capabilities, in the field of economic policy, without corresponding positive action at the Union level is apt to lead to democratic deconsolidation of national and European institutions and eventually to threaten the integration process itself.

Democratic consolidation according to Gunter et al (1995) is achieved when there is widespread legitimation of institutional behavior and the internalization of rules of conduct and behavioral norms derived from the functioning of these institutions. In the case of the Union, the combination of a "policy vacuum" at the European level coupled with the attack on member state capabilities to initiate positive action, have alienated the individual from a political process for which he (or she) has no clear comprehension.

To the average citizen the political system appears to lack accountability, transparency, policy effectiveness. This is made worse by the fact that economic decision-making, entrusted to Community institutions which appear to be incapable to initiate positive legislation, or joint fiscal action, is increasingly perceived to be influenced by lobbies and organized commercial and business interests that engage in rent-seeking activities through their influence on legislation or policy guidelines.

In the context of an institutionally weak Europe, dominant elites of the consistent units often present themselves as agents of specific constituencies, resisting the development of horizontal networks among national parliaments or the demoi. Instead, acting on behalf or the "wider Community interest," they tend to promote vertical integration as a means of retaining ultimate authority within their domestic subcultures. As Tsinisizelis and Chryssochoou (1997) point out, this tendency towards inter-elite accommodation, and controlled pluralism, is conditioned by the extent to which a delicate balance of interests can be struck among the consistent unit. Under "consociation," as this process has come to be known, democratic deconsolidation can occur easily if the balance of interests among elite cartels is disrupted.

This introduces a further element of instability in the present day functionary of European institutions.

What is the solution to the that impasse that threatens democratic persistence and European integration at the same time?

First, these has to be a broad realization that there is no economic decision which does not involve costs and benefits to specific groups, even the decision not to act or legislate has important political repercussions.

Secondly, as EMU is likely to become a reality in a few years, there is an urgent need for a reorganization of competences across institutions for appropriate steps to empower them to exercise their respective functions effectively. For example, we collectively need to decide if fiscal and redistributive policies are better served by national or European institutions; if fiscal policy can be exercised more effectively at the national level, then the convergence criteria need to be appropriately modified, if not then the Community's own resources and the Budget need to be expanded to allow for the development of a unified tax and transfer system.

Finally, as mass legitimation is being increasingly undermined there is an urgent need to address the demands of European citizens for protection of fundamental economic and social rights such as the right to employment, the right to a minimum income if employees cannot be secured and the right of access to basic social services such as education and health. We thus need to decide not only on competencies but also on the content of European policy.

If the implementation of social and economic liberties and quality of the democratic process is intimately tied to the degree of inequality and of social cohesion in a society, then Europe need for its own sake to go beyond convergence and to change the policy mix, allowing for a more coordinated expansion of democracy through investment and trade at the European level coupled with more active structural employment and social policies at the national level.

References

EECE. 1962. *The Commission's Action Programme*. Brussels: EC.

European Economy.1986. *Annual Economic Report for 1986*. Brussels: EC.

European Economy.1988. *Annual Economic Report for 1988*. Brussels: EC.

European Union. 1997. *Making Sence of Amsterdam Treaty*, Brussels: The European Policy Centre.

Gordon, R. 1987. "Wage Gaps vs. Output Gaps: Is there a Common Story for all of Europe," *NBER Working Paper*, No 2454, December.

Gunther, Diamandouros and Puhle. 1995. *The Politics of Democratic Consolidation: Southern Europe in Comparative Perspective* John Hopkins University Press.

Held, David. 1987. *Models of Democracy*, Polity Press.

Katseli, Louka. 1989a. "The Political Economy of European Integration: From Euro-sclerosis to Euro-corporatism." *CEPR Discussion Paper* Series No 317, October 1989.

_____. 1989b, "The Political Economy of Macroeconomic Policy in Europe" in P. Guerrieri and P.C. Padoan, eds. *The Political Economy of European Integration*. Wheatsheaf.

Solow, Robert. 1991. *The Labor Market as a Social Institution (Royer Lectures)* Oxford: Blackwell.

Triffin, Robert. 1960. *Gold and the Dollar Crisis*, New Haven: Yale University Press.

Tsinisizelis, Michael and Chryssochoou, Dimitris. 1995. *From Gesellschaft to Gemeinschaft? Confederal Consociation and Democracy in the European Union*. Institute of Federal Studies, Leicester University Press.

_____. 1997. "The European Union: Trends in Theory and Reform". in Schmitter, M. (ed.), *The Political Theory of European Constitutional Choice.* London: Routledge.
Tsinisizelis, Michael. Yfantis, Kostas and Chryssochoou, Dimitris. 1997. *Rethinking Maastricht: Theory, Process and Change.* Manchester: Manchester University Press.
Tsoukalis, Loukas. 1977. *The Politics and Economics of European Monetary Integration,* George Allen and Unwin.

9 Catching Up or Falling Behind: Regional Economic Performance and the Trajectories of Regional Economic Development in the EU

MICHAEL DUNFORD

Introduction

A central question in studies of regional economic development is why do certain cities, regions and countries grow at different speeds and why do they achieve different levels of economic prosperity and well-being. Interest in this question has however varied. Classical economists were essentially interested in growth and distribution, though there were different views about the outcome of growth processes, with some (such as Malthus) seeing industrialization as a process that was inherently uneven and that could lead to cumulative growth and decline, whereas Ricardo envisaged a smooth process of growth leading to a stationary state with zero growth and no institutional or technological change due to the decreasing marginal returns associated with agriculture (Boyer, 1997). With the neoclassical revolution in economics attention shifted away from questions of growth and development to questions of the allocation of a given volume of resources. Growth questions re-emerged in the 1940s when some of Keynes' followers sought to extend his ideas to the long-run and developed models which indicated that market forces acting on their own would not lead to full employment in the long run (Harrod, 1939; Domar, 1946; Robinson, 1956). In the view of these neo-Keynesian authors the dynamic equilibrium of consumption and investment decisions would result in an unstable macroeconomic development path: "either the economy experienced explosive growth, or it was trapped in a cumulative and self-defeating depression" (Boyer, 1997, 34). To neoclassical economists these neo-Keynesian models rested on restrictive assumptions, of which the most important was that of a fixed relation between the factors of production. Encouraged by the regular character of postwar expansion, neoclassicists such as Solow and Swan consequently developed alternative models that predicted a much more peaceful and regular growth process and eliminated Keynesian problems of long-run unemployment and economic instability: "if all markets are competitive and if the same technology is available in each country, every economy would grow at the same rate – a growth rate imposed by technical change and corrected by demographic trends". Under these idealized conditions neoclassical theory provides a simple rationale for economic convergence of growth rates.

The difficulties with these models included their prediction of convergence for which there was clear counter-evidence, their prediction that in the absence of exogenous technical progress there would be no growth in the long-run and their limited explanatory power in empirical research. Alternative perspectives, more in the Keynesian tradition, were developed by Kaldor and others (see Kaldor, Targetti and Thirlwall, 1989a; 1989b). In these models long-run growth was possible as a result of endogenous technical progress and changes in the distribution of income. These ideas remained, however, on the margins of academic research.

In the 1970s with the growth slowdown neoclassical work declined in fashion. Authors inspired by Schumpeter and Kaldor emphasized the importance of technology gaps between countries in explaining disparities in development paths. Some of this work emphasized the importance of the potential for catch-up centered on the technology gap, and the nature of the prerequisites for exploiting this potential. These authors were dissatisfied with the neoclassical assumptions about the automatic character of technical change and the view that it was independent of investment or technology policies: 'If, for example, a country does not save and consequently under-invests, can it benefit from the same opportunities as a more innovative and virtuous country. Probably not, because learning by doing will be less efficient and the lack of domestic technological expertise may make it hard to capture advances in basic knowledge and technology'

(Boyer, 1997, 35). Others pointed out that technology gaps do not necessarily lead to convergence but may be consistent with a diverging pattern (Dixon and Thirlwall, 1975).

In the mid-1980s there was a renewal of interest in these questions in the ranks of neoclassical economics with the development of the new growth theories in which technology and human capital were made endogenous.

Quite quickly convergence theories were given a further stimulus by several factors. The first was increasing globalization and its suggestion that there is a strong trend towards convergence (the idea that companies adopt similar technologies, that their is a trend towards a closer alignment of consumption patterns and life-styles and that the development of global financial markets is leading to an alignment of national economies and government policies). The second was the collapse of the Soviet system.

What this brief account of the evolution of ideas about growth and convergence indicates is that the dominant interpretations involve an oscillation between models that predict regular growth and convergence on the one hand and models that suggest that growth is unstable and can reinforce as well as reduce inequalities. In this paper I shall argue that making sense of the historical record involves a recognition of the fact that there are always two divergent tendencies. At every point in time there are both trends towards an equalization of conditions of production and exchange and, at the same time, forces leading to a differentiation of conditions of production and exchange. In capitalist economies competition is a force which leads those enterprises whose productivity is less than average and whose costs are above average to close the gap on the market leaders or to disappear; at the same time the quest for surplus profits leads to a constant differentiation of production and exchange as enterprises seek to innovate and/or reduce costs. The outcome of these two tendencies will depend on the balance between these forces and the conditions in which they unfold and will vary over time and space. Also the forces for convergence are rarely powerful enough to homogenize economic structures and performance.

These concerns are at the root of this paper whose title draws on the work of Abramovitz (1986) to insist that while convergence has received much recent attention, making sense of economic development requires that attention also be paid to processes of differentiation and in particular to the falling behind experienced by less developed areas and the forging ahead of the most developed. The aim is to identify certain trends and to help develop a framework that can account for catching up (convergence) and falling-behind (divergence).

There is a second dimension to this debate in that there are disagreements as to whether or not supply side or demand side (including the external trade of national and regional economies) are the most important determinants of their growth performance. As Dalum, Laursen and Verspagen (1996) have argued:

> Krugman (1994) has forcefully argued that the issue of competitiveness, which underlies the idea that growth is determined by the performance in international product markets, does not make sense from a theoretical point of view. Underlying his view, as well as the point of view expressed in most mainstream work based on a 'Solow-type theory' approach, is that growth is determined by supply-side factors, which are basically determined by domestic factors, such as the growth rate of the population or the labor force, factor prices, the savings rate, and, in more recent 'new growth' models, the generation of technology. In this approach, the impact of trade is not so much on economic growth, but instead on welfare, and works through the allocation of production factors, and factor prices. Outside the mainstream, there are several approaches which stress the interaction between international factors and domestic growth performance. In the Keynesian tradition, Kaldor (1966, 1970) and Thirlwall (1979) have argued that exports and trade performance are the main determinants of growth .... Their approaches, which characterize growth as 'export-led,' or as 'balance of payments restricted,' stress the impact of demand on growth. The recent 'evolutionary' literature on economic growth ... takes technical change as the main determinant of growth, but reserves an important role for demand in the form of exports and imports. Finally, models of open economies in the so-called 'new growth theory' argue that trade matters for growth.

To these ends I shall examine some of the ways in which the recent trajectories of the regions of the EU can be explained, outlining the roles of supply and demand-side factors, and emphasizing the historically-changing nature of growth and convergence.

The Scale of Regional Inequality

As a result of the economic strength of its largest Member States and its progressive widening to include new members, the European Union has emerged as one of the three major economic powers in the world economy in spite of the fact that rates of European economic growth since the mid 1970s have stood at one half of those achieved in the post-war 'golden age' which lasted until the mid-1970s. Europe's economic potential, while considerable in global terms, is far from equally distributed as is indicated by the fact that within the EU there are substantial disparities in economic development.Figure 1 indicates the scale of these disparities in 1994 by plotting PPS estimates of regional per capita GDP for NUTS 2 regions in fifteen Member States, themselves ranked from left to right according to their national GDP per head. In that year output per head in NUTS Level II regions measured in PPS varied from 196 to 37.7 per cent of the EU average, while in ECU the extreme values were 227 and 31.

The ten per cent band or decile of the population of the Community that lived in the least prosperous areas had an average GDP per head of 58. A further ten per cent lived in areas with an average of 71. More than 19 per cent of the population of the EU lived in (Objective 1) areas with a per capita GDP of less than 75 per cent of the Community average: included were all of Greece, Portugal outside of Lisbon, the French overseas départements, the former German Democratic Republic, 10 of 18 Spanish NUTS II regions, 5 of the regions of the Italian Mezzogiorno, Burgenland in Austria and South Yorkshire in the UK. Just outside were the Canaries, Merseyside, Corsica, Molise and Flevoland in the Netherlands. In most of these areas the share of income from low-productivity agricultural sectors was large, and unemployment was high. A further 36 per cent lived in areas with a per capita GDP of less than the Community average. Included are many rural areas and areas affected by the decline of employment in mining, steel, textiles and shipbuilding with above-average unemployment rates. At the other end of the spectrum ten per cent of the population of the Community lived in areas with an average of 153. Included were Hamburg (196), Brussels (183), Darmstadt (178), Luxembourg (169), Ile de France (161), Oberbayern (161), Vienna (158), Bremen (156), Greater London (147), Stuttgart (139), Antwerp (139), Grampian (136) in Scotland and Lombardy (131). A large share of the regions in this group were West German, and most were metropolitan economies clustered around an axis (the so-called "blue banana") that extended from Greater London through Belgium and the Netherlands along the Rhine and into Lombardy and Emilia Romagna in the north of Italy which lie just outside the top 10.[1]

While the 1996 enlargement saw the accession of three Member States whose per capita GDP is close to the EU average, the next will probably see a significant increase in disparities and will have important consequences for the 132 million people who reside in Objective 1 areas and the 62.8 million inhabitants of the four Cohesion countries (Greece, Portugal, Spain and the Republic of Ireland).

Short of major increases in expenditure, or a redefinition of the rules of structural policy (on the lines for example of the Agenda 2000 (CEC, 1997) proposals) any enlargement to the east will in particular lead to a descheduling of a substantial number of Objective 1 areas as they will no longer fall beneath the 75 per cent of EU GDP threshold and will change the relative position of Cohesion countries. Candidates for membership include Poland with a population of 38.2 million people and a per capita GDP in the early 1990s of 36.4 per cent of the EU average, Hungary with 10.6 million and 40.5 per cent, the Czech Republic with 15.6 million and 45.7 per cent, Romania with 23 million and 23.7 per cent and Bulgaria with 9 million and 32.9 per cent. Regional disparities may therefore assume yet more significance in the years ahead.

FIGURE 1   Gross domestic product per head (in PPS)
by NUTS II region in 1994

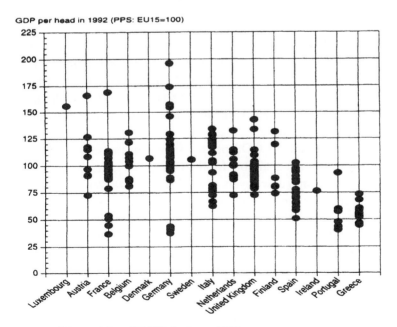

Source: elaborated from REGIO database, 1996.

Components of Territorial Disparities

To help identify the causes of disparities, differentials in development can be divided into two elements: an element that depends on productivity differentials; and an element that depends on differential in the employment rate (the per centage of the population in employment). More formally:

$$\frac{\text{Gross Domestic Product}}{\text{Resident Population}} \equiv \frac{\text{Gross Domestic Product}}{\text{Resident Population}} \times \frac{\text{Gross Domestic Product}}{\text{Resident Population}}$$

Differences in productivity measure the average wealth created per person employed which may vary due to productivity differences within a single sector or to differences in sectoral/functional specialization. Differences in the employment rate, defined as the share of the population in employment, reflect variations in the capacity of an economic system to mobilize its human potential (see Dunford 1996). The employment rate depends on a number of factors: the age profile of an area's population, conventions concerning retirement and schooling; the share of the population in active age groups that is inactive or whose work is hidden which depends on gender roles, the extent of early retirement, sickness and hidden unemployment; and the scale of unemployment.

In order to identify the relative roles of variations in productivity and the employment rate the data for each region is plotted on a graph which records the value added per person employed on the vertical axis (measured in ECU and not at Purchasing Power Standards) and the employment rate on the horizontal axis. Each variable is measured as a percentage of the EU average (see Figure 2).

The areas with the lowest GDP per head were in the main in Greece and Portugal. (Data was not available for the French overseas départements which also had particularly low levels of GDP per head). What is clear in the case of Greece (with the exception of Kentriki Ellada in the west) and mainland Portugal however is the fact that their employment rates were close to the EU average (92 to 102 per cent). (Of the Cohesion countries their unemployment rates were also comparatively low). Yet their levels of productivity (measured in PPS) were equal to 65 to 72 per cent of the EU average.

FIGURE 2   Employment and productivity rates in
NUTS I EU regions in 1993

A.

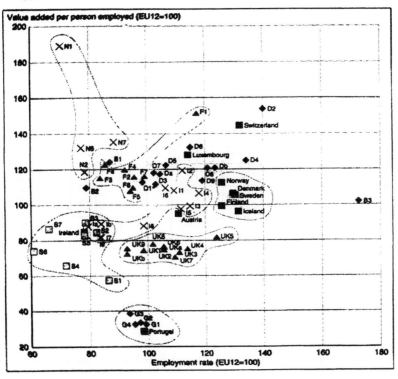

1986

B1	Vlaams Gewest	S1	Noroeste	I8	Abruzzi-Molise
B2	Region Wallonne	S2	Noreste	I9	Sud
B3	Bruxelles-Brussel	S3	Madrid	IA	Sicilia
R9	Danmark	S4	Centro	IB	Sardegna
D8	Baden-Württemberg	S5	Este	R6	Luxembourg
D9	Bayern	S6	Sur	N1	Noord-Nederland
DB	Berlin	S7	Canarias	N2	Oost-Nederland
DC	Brandenburg	F1	Ile de France	N7	West-Nederland
D4	Bremen	F2	Bassin Parisien	N5	Zuid-Nederland
D2	Hamburg	F3	Nord-Pas-de-Calais	P1	Continente
D6	Hessen	F4	Est	P2	Açores
DD	Mecklenburg-Volpommern	F5	Ouest	P3	Madeira
D3	Niedersachsen	F6	Sud-Ouest	UK1	North
D5	Nordrhein-Westfalen	F7	Centre-Est	UK2	Yorkshire and Humberside
D7	Rheinland-Pfalz	F8	Mediterranée	UK3	East Midlands
DA	Saarland	F9	Départements d'Outre-Mer	UK4	East Anglia
DE	Sachsen	R8	Ireland	UK5	South East
DF	Sachsen-Anhalt	I1	Nord Ovest	UK6	South West
D1	Schleswig-Holstein	I2	Lombardia	UK7	West Midlands
DG	Thueringen	I3	Nord Est	UK8	North West
G1	Voreia Ellada	I4	Emilia-Romagna	UK9	Wales
G2	Kentriki Ellada	I5	Centro	UKA	Scotland
G3	Attiki	I6	Lazio	UKB	Northern Ireland
G4	Nisia	I7	Campania		

B.

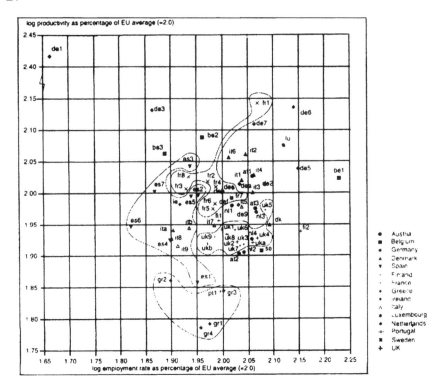

Source: elaborated from data from the REGIO database and DGXVI employment data.

The situation in Spain and the Republic of Ireland was rather different. Generally speaking employment rates were low varying from 91 per cent in Northern Spain (ES1 and ES2) to 67 per cent in the South (ES6). In Ireland the employment rate stood at 84 per cent. The rates of productivity were much closer to the EU average than in the cases of Greece and Portugal varying from 112 per cent in Madrid to 73 per cent in North West Spain but with most areas clustered in the upper half of this range. In the Republic of Ireland productivity was equal to the EU average.

Close to this cluster were also the regions of Southern Italy: Campania (IT8); Puglia, Basilicata and Calabria (IT9); Sicily (ITA); and Sardinia (ITB). In all of these areas productivity was between 82 and 89 per cent of the EU average, while employment rates were 80 to 87 per cent of the average. Abruzzo and Molise (IT7) were somewhat detached from this group in that their employment rate (97 per cent) was just short of the average, although their productivity level (89 per cent) was quite close to the other parts of the Mezzogiorno. This region lay between the Mezzogiorno and the Center-North. In the Center-North productivity was greater than the EU average (varying from 95 per cent in the Central region to 115 per cent in Lombardia), while employment rates were 4 to 17 per cent above average. The differential positions of the two parts of the country graphically confirms the existence of two different economic and social worlds in Italy. Austria interestingly occupies a position that is close to that of the Centro region (IT5) in Italy and the North East (IT3) which in the past was under Austrian control.

The position of the United Kingdom (UK) is also particularly striking. Generally speaking UK productivity is low, ranging from 82 to 96 per cent of the EU average. Employment rates were, on the other hand, much more varied and were in most cases in excess of 100 per cent: the lowest scores were 95 per cent in Northern Ireland, while the highest was 123 per cent in the South East, and the next highest was 118 in East Anglia. Overall comparatively high rates of employment partially compensate for low productivity.

The Nordic countries are associated with substantially higher rates of employment: 125 per cent in Denmark and 121 per cent in Sweden, but due to recent employment loss just 100 per cent in Finland. In Denmark (90 per cent), Finland (92 per cent) and Sweden (82 per cent) productivity lay below the EU average. GDP per head seems therefore to have been relatively high largely as a result of the high degree of mobilization of the human potential of the Nordic countries.

Hamburg (DE6), Hessen which contains the city of Frankfurt and to a lesser extent Bremen (DE5) have high productivity and employment rates, though the figures for Hamburg and Bremen are difficult to interpret due to the significance of commuting. In the rest of Germany, employment rates are high (125 and 126 per cent) in the southern Länder of Baden-Württemberg (DE1) and Bayern (DE2). Rates of productivity in these two Länder are close to those in the northern Rhinelands and North Sea coast (98 to 103 per cent) but the latter are characterized by employment rates in the order of 101 to 110 per cent.

With the striking exception of Ile de France and to a lesser extent the Centre-East, the French and Belgian regions display close-to-average productivity rates but less than average employment rates. French provincial productivity rates range from 96 per cent in the Ouest to 107 per cent in the Méditerranée. Employment rates range from 86 per cent in the old industrial region of Nord-Pas-de-Calais to 105 per cent in the Centre-Est (Rhône-Alpes and Auvergne) in provincial France. The Ile de France stands out from the rest of France as a consequence of its higher employment rate (118 per cent) and in particular of its rate of productivity (139 per cent). Belgium is characterized by high rates of productivity, and rates of employment that are on average low (96 per cent). In Belgium therefore the strong positive impact of productivity on relative GDP per head is in part offset by the downward pressure exerted by comparatively low rates of employment.

The Netherlands is a country whose position has changed from the top left to bottom right hand quadrant. In 1993 rates of productivity ranged from 87 (Zuid-Nederland) to 99 per cent (Noord-Nederland), while employment rates ranged from 106 to 118.

Trends in Inequality

Data on long-term trends in territorial inequality in the EU indicates that disparities in regional development and inequalities in the distribution of income, which diminished in much of the 1960s and early 1970s, have subsequently increased though trends do differ from Member State to Member State. Figure 3, for example, plots several indicators of inequalities in Gross Domestic product per inhabitant in the first twelve Member States. The graph shows strong convergence until the mid-1970s. In the case of Member States, convergence gave way to divergence until the early to mid-1980s depending on the indicator used. From the mid-1980s until 1990 the Member States converged. At the start of the 1990s there was a further upturn in most measures of inequality with levels close to their 1974 level: over the period from 1974 to 1992 there was no overall reduction in disparities.

EU data on trends in regional inequalities are set out in Table 1. The indicator of regional inequality used is the sum of the absolute deviations of regional per capita GDP (measured at Purchasing Power Standards) expressed as a percentage of the mean. The data in the upper half of the table relates to NUTS I regions while the lower half relates to NUTS II regions.

A number of investigators have identified convergence in national series until the mid-1970s. The data in Table 1, which relates to the late 1970s and 1980s, indicates that in most Member States divergence occurred. Convergence was confined to Greece, the Netherlands after 1986, and, if the latest REGIO data are used, Italy in the 1990s. In the UK disparities increased at NUTS I level from 8.8 per cent in 1977 to 11.5 in 1991 and at NUTS II level from 12.6 to 14.4. In France there was an increase at NUTS II level from 15.9 to 18.7. In Spain there was an increase from 14.7 in 1980 to 17.5 in 1991.

FIGURE 3   **Trends in Inequality Between Member States**

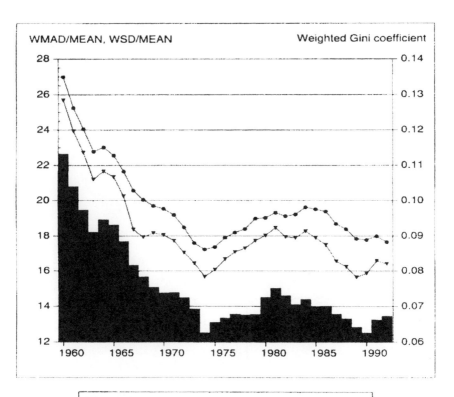

TABLE 1   Regional inequality in the European Union: WMAD/MEAN

NUTS I	Number of regions	1977	1978	1979	1980	1981	1982	1983	1984	1985	1986	1987	1988	1989	1990	1991
Germany	11	7.8	7.6	7.5	7.5	7.5	7.6	8.0	8.2	8.4	8.5	8.8	9.1	9.6	10.0	10.3
France	8	15.6	15.8	15.3	15.5	15.9	16.9	17.7	17.2	18.1	17.7	18.5	18.8	18.7	18.6	18.6
Italy	11	22.1	22.6	21.8	22.6	22.3	22.1	20.7	20.8	21.9	22.4	22.3	22.8	23.0	22.9	23.0
Netherlands	4	11.1	10.5	10.7	11.5	13.2	13.4	13.3	13.6	13.5	10.7	8.6	9.0	8.0	7.3	6.8
Belgium	3	10.8	10.7	10.7	11.5	12.5	12.2	11.4	11.4	11.7	11.7	12.4	12.5	12.6	12.6	12.6
Luxembourg	1															0.0
United Kingdom	11	8.8	9.6	10.5	10.7	11.0	10.3	10.9	11.2	11.1	11.6	12.0	12.5	13.0	12.5	11.5
Republic of Ireland	1															0.0
Denmark	1															0.0
Greece	4			13.8	8.8	5.7	4.7	6.4	4.4	3.8	5.4	5.1	4.7	4.8	5.5	7.8
Spain	11				14.0	15.1	14.6	14.6	14.7	16.3	17.0	17.1	16.9	17.7	18.0	17.5
Portugal	3															0.0
EU	63				19.0	20.8	20.5	20.2	20.6	20.8	20.7	20.0	19.9	19.8	19.7	19.9

NUTS II	Number of regions	1977	1978	1979	1980	1981	1982	1983	1984	1985	1986	1987	1988	1989	1990	1991
Germany	31	15.9	16.1	15.8	12.7	13.0	13.4	13.7	13.9	14.2	14.2	14.0	14.0	14.3	14.8	14.9
France	21/22 from 1982			15.8	15.8	15.9	17.0	17.7	17.3	18.1	18.0	18.8	18.9	18.8	18.8	18.7
Italy	20	22.5	23.0	22.0	22.6	22.4	22.1	20.7	20.9	22.0	22.6	22.5	22.9	23.1	23.1	23.1
Netherlands	9/12 from 1986	12.9	12.8	12.8	13.3	14.9	14.5	14.7	15.3	16.5	12.8	10.8	10.6	9.4	9.0	8.9
Belgium	9	13.4	12.8	12.7	13.3	13.4	13.4	12.1	13.0	13.2	12.2	12.4	12.3	12.2	12.2	12.2
Luxembourg	1															0.0
United Kingdom	34/35 from 1987	12.6		13.6	13.9				14.4			15.1	15.2	15.4	15.0	14.4
Republic of Ireland	1															0.0
Denmark	1															0.0
Greece	13			15.9	13.0	8.7	7.5	9.2	7.7	7.3	8.5	9.3	9.1	8.2	9.0	10.2
Spain	18				14.7	16.1	16.0	15.5	15.3	16.6	17.1	17.1	17.0	17.8	18.0	17.5
Portugal	5				23.2	23.2	23.8	23.2	22.6	22.0	24.8	28.3	24.4	24.2	25.5	25.5
EU				21.6	22.7		23.3	23.1	22.0	23.8	23.6	21.5	21.5	21.2	21.1	21.5

133/134 in 1982–3 and 1985/137 in 1986/ 165 in 1981 and 1984/ 170 from 1987

At a European Union level it is difficult to measure trends due to the absence of data for particular countries in particular years. A far from ideal solution is to drop regions for which values are missing. The complete data shows however that over the period as a whole there was little change in the scale of regional disparities. At a NUTS- I level, the measure of disparity stood at 19.0 in 1980 and 19.9 in 1991. At a NUTS II level, it did not change much after 1980 though the change in the number of regions for which data exist make it difficult to measure changes in inequality in the EU at this particular scale: for the 130 regions for which there is data for all years the index rose marginally from a value of 21.7 in 1980 to 22.5 in 1991 peaking at 24.1 in 1985.

A Disaggregation of Trends in Output per Head

To what extent are these changes in disparities a result of differences in changes in rates of productivity and in employment rates? Are inter-regional productivity differentials increasing or decreasing? Are variations in the employment rate increasing or decreasing? Are areas that are economically weaker comparatively unsuccessful in their attempts to re-employ people who lose their jobs as a result of structural change or to provide alternative employment possibilities for new generations entering the job market for the first time? Does inter-regional migration serve to adjust the changing regional supply of and demand for labor?

To answer some of these questions, trends in the rates of productivity and employment were analyzed in Figure 4, which records the trajectories of change of the twelve Member States. Of the Cohesion countries, Ireland and Portugal both show significant convergence in rates of productivity, but at the expense of divergence in rates of employment. Spain's overall position also improved but in different ways: until 1986 rates of productivity converged, while rates of employment diverged; in 1986-1990 the employment rate improved at the expense of divergence in rates of productivity; while in 1990-91 sharper convergence in rates of productivity coincided with a less pronounce loss of ground in employment rate terms.

Of the stronger economies, Belgium and in particular France strengthened their position in rate of productivity terms but at the cost of a deterioration in their rates of employment. Italy, the former Federal Republic of Germany and to a lesser extent Denmark went through two phases returning in 1991 to a relative position close to the one occupied in 1980. In the case of the United Kingdom, in 1987-91 an improved employment rate was achieved at the expense of a deterioration in its rate of productivity compared with the European average.

There are few signs of a virtuous cycle in which relative rates of productivity and employment increase. Instead there is some evidence of a trade-off with the achievement of gains in relative productivity at the expense of employment and vice versa.

**FIGURE 4 Trends in inequality in productivity and employment
rates in 1980-91**

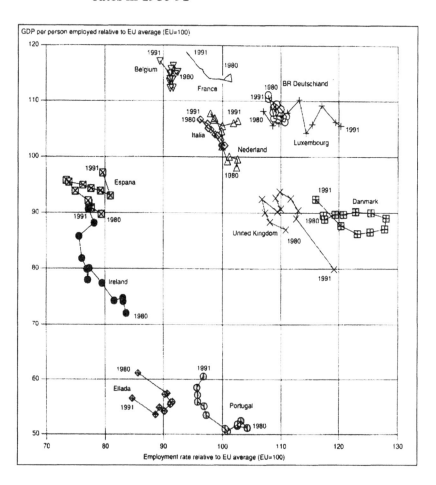

Re-Employment and Industrial Restructuring

The identification of this trade-off is particularly important for any analysis of the impact of economic change on producer welfare and is endorsed in micro-economic studies of change in local labor markets in Europe. An important example is provided by study by Beatty and Fothergill (1995). The study examined the impact of job loss in Travel to Work Areas in England and Wales dependent on employment in the coal industry. What it showed was that for every increase of 100 in the supply of male labor, due to the loss of jobs in coal and the net increase in the size of the workforce (the difference between the number of young people who joined the job market and the number who reached retirement age): 33 emigrated; 31 either found alternative work, commuted to work outside the are or were employed on a government scheme; 33 dropped out of the workforce, with many being classified as "permanently sick," Almost no increase in unemployment was registered, but there was a significant growth in male non-employment. This reduction in labor force participation will, other things being equal, add to disparities in development. The example of the coal industry might be thought to have some special characteristics, but the point is a general one.

Development depends not just on the productivity of an area's economic activities but also on the degree to which an area's human potential is mobilized, while trends in its economic performance and in inequality depend on the dynamics of labor force mobilization. As the coal area study indicates, the rate of employment depends upon a number of factors: the age profile of an area's population and conventions concerning retirement, schooling and learning; the share of the population in active age groups that is inactive or whose work is hidden which itself depends on gender roles, the scale and character of child care provision and welfare support, the extent of early retirement, sickness and hidden unemployment and the scale of the informal sector; and the scale of unemployment. All of these factors are moreover shaped by the institutional compromises that characterize particular countries, cities and regions as well as by the structure and dynamics of their economies.

Employment Rate Differentials and Unemployment

Amongst the causes of differences in labor force mobilization is the existence of very sharp variations in unemployment. In April 1992 in the EU, unemployment stood at 9.4 per cent compared with 8.5 per cent in April 1991 but differed sharply from one region to another. In Southern Italy and Spain there were many areas with unemployment rates in excess of 20 per cent (Andalucia 27 per cent, Extremadura 26.3 per cent, Sicilia and Basilicata 21.8 per cent and Campania 21.3 per cent). At the same time less than 5 per cent of the workforce was out of work in the south of Germany, Luxembourg, some parts of northern Italy and Portugal outside of the Lisbon area and the Alentejo. 8 per cent of men were out of work compared with 11.5 per cent of women and 18.1 per cent of people under 25. Geographical variations were once again substantial. Amongst under 25 year-olds unemployment exceeded 50 per cent in many parts of the Italian Mezzogiorno (72.7 per cent in Caltanissetta and over 60 per cent in Napoli, Enna and Agrigento), exceeded 30 per cent in two-thirds of Spanish Level II regions, averaged 26.2 per cent in Ireland and reached 25 per cent in certain Belgian and French regions (EUROSTAT 1993).

At each point in time differences in the magnitude of unemployment help explain variations in GDP per head. An understanding of these differences requires, however, that some attention be paid to the dynamics of unemployment. Figure 5 accordingly records the evolution of unemployment in five European countries measuring unemployment in year t on the vertical axis and in year t-1 on the horizontal axis two factors warrant particular attention.

As Figure 5 shows unemployment varies with the economic cycle. As it also shows however the point around which unemployment revolves in all of the countries except Sweden increased after each of the major shocks since the end of the post-war "golden age" of full employment and comparatively high growth. Two features of the trends depicted in Figure 5 deserve attention. First in the 1964-74 unemployment averaged 0.9 per cent in West Germany, 2 per cent in Sweden, 2.3 per cent France, 2.9 per cent in the United Kingdom and 5 per cent in Italy (though with significant North-South differences). After the oil crisis unemployment increased sharply in all countries though in Sweden it subsequently returned to its previous equilibrium averaging 2.3 per cent in 1975 to 1991. In West Germany and the UK there were new short-lived equilibria in the late 1970s (averaging 3.4 and 5.5 per cent respectively), while in France and to a lesser extent Italy unemployment crept steadily upwards. In 1986 the gaps were wider (2.7 per cent in Sweden, 6.4 per cent in West Germany, 10.4 per cent in France, 10.5 per cent in Italy and 11.2 per cent in the UK). In the early 1990s unemployment soared in Sweden, while in the other countries a new equilibrium of mass unemployment seemed to be in place (see Freeman and Soete 1994). Second the amplitude of the cycles represented in Figure 5 varies indicating that the degree of instability also differs significantly from one country to another.

The rise in unemployment indicates that cohesion should not be viewed solely in terms of differentials. The absolute levels of unemployment and non-employment and the differentiation in income and life chances that they generate are critical determinants of the cohesiveness of a society especially as in mixed economies social integration occurs fundamentally through work.

FIGURE 5   Unemployment in the United Kingdom, Italy, France, Sweden and West Germany 1964-93

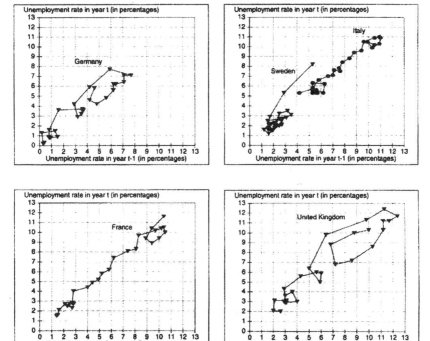

Source: elaborated from data in Central Statistical Office (1994) Economic trends and MI-DAS after Ormerod, 1994.

Trends in Income Inequality

A recent study of developments in the distribution of disposable income in
seventeen OECD countries (OECD 1995) showed that there was a rise in
inequality in the 1980s for the majority of countries. Increases in measured
inequality were the largest in the Netherlands, Sweden and in particular in
the United Kingdom and United States (see Table 2).

TABLE 2: Trends in income inequality in OECD countries

Country	Year	Gini coeff.	Year	Gini coeff.	Change in Gini coeff.
Finland	1990	21.5	1987	20.7	0.8
Sweden	1987	22.0	1981	19.9	2.1
Norway	1986	23.4	1979	22.2	1.2
Belgium	1988	23.5	1985	22.8	0.7
Luxembourg	1985	23.8			
Netherlands	1987	26.8	1983	24.7	2.1
Canada	1987	28.9	1981	28.6	0.3
Australia	1985	29.5	1981	28.7	0.8
France	1984	29.6	1979	29.7	-0.1
Un. Kingdom	1986	30.4	1979	27.0	3.4
Italy	1986	31.0			
Switzerland	1982	32.3			
Ireland	1987	33.0			
United States	1986	34.1	1979	30.9	3.2

Source: OECD (1995).

At the more recent dates for which there was data relative inequality
was smallest in the Scandinavian countries, Benelux and Luxembourg and
greatest in the United States, Ireland and Switzerland. (These figures are a
result of a complex set of factors that include changes in the distribution of
earnings and workforce participation, aging of the population, changes in
household structures, changes in taxation and income transfers with in several countries reductions in taxes in upper incomes and reductions in the

level and coverage of benefits and increases in the return to capital as well as changes in the ownership of assets in part as a result of privatization).

Competitiveness and Cohesion

This analysis of trends in disparities suggests that there was a turning-point in the mid-1970s. After 1974, growth was slower, and, for a decade, divergence occurred, though in the mid-1980s it gave way to renewed convergence. Disparities in GDP per head in 1991 were close to their mid-1970s level.

A disaggregation of disparities in GDP per head into productivity and employment rate differentials suggests that in the 1980s there was a trade-off between increases in the relative rates of productivity and employment: in some areas relative rates of employment improved as a result of the expansion of relatively low productivity activities, while in others relative productivity increased but without a sufficiently fast rate of output growth to sustain relative employment rates. This trade-off is suggestive of a fundamental dilemma as a realization of the gains of integration requires that the resources released as a result of restructuring are re-employed in activities where their contribution to output is greater.

A possible explanation of this dilemma lies in the increased internationalization of the economies of Member States and the intensification of international competition. Greater competition would normally result in a reduction in prices relative to incomes so that the consumers and users of goods and services gain. In so far however as producers are not re-employed (1) gains will be offset by greater welfare expenditures and an greater burden on government social security finances and (2) the multiplier effects of reduced incomes and expenditures of those who do not find new employment will have a depressive effect on output and employment. As adjustment is not instantaneous increases in competition in sectors that were formerly protected and in activities in which productivity growth exceeds the rate of output growth a short-term effect of change will be greater unemployment and non-employment.

If solidarity and compensation mechanisms are insufficiently strong there will be losers and problems of cohesion unless and until these resources are re-employed. A re-employment of resources is required, however, not just to ensure cohesion but also so that potential gains are realized. If the resources released (or the new generations that join the job market) are not re-employed in activities in which their contribution to output is greater than in the activities they left the medium-term gains remain potential rather than actual. In this sense improved cohesion is a prerequisite for the achievement of efficiency gains and growth.

What the evidence of the increase in unemployment and non-employment disparities and of the stabilization or increase in the magnitude of some disparities in income (along with the overall growth of unemployment and the slowness of output growth) suggest is that this adaptation is not taking place.

Conclusions

In capitalist economies there are constantly processes of differentiation and equalization of the conditions of production and exchange. Competition compels the less productive to change, while technology gaps offer opportunities to accelerate growth, but convergence and catch-up are processes that depend also on a wide range of social, political and institutional factors that permit the exploitation of this potential and on the character of the wider environment and are far from automatic consequences of market-adjustment. The evidence of the recent past suggest that convergence on one indicator or at one scale can coincide with divergence on/at others and that there are strong forces leading to greater inequality. What this chapter also suggests is that greater inequality is often a reflection of a failure to mobilise resources and an important determinant of poor economic performance (measured in term of living standards rather than profitability).

Note

1. To be in the ten per cent band or decile that lives in the regions with the highest levels of per capita output does not imply, however, that a household or individual is rich: it is average output that is large, and household income depends first on whether the income associated with a region's output of goods and services accrues to the region's inhabitants, and second on the personal distribution of income within the region.

References

Abramovitz, M. 1986. "Catching up, forging ahead and falling behind." *Journal of Economic History*, 46, 385-406.

Beatty C. and Fothergill S. 1996. "Registered and hidden unemployment in areas of chronic industrial decline: the case of the UK coalfields." *Regional Studies*, 30.

Boyer, R. 1996. *The seven paradoxes of capitalism ... Or is a theory of modern economies still possible*. Seminar given at the University of Wisconsin-Madison, 18-19 November.

CEC. 1996. *First Report on Economic and Social Cohesion 1996. Preliminary Edition.* Luxembourg: Office of Official Publications of the European Union.

Dalum,B., Laursen, K. and Verspagen, B. 1996. "Does Specialization Matter for Growth?" Paper is available electronically from http://meritbbs.unimaas.nl/tser/tser.html.

Dixon, R.J. and Thirlwall, A.P. 1975. "A Model of Regional Growth–Rate Differences on Kaldorian Lines." Oxford Economic Papers, 11, 201-214.

Domar, E. 1946. "Capital expansion, rate of growth and employment." *Econometrica*, 14 (April), 137-47.

Dunford M. 1993. "Regional disparities in the European Community: evidence from the REGIO databank." *Regional Studies*, 27, 8, 727-43.

_____. 1994. "Winners and losers: the new map of economic inequality in the European Union." *European Urban and Regional Studies*, 1, 2, 95-114.

_____. 1996. "Disparities in Employment, Productivity and Output in the EU: the Roles of Labor Market Governance and Welfare Regimes." *Regional Studies*, 30, 339-357.

EC (European Commission). 1996. *The spatial consequences of the integration of the new German Länder into the Community*. Luxembourg: Office for Official Publications of the European Communities.

EUROSTAT. 1993. "Unemployment in the regions of the Community in 1992." *Rapid Reports: regions*, number 2

_____. 1995. "Per capita GDP in the European Union's regions." *Statistics in focus: regions*, number 1

Fagerberg J., Verspagen B. and Caniëls M. 1997. "Technology, Growth and Unemployment across European Regions," *Regional Studies*, 31, 5, 457-66.

Freeman C. and Soete L. 1994. *Work For All or Mass Unemployment*. London: Pinter.

Harrod, R. 1939. "An essay in dynamic theory." *Economic Journal*, 49 (June), 14-33.

Kaldor, N. 1966. *Causes of the slow rate of growth of the United Kingdom*. Cambridge: Cambridge University Press.

_____. 1970. "The case for regional policies." *Scottish Journal of Political Economy*, November.

Kaldor, N., Targetti, F. and Thirlwall, A.P. (eds.) 1989a. *The essential Kaldor*. London: Duckworth.

_____. 1989b. *Further essays on economic theory and policy*. London: Duckworth

Krugman, P. (1994) "Competitiveness: a dangerous obsession." *Foreign Affairs*, 73, 2, 28–44.

OECD (Organization for Economic Cooperation and Development). (Annual). *National accounts of OECD countries*. Paris: OECD.

_____. (Annual). *Labor force statistics*, Paris: OECD.

Robinson, J. 1956. *The Accumulation of Capital*. London: Macmillan.

Schumpeter, J. A. 1934. *The theory of economic development: an inquiry into profits, capital, credit, interest, and the business cycle.* Translated from the German by Opie, R. Harvard economic studies no. 46. Cambridge, Mass.: Harvard University Press.

Thirlwall, A. P. 1979 "The balance of payments constraint as an explanation of international growth rate differences." *Banca Nazionale del Lavoro,* 32, 45–53.

10 European Unemployment: Myths and Realities[1]

THEODORE PELAGIDIS

Introduction

According to official figures, around 12% of the working population of the European Union is unemployed. Eighteen million European citizens, five million of them under twenty-five, are officially looking for work. Relevant research institutes around Europe inform us that the number of unemployed is continuing to rise. It is estimated that over the next two years at least another half million people will join the ranks of the unemployed.

The precipitous rise in unemployment in Europe has caused huge social problems in recent years. The rupture of the social cohesion, the marginalization of a large part of the labor force, the fall in living standards for a significant number of European citizens, has shaken the faith of Europeans in the European ideal of Social Europe, such that in a number of countries the supporters of Economic and Monetary Union (EMU) now constitute a minority.

The rise of unemployment confirms those who are skepticists about the way the "new Europe" is constructed and the way the EURO is established in particular. The aforementioned skepticism, based on the theory of Optimum Currency Area (OCA), focus on the mediocrity of the treaties of Maastricht and Amsterdam (Pelagidis 1997b, 1997c), where the emphasis is exclusively paid on "inflation targeting" and public deficits reduction rather than on growth and employment.

However, the majority of the authors in the relevant literature, instead of blaming economic policies implemented since 1992, attribute the European disease of unemployment – and lost production as a consequence — on factors such as technology, "globalization", labor market rigidities and the — so believed — generous welfare European States. More specifically, an influential section of academic and political opinion places the blame on three factors:

a) the nature of the new technologies and more generally the new type of development described as "jobless growth." Some economists view the unemployment problem as a result of skilled-biased technological change in particular (Lawrence 1994, Krugman 1995, Baldwin and Cain 1997). It is argued that there is a shift in the demand for skilled workers within industries, which can be explained by skilled-biased technological change. As a result, there is a decline in relative wages of the least educated workers, along with increased unemployment of these workers and of the low-skilled in particular.

b) the inflexibility of the European labor market, the high living standard of European working people, welfare programs and firing costs (Bean 1994) and above all high wages, both direct and indirect (in the form of social expenditure). Many of these inflexibilities have to do with institutional regulations (Wyplosz 1997) and are understood as the outcome of political influence by incumbent employees ("insiders"). According to this view, labor market rigidities allow "insiders" to achieve indirectly monopoly power in wage setting. Thus, unemployment levels are considered as a direct result of the powerful political influences exerted by people who already have jobs (Saint-Paul Gilles 1996, 1997). Conventional wisdom also mentions employment protection legislation and generous welfare benefits in Europe, which preserve rigidities and slow response of wages and prices to demand disturbances and thereby increase unemployment.

c) the increase of international trade and intensification of international competition, in other words, the effects of the so-called "globalization." It is claimed that the imports of products from developing countries with low labor costs undermine the international competitiveness of European products (Wood 1995). As a result, industries close-down and unemployment rises, especially that of least educated workers (Baldwin and Cain 1997).

Are the above factors really the cause of the high rates of unemployment in Europe?

Pretexts For European Unemployment

Technological Unemployment

First, unemployment is not, as claimed, a world-wide phenomenon. In Japan it fluctuates at about 3%, while in the USA it is approximately 4.5% (OECD 1997, A4) and falling. It is well-known that both the United States and Japan are in the forefront of technological innovation. By contrast, Europe is characterized by low levels of investment, low levels of expenditure on Research and Development (R&D) and a particularly slow rate of application of new technologies (see Tables 3 and 5 below). As a result, as has been pointed out in a relevant study carried out on behalf of the European Commission (1996), over the last thirty years the European Union has created only half as many new jobs as Japan and a fifth as many as the USA. Europe's technological backwardness is very faithfully reflected in the high cost of production of those services related to entrepreneurial activity and traditionally linked to state investments, such as communications and transport.

The logical conclusion then is that unemployment is a European phenomenon and a reflection of the technological backwardness of the EU and its resulting inability to match the performance of its competitors in meeting its potential, increase in productivity and ability to create new job opportunities (Vergopoulos 1995). Technological backwardness and the resulting sluggish rates of growth of the gross domestic product (GDP) are responsible for the high levels of unemployment. It is worth pointing out that the average rate of GDP growth between 1992 and 1996 was only 1.5%, while in the US was around 3%.

Wages and the Welfare State

The argument that direct wage payments are higher in the European Union than anywhere else would be supported only if it were the condition in all member states of the EU. But in Greece, for example, as we have demonstrated elsewhere (Pelagidis 1997a), labor costs, real wages and their share as a percentage of GDP are at very low levels. None of this is inconsistent with official unemployment rates exceeding ten percent (OECD 1997).

Any tendency in real wages (Dw-Di where w = wages and i = inflation) to exceed the rate of growth in productivity (production per hour or Dq-Dh) should logically, in accordance with the above argument, be reflected in an increase in the share accruing to labor (Ds) in the European Union (Gordon 1996). With labor cost increasing relative to its marginal product, if the share accruing to labor were to increase, profit levels should have been depressed, demand for labor should have diminished and unemployment should have increased (Gordon 1996).

TABLE 1   Adjusted wage share; total economy
(% of GDP at factor cost)

	71-80	*81*	*85*	*90*	*91*	*92*	*93*	*94*	*95*	*96**	*97***
EU	75.4	76.7	73.0	70.7	70.9	71.0	70.8	69.5	68.8	68.7	68.4
USA	72.1	71.7	71.0	71.8	72.6	72.4	72.0	72.1	71.9	71.3	72.4
Japan	78.0	78.6	74.6	74.1	74.1	74.2	72.9	72.1	71.7	74.3	72.4

Source: European Economy (1995), *European Economy (1996b), **European Economy (1997a).

The figures given by European Economy (1995, 1996b, 1997a) it emerges that in spite of the arguments focusing on the high wage levels in the European Union, the share of wages as a proportion of GDP has steadily declined since the early 80s (*see Table 1*). From 76.7% in 1981 it has fallen to 68.7% in 1996 and to 68.4 % in 1997, while in the United States it remains stable at 71 to 72%.

The average annual increase in real wages in Europe between 1992 and 1996 was around 0.7%, while the corresponding increase in productivity has been 2.0% (Eurostat & DG 1996). If we add to these the reduction of the labor share of income then we are clearly led to the conclusion that real wages and what is characterized as inflexibility in the labor market are not responsible for the increase in unemployment and poverty in Europe.

As far as the social wage is concerned, and the European welfare state in the wider sense, it should firstly be pointed out that unemployment in the European Union is a phenomenon of the past ten years. Throughout the post-war period, low rates of unemployment were eminently compatible with a welfare state that was even looked upon as a competitive advantage for Europe, as it was conducive to the production of the high-quality competitive products that predominated on the international markets. Why should this be considered a burden?

Trade and "Globalization"

"Globalization" of the economy and internationalized competition are used to explain the fact that conditions today are different. The opening of national economies and the increase in the volume of trade internationally have push European salaries down, because they have to compete with the low labor costs of countries outside the European Union. It is argued that European businesses close and investments are canceled because of the relative inflexibility of European wages.

The above arguments seem less convincing if we take into account that as a proportion of GDP, the level of trade between member countries in the OECD from 1982 to 1994 remained stationary at around 10% (OECD 1996, A71). And in Europe generally (not narrowly restricted to the countries of the EU) since the beginning of the 1980s, trade has remained at the same level of about 14% of European GDP. As for EU trade with OECD members, the equivalent proportion has risen only minimally to around 17%. It is particularly significant that with low labor cost countries such as China, Taiwan, Hong Kong, Singapore, Malaysia, Thailand and Korea, it accounts for only about 1% of GDP (OECD 1996, A71). EU exports to Asia generally, a low labor cost region, increased from 4.5% in 1989 to 7.1% in 1995, while imports rose to some extent, but less, from 5.3% in 1989 to 7.5% in 1995 (IMF 1996). It is also worth pointing out that the EU imported more investment capital from the United States (8.5 billion ECU) and Japan (1.4 billion ECU) than it exported (the United States, 6.4 billion ECU; Japan, 0.3 billion ECU) (Eurostat 1997).

The rise in unemployment cannot therefore be explained by the supposed increase in the volume of European trade with OECD members, and even less by the penetration of the European market by low-labor-cost goods. The percentages are, as we have seen, too low to explain, apart from the relative increase, the high level of unemployment in Europe.

Causes of European Unemployment

Even if wages or social expenditure – with the resulting public deficits – were prohibitive for the profitability of European businesses, one could well ask what the effects on the already weak increase in real total domestic demand in the EU would be of reducing them.

The increase in overall domestic demand in the EU from 1995 to 1996 was only about half that in Japan and much lower than in the US (*see Table 2*). More generally, in the first years of the present decade, the average increase in total domestic demand in the EU was only about 1% (European Economy 1996b).

TABLE 2   Demand (annual percentage increase 1995-1996)

	EU	*USA*	*Japan*
Private Consumption	1.7	2.5	2.4
Public Consumption	0.8	-0.9	2.1
Investments	2.3	5.3	3.2
Total Domestic Demand	1.4	2.2	2.6

Source: OECD (1996), A57.

Because of fiscal and monetary policies of excessive austerity in Europe, total demand has not increased in proportion to the increase in the workforce and thus of the labor supply. The problem relates to the inadequacy of the money supply in Europe – Germany being the number one culprit – which pushes real interest rates to high levels, thus undermining the increase in investments and income (Pelagidis 1997b, 1997c). Particularly interesting are the figures for investments in EU members, which are appreciably lower than those in Japan, and less than half of those in the United States (*see Table 3*), with negative consequences on GDP growth.

Given that European companies sell about 90% of their products on the European market, a further contraction in overall demand, and particularly in public and private consumption, would be even more damaging for prospects of increases in production and productivity.

It should be noted particularly that, technologically backward or otherwise, Europe has anything but a deficit in its trade with other countries of the world. European Union trade with countries outside Europe is in surplus, equivalent to approximately 1% of its GDP.

TABLE 3   **Real gross fixed capital formation
(cumulative % 1992-1996)**

	Private, non-construction	*All sectors*
USA	35.1	28.9
Japan	-13.7	1.9
EU	-0.4	0.3

Source: OECD (1996), A9, A8.

The rise in nominal wages over the period 1992-1995 has been under 4%, with real per unit labor costs declining sharply (European Union 1995). Both the trade balance and the balance of current account have seen a growing surplus in recent years, while the corresponding figures for the United States have tended in exactly the opposite direction (*see Table 4*).

TABLE 4   **Trade balances and balances of current account**

	1992	1993	1994	1995	1996*	1997*
	*Trade balances in $ billions***					
EU	-9.5	70.9	99.1	122.2	156.1	155.5
USA	-96.1	-132.6	-166.4	-177.6	-187.3	-200.5
Japan	132.4	141.6	145.9	138.9	96.91	109.0
	Balances of current account in $ billions					
EU	-78.3	8.9	10.5	58.4	83.3	87.9
USA	-67.8	-103.9	-155.7	-147.8	-149.5	-157.4
Japan	117.4	131.5	129.2	111.9	68.8	92.1

* For 1996 and 1997: European Economy, Supplement A, no.5 (Brussels: European Union, 1997, 24; Note: According to Eurostat services, the EU enjoyed an 11 billion ECU surplus for the first half of 1996 in its commercial transactions with third countries. (In ECU: EU 1995 = 24.2 billion; 1996 = 46.3 billion); [1 ECU=1.08$]
** Figures are FOB-FOB.

Source: European Economy (1996a), 24.

**TABLE 5   Per unit labor costs in the business sector
(cumulative % 1992-1996)**

	Nominal Cost	*Inflation**	*Real Cost*
USA	9.8	12.6	-2.8
EU	9.7	17.2	-7.5
Japan	1.8	2.9	-1.1

Source: OECD (1996), A16, A18. *Deflator of private consumption.

On the other hand, labor costs in the business sector have contracted three times faster in the EU than they have in the US (*see Tables 5 and 6*), while on the technological front, as we said previously, not only have investments and capital formation stagnated, but expenditure on Research and Development (R&D) is even further behind United States and Japan (*see Table 7*).

**TABLE 6   EU: relative unit labor costs in common
currency against nine -non EU- OECD
countries, 1961-1973=100**

	1992	*1993*	*1994*	*1995*	*1996*	*1997**
Unit labor costs	107.8	94.5	91.5	94.9	97.3	99.9
Annual % change	3.8	-12.4	-3.1	3.7	2.6	1.2

Source: European Economy (1996). *European Economy (1997).

TABLE 7   R&D expenditures as % of GDP (1996)

	Overall Economy	*Industry*
EU	1.9	1.0
USA	2.5	1.6
Japan	3.0	2.2

Source: European Commission (1996).

The result of the low rate of R&D Expenditure is, as the European Commission (1996) itself reports, much higher production costs in the EU than in the US and Japan, particularly in basic production coefficients such as energy, communications, and transport. Moreover scientific research personnel constitute 0.47% of the workforce in the EU compared with 0.74% in the US and 0.80% in Japan.

The foregoing leads to the conclusion that the EU, thus far, has taken advantage of the benefit of cheap labor to enter international markets at the expense of other countries, without converting these profits into new jobs, since it is precisely the advantage of the low percentage of the workforce in employment that secures these profits. This explains why over the last twenty-five years the European Union has created 50% fewer new jobs than Japan and less than 20% than the US (European Commission 1996).

To sum up, the backwardness of Europe in the critical sectors of investment, capital formation, R&D and job creation has led to a rise in unemployment in Europe at the levels of the '30s.

Policy Guidelines for a Social Europe

The "Alternative Europe" (*"l'autre Europe"*), the "Social Europe," is not an economically nonviable Europe. Quite the contrary. It is a Europe that must emphasize that high levels of employment and the high living standards of its citizens constitute competitive advantages, truly indispensable prerequisites for the production of superior-quality products and international market supremacy.

In Europe as a whole, policy measures for employment are being actively pursued. For example, in Germany, companies providing jobs for unemployed workers are given an 80% subsidy for the first six months and 60% for the second, while in France the employer is exempted from social insurance contributions for a period ranging from six to eighteen months. In other countries such as Greece, state expenditures to administer employment and placement services, as well as promote measures for dealing with youth unemployment, are significantly lower than elsewhere in the EU. It is worth noting that the Greek Ministry of Labor favors subsidization of the unemployed and the upgrading of their qualifications so as to facilitate their attempts to find work.

All of this would be well and good if the unemployment was due to workers lacking the appropriate qualifications to be appointed to a relative abundance of positions. But this is not the case. Very few new jobs are actually being created, since there has been no appreciable increase in the level of production (1.5% average growth in GDP in the EU between 1992 and 1996, compared with 3.0% in the US). The new jobs created are being outstripped by the growth in the workforce.

Because of the excessively tight economic policies in Europe, mainly as a result of high German interest rates and restrictive money supply policies, the increase in total demand (an average of 1.1% annually between 1992 and 1996) does not keep pace with the numerical growth of the workforce and the increase in productivity. Growth in the real money supply, as demanded by F. Modigliani (1996), the Nobel prize winner, would push real interest rates low enough for investments and GDP to revive and the rate of job creation to accelerate to a point where the present high rate of unemployment would start to level off.

A slight relaxation of monetary policy would be enough to bring down real interest rates and, with them, the cost of debt servicing. This would lead to a corresponding increase in the real rate of investment growth and GDP, so that drastic expenditure cuts and high primary fiscal surpluses (i.e. pro-cyclical economic policies), which merely undermine economic development, would no longer be perceived as necessary. Tax revenues would rise with the expansion of the tax base and real GDP could begin to approximate the "potential output," that is, the "expanded product" that would be available if we made full use of the forces of production currently being restrained and depressed, which is estimated at approximately 10% or more for the 1992-1996. This would moderate the level of unemployment, strengthen the balance of current accounts, and stabilize the national currencies in the money markets. By contrast, as long as inflation and the public deficit are dealt with through further cutbacks on consumption and expenditure, the cost of restraining price rises and reducing indebtedness will grow ever more disadvantageous in terms of unemployment, lost output and ultimately the process of convergence.

The logic of the "Stability Accord," decided upon in Dublin (December 1996) and ratified in Amsterdam (June 1997), in effect bans with the force of police ordinances any exercise of anticyclical economic policy and in its place institutes an absurd dialogue on the place of the decimal points in the fiscal deficits.

The political message from the European electorates (France, Great Britain, Italy and Greece) points to the so-called "*l'autre politique*" and "*l'autre Europe*" or, in other words, an end to the process of building the

Europe of the bankers and the backward-looking and conservative "establishment." For those who subscribe to the European ideal of development, social cohesion, and solidarity, this economic policy of full employment represents a viable answer to the popular call for the transformation of Europe's high standard of living into a competitive advantage by a more satisfactory means than Germany's tragic anachronism of achieving competitiveness through a passively flexible labor market, hard currency and zero inflation.

Note

1. An earlier version of this paper has been presented in the International Symposium "Rethinking Democracy and the Welfare State", held in Delphi, Greece, 2-5 October 1997. For helpful comments I thank K. Vergopoulos, R. Wolff, L. Katseli, M. Dunford, J. Huffschmid, J. Milios and other participants of the Delphi Symposium. The paper also appears in: *Challenge. The Magazine of Economic Affairs*, May/June 1998.

References

Baldwin, R. and Cain, G. 1997. "Shifts in US Relative Wages: The Role of Trade, Technology and Factor Endowments." CEPR Discussion Paper Series No.1596.
Bean, C. 1994. "European Unemployment: A Survey." *Journal of Economic Literature* 32(2), June, 573-619.
European Union. 1995. *Bulletin of EU*, No.12, Brussels: EU.
European Commission. 1996. *Report of the Committee for Competitiveness*, Brussels: EU.
European Economy.1995. *Annual Economic Report for 1995*, No.59, Brussels: EU.
_____. 1996a. *Supplement A*, No.5/6, Brussels: EU.
_____. 1996b. *Broad Economic Policy Guidelines*, No.62, Brussels: EU.
_____. 1997a. *Annual Economic Report for 1997*, No.63, Brussels: EU.
_____. 1997b. *Supplement A*, No.5, Brussels: EU.
Eurostat. 1997. *Statistics in Focus: Money and Finance #3*. Brussels: EU.
Eurostat and DGII. 1996. *EC Economic Data Pocket Book*, n.8/9, Brussels: EU.
Gordon, R. 1996. "Macroeconomic Policy in the Presence of Structural Maladjustment," CEPR Discussion Paper Series No.1493.
IMF. 1996. *World Economic Outlook, May*, IMF: Washington, D.C.
Kapstein, E. 1996. "Workers and the World Economy." *Foreign Affairs*, Vol.75, No.3, May/June, 17-37.
Krugman, P. 1995. "Technology, Trade and Factor Prices." NBER Working Paper No. 5355, November.
Lawrence R. 1994. "Trade, Multinationals and Labor." NBER Working Paper No. 4836, August.
Modigliani, F. 1996. "The Shameful Rate of Unemployment in the EMS: Causes and Cures," *The Economist* 144, No.3, 363-376.

OECD. 1996. *Economic Outlook*, No.59, June, Paris: OECD.
_____. 1997. *Economic Outlook*, No.61, June, Paris: OECD.
Pelagidis, T. 1997a. "La 'Flexibilite' du Travail dans le Secteur du Textile et de l'Habillement en Grèce du Nord: une Etude Empirique," *Relations Industrielles*, Vol.52, No.1, 114-137.
_____. 1997b. "Europe at a Monetary Crossroads: Problems and Prospects," *Cahiers Economiques de Bruxelles*, No.152, 451-486.
_____. 1997c. "Divergent Real Economies in Europe," *Economy and Society* Vol.26, No.4, 546-559.
Saint-Paul Gilles. 1996. "Understanding Labor Market Institutions: A Political Economy Perspective," CEPR Discussion Paper Series No.1438.
_____. 1997. "The Rise and Persistence of Rigidities," CEPR Discussion Paper Series No. 1571.
Vergopoulos, K. 1995. "Unemployment Destabilizes Europe," *Avgi*, 4 June, 10 (in Greek).
Wood, A. 1995. *North-South Trade, Employment and Inequality: Changing Fortunes in a Skill-Driven World*, London: Clarendon Press.
Wyplosz, C. 1997. "Notes on Unemployment in Europe," CEPR Discussion Paper Series (forthcoming 1998).

PART D
THE END OF THE WELFARE
STATE IN EUROPE ?

11 Diminished Profitability and Welfare Decline (Reflections on the Irreformability of Capitalism in the 1990s)

JOHN MILIOS

Introduction: The Crisis of Conservative Policies and the Ineffectuality of the Left

In the eighties or early nineties, conservative parties obtained the support of the middle classes in many Western capitalist countries and won elections on the strength of a clear "liberal" political slogan: "Let market forces act freely. Give us, the conservatives, the chance to fight all forms of bureaucratic, corporatist or monopolistic distortions of the market mechanism, and the economy will once again achieve the high growth rates of the past." This conception was then concretized in a restrictive economic program aimed at curtailing wages and social spending, deregulating markets – including, of course the labor market – and privatizing public enterprises.

However, today's austerity is futile unless society can be persuaded that it is paving the way for tomorrow's prosperity.[1] As the promised economic prosperity fails to eventuate, liberal ideologies meet with diminishing public acceptance. Conservative parties, after a period in office – lengthy in the case of Britain and Italy, shorter in for example France or Greece — have accordingly lost elections to center-left parties.

What deserves further investigation, though, is the inability of center-left governments to implement an alternative strategy for overcoming poor economic performance and social crisis. What the parties constituting these governments promised to the electorate in order to return to power was simply the same conservative policy of restriction, aimed at achieving price stability, cutting the public deficit, reducing debt, etc. (all of this codified in EU countries as a policy framed in accordance with the Maastricht convergence criteria), leavened by a degree of "social sensitivity," i.e. measures of social protection for the low-income or marginalized sectors of the population.[2]

What took place, is a retreat of the political and ideological visions of the (ruling) Left, which manifests itself also in a conservative shift of the majority of left intellectuals. These intellectuals confine themselves now to the continuous reiteration of the simple thesis that full deregulation can never exist and that therefore center-left are more effective than conservative governments.[3]

One apparent attempt to create an integrated alternative vision to the pragmatic administration of existing relations is "stakeholder capitalism," a policy conception involving a critique of conservative positions which was formulated and broadly discussed in Britain in the two years leading up to the 1997 general elections. The "stakeholder capitalism" approach on the one hand utilizes many of the ideas or arguments also put forward by nearly every center-left governing party of recent years, and on the other attempts to mold them further into a political and social plan for reforming contemporary capitalism (in Britain). However, in my opinion it represents the mere semblance of an alternative to conservative policy. Its claim to be able to achieve the same goals by other means is altogether fantastic.

In the section that follows I will undertake a brief presentation of the "stakeholder capitalism" approach, followed in the next three sections of the paper by a critique of the approach in question. I will then attempt to determine the reasons for the stability of conservative policy and to analyze the factors underlying poor economic performance. In the final section of the paper I will address questions bearing on the future of the welfare state and the political strategy of the Left.

Visions of a "Decent Capitalism"...

The central idea of center-left governments of the mid- and late-nineties is that economic prosperity and social cohesion cannot be achieved simply through the unfettered functioning of markets. The actual problem is, however, to establish a clear demarcation of the limits – and to determine the proportions and the character – of state regulation. In this context, center-left governments, persisting in policies that give priority not to reducing unemployment but to stabilizing prices, curtailing public deficits, promoting "labor-market flexibility" and privatizing public enterprises, appear as "moderate" exponents of conservative policy, "monetarism with a human face" as it were. These policies therefore suffer from a lack of strategic vision, of a *hegemonic social ideology,* which would be different from center-right pragmatism. The "stakeholder capitalism" perspective was formulated in Britain as a way out of this strategic embarrassment. According to its supporters it can "give the intellectual leadership back to the Left for the first time in twenty years" (Kelly et al, 1997, 238).

Stakeholding implies social inclusion, citizenship, co-operation and the social contract and is meant to foster such ideas as functioning principles of contemporary capitalism. What differentiates this project of stakeholder capitalism from other attempts[4] to embellish capitalism, promoting it as a social system favoring a "harmony of interests" among social classes or individuals, is that its supporters do not restrict themselves to defending these ideas, but use them as the starting point for a critique of existing relationships and structures, which supposedly prevent the ideas from being implemented. "Stakeholder capitalism" therefore appears as an adversary to existing capitalism under conservative hegemony, not engaging in apologetic declarations but on the contrary demanding change. The fact that the whole project is embedded in the theoretical approaches and analytical notions put forward by some of its supporters naturally has a bearing on the dynamics of this posture.

The publication in 1995 of the first edition of *The State We're In,* by Will Hutton, might be considered the starting point of the campaign for stakeholder capitalism and the discussion related thereto. Hutton, now editor of *The Observer* and at that time economics editor of *The Guardian,* in 1996 brought out a second revised edition of the book, which had remained on the paperback best-seller list for more than six months and had been broadly discussed in newspapers as well as in articles published in referred journals. The concept of stakeholder capitalism was adopted by

Tony Blair during the 1997 election campaign, having already been incorporated into British trade union documents (such as *Your Stake at Work - TUC Proposals for a Stakeholder Economy*, 1996).

One of Hutton's main ideas, implied also in the title of his book, is that capitalism is inconceivable independently of its institutional edifice, and more specifically of the state. His critical analysis targets British capitalism as it took shape during the period of Conservative rule after 1979. He writes: "If a well-functioning market economy requires skilled workforces, strong social institutions like schools and training centers, and a vigorous public infrastructure, these cannot be achieved if the governing class cannot understand the values implicit in such bodies" (Hutton 1996, 25). This idea embodies a critique of the notion of "globalization" and its political implications, i.e. the proposition that the internationalization of capital and the economic interdependence of international markets have developed to such a point that they make all forms of national economic policies (if different from the conservative dogmas of deregulation and "flexibility") impossible. As Hutton himself puts it: "the world is not *that* global" (Hutton, in Kelly et al 1997, 7) Or, formulated another way, "capitalism is not simply and exclusively an economic system but a socio-political system whose content and structure is formed and moulded by its history" (D. Kelly, in Kelly et al, 49).

However, what lends Hutton's book its broad intellectual authority is its incorporation of a twofold critique of mainstream conceptions: on the one hand a codified theoretical critique of neoclassical economic postulates concerning the way the (capitalist) economy functions, on the other a polemic against the policies followed in Britain under Conservative governments and so of the way that British capitalism has developed.

Hutton disputes the key tenets of neoclassical economic theory (the notion of economic rationality, the doctrine of rational expectations, the law of diminishing returns, the theory of general competitive equilibrium), preferring a Keynesian approach according to which a correctly regulated financial system constitutes a prerequisite for increased investment, which in turn represents "the key motor of the economy's prosperity because it has a snowball effect, what Keynes called the multiplier" (Hutton 1996, 242). If the financial system's inherent tendency to liquidity is not retarded by state policies, it may act counter-productively and thus destabilize the market economy. This means, according to Hutton "that unmanaged capitalism is inherently unstable as a system and that successful enterprise is a social rather than an individualist act" (Hutton 1996, 237, see also Hutton 1994).

At the level of concrete analysis of British capitalism, Hutton criticizes the effects of conservative policies such as dogmatic monetarism and above all the deregulation of financial markets. He claims that such policies granted supremacy to stock markets and the financial system at the expense of the British economy as a whole, eroding the country's productive capacity, which is directly linked to industry and investment. As a result, an extremely diffuse ownership structure evolved whereby a hundred and sixty insurance companies and pension funds own seventy percent of the shares in British enterprises, putting pressure on managers to pay high dividends (in order to avoid takeovers) and thus reducing the funds available for investment. The short-termist culture of financial markets is in this way transmitted to the entire economy, displacing long-term investment and growth strategies. The attitude of owners is characterized by a counterproductive "lack of commitment to and responsibility for their assets (...) because they are always ready to walk away from the companies they own by selling their shares" (Hutton 1996, 157).

British capitalism thus loses, according to Hutton, its ability to increase productivity, to introduce innovation in the means of production, to achieve high growth rates, to create new jobs, to distribute prosperity throughout the whole of society. Inequality and social marginali-zation then occurs, as a consequence of "the spiral of corporate downsizing and de-layering, and the displacement of risk onto the labour force" (Hutton in Kelly et al 1997, 4). The end result is a thirty/thirty/forty society, with thirty percent of the population unemployed and marginalized, thirty percent insecure and "newly marginalized" and only forty percent of the population holding a secure and stable job.

The project of "stakeholder capitalism" aims at curing all these shortcomings of (British) capitalism. Hutton and all other exponents of the "stakeholder capitalism" concept believe that this is possible. "Thus the great challenge of the twentieth century, after the experience of both state socialism and unfettered free markets, is to create a new financial architecture in which private decisions produce a less degenerate capitalism. The triple requirement is to broaden the area of stake-holding in companies and institutions, so creating a greater bias to longterm commitment from owners; to extend the supply of cheap, longterm credit; and to decentralize decision-making. The financial system, in short, needs to be comprehensively republicanised" (Hutton 1996, 298).

"Stakeholder capitalism" thus appears as a vision of a new, cooperative and socially decent form of capitalism. This form of capitalism is moreover considered to be the only one that can be successful. In Hutton's words "there is clearly a huge interest in trying to construct a way in which a moral community can coexist with a successful capitalism" (Hutton in Kelly et al 1997, 8). "Successful capitalism demands a fusion of co-operation and competition and a means of grafting such a hybrid into the soil of the economic, political and social system" (Hutton 1996, 255).

... Fudge and Fudge Again

The concept of stakeholder capitalism implies that it is possible politically and ideologically to shape a structural unity, i.e. a unity of interests on a stable and long-term basis, among individual workers and "their" enterprise. From such a perspective the worker is seen as a part of the capitalist enterprise, as committed to it, as included in the enterprise.[5]

The "stakeholder capitalism" approach thus attempts to refute the notion of capitalism's inherently exploitative and contradictory character – the notion that it constitutes a system of class power and class exploitation (extraction of surplus value) of the laboring class by the capitalist class. It is aware of the reality of inequality and social exclusion (what Hutton describes as a "thirty/thirty/forty society") but attributes it to the hegemony of the "counterproductive" financial system (and its capital) and to conservative policies of market deregulation, not to the class structure of the capitalist economy.

To my mind this approach constitutes a theoretical and ideological retreat from classic social-democratic positions in favor of liberal-individualist ideas. Social Democracy traditionally conceived of working people and the labor movement as an entity, a social class and a social force defined by its own special class interests and goals, even if under certain circumstances or in certain conjunctures these interests were seen as being compatible with those of specific capitalist fractions or of the capitalist class as a whole. In the case of stakeholder capitalism the working class, with its special class interests, is considered non existent and the analysis focuses on *individual workers*,[6] whose interests are regarded as integrated (or requiring integration) into "their" company's interests and goals. This theoretical and ideological theses have specific political consequences: "I am not an advocate of (...) industry-wide collective bargaining (...) Instead I conceive of the workforce as, in European terms, a social partner who will bargain and operate at the level of the firm and the industry. This is not a return to old-style corporatism" (Hutton in Kelly et al 1997, 7).

Apart from this, the question arises as to whether, and to what extent, the "stakeholder capitalism" agenda is feasible, i.e. if it is actually possible to bring into effect a plan of co-operation and mutual commitment between labor and "productive capital" (enterprises) for a reform of state institutions and a challenge to the hegemonism and unaccountability of financial markets. The feasibility of the "stakeholder capitalism" strategy has been disputed by both right and left.[7]

The whole concept of "stakeholder capitalism" can be disputed not only because it arbitrarily assumes a stable commitment of workers to "their" enterprise, but also because it is founded on the undocumented assumption of a "structural" contradiction between the "hegemonic" financial and the industrial ("productive") capital. This contradiction is regarded, as already shown, as an outcome of monetarist economic policies which transmitted the short-termist culture of financial markets to the entire British economy.

However, the expansion or contraction of the financial markets depends on the economic conjuncture and the (upswing or downswing) phase in capital accumulation (the phase of the economic cycle) and not on the "entrepreneurial culture" in one or the other country. It was Karl Marx who has shown, in Part V of Volume 3 of *Capital*, that the expansion of credit and of financial speculation is closely related with the periodic economic depressions: An increase in profits (due to a suppression of the wages fund), which takes place in a conjuncture of low rates of capital accumulation (depression), boosts the financial sphere and speculation, long before an upswing trend in the economic cycle is made possible (through restructuring of the capitalist production). (See Marx 1981, Ch. 32). On the basis of this analysis, Paul Mattick pointed out, almost 30 years ago: "This (the Keynesian, J.M.) distinction between 'industry' and 'finance,' between 'productive' and 'parasitical' capital is as old as capitalism itself and gave rise to a pseudo-struggle against 'interest-slavery' and irresponsible speculators (...) Speculation may enhance crisis situations by permitting the fictitious over-evaluation of capital, which then cannot satisfy the profit claims bound up with it" (Mattick 1969, 23-24).[8]

Share prices increased as more and more money-capital moved into the stock markets, as a result of a contraction of the spheres of profitable investment in the "real" economy. What the "stakeholder capitalism" approach construes as the negative element in the hegemonic role of finance capital (undermining owners' "commitment to and responsibility for their assets," Hutton 1996, 157) has to do not so much with shareholders' expectations that they will earn high dividends as with the fast changing value of the shares themselves, i.e. with the expectations of "financial investors" that they will be able to buy shares cheap and sell them dear, or to hold shares of high and increasing value. It is this process that has driven share values in most capitalist countries to levels no longer corresponding to the actual performance of rise in output of the "real" economy.[9]

The "hegemony" of the financial markets does not derive from some inherent contradiction between productive and financial capital, but from the slow-down in the rate of *productive* capital accumulation. As Karl Marx puts it, "accumulation is the independent, not the dependent, variable" (Marx 1981, 679).

Aspects of Germany's "Social-Market": The Supremacy of Finance Capital and Policies of Downsizing Enterprises

In order to defend their arguments, the supporters of the stakeholding idea would need to undertake on the one hand a theoretical analysis of the social structures, classes, antagonisms and tensions in a capitalist society and on the other to examine the dynamics of stakeholding through history. Instead, Hutton argues with the simplistic affirmation that *"stakeholder capitalism" already exists, in contemporary Germany and its neighboring countries (Austria, Switzerland, the Netherlands...).*

Hutton's reflections are based on a twofold assertion: a) that radically different forms of capital do exist,[10] and that the "German form" of capitalism is actually a "stakeholder capitalism." Through this sleight-of-hand he transforms the "stakeholder capitalism" agenda from a universal promise of creating a humane capitalism ("the great challenge of the twentieth century, after the experience of both state socialism and of unfettered free markets" (Hutton 1996, 298) to the banal pragmatism of adopting the (supposedly different from the British) "German model" of capitalism in Britain. He therefore becomes a run-of-the-mill apologist for actually existing (German !!!) capitalism:

> Capital and labour operate in partnership (...) It is a social market (...) there is a compromise in favour of concerted and co-operative behaviour aimed at boosting production and investment. Labour has to recognise the legitimacy of capital, and capital the rights of labour (...) Wider economic policy is the out-

come of negotiations between the various social partners (...) In order for managers and workers to run enterprises collaboratively, financial stakeholders have to concede that they cannot maximise their returns in the short run (...) The rentier tradition is very weak in Germany (Hutton 1996, 262-68).

However, his simple assumption that there is still such a thing as "the German miracle" (the miracle of the "Social Market") cannot disguise the fact that since 1994 all kinds of indices that he considers crucial for the determination of the prevalent "form of capitalism" (growth rates of the GDP and of gross fixed capital formation in equipment, change in the number of employed and in the unemployment rate) have deteriorated in Germany to such an extent that they now rate below the corresponding figures for the British economy (EU 1997).

The rate of unemployment, for example, hit a new post-war record in Germany in July 1997, as the national figure exceeded 11.3% (18.2% in Eastern and 9.8% in Western Germany, *Financial Times*, August 7 1997).[11] Moreover, for all Hutton's assertions, the behavior of the German stock market is not qualitatively different from that of its British counterpart.

It is characteristic that until the mid-eighties more than 42% of shareholder value in Germany was in the hands of the companies themselves, often through cross-holdings of shares among enterprises. This situation has changed rapidly since the late eighties or early nineties. More than forty percent of investors in the Frankfurt stock market are now non-Germans (Japanese and European banks, American pension funds, etc.) so that what has now emerged in Germany is a dispersed pattern of shareholder value similar to that prevailing in Britain.

In Germany, as in Britain, shareholders and company managers work together quite harmoniously to ensure that the latter follow policies that enhance the confidence of the financial markets, thereby ensuring increases in the shareholder value of companies. What are these policies? They are policies of radical income redistribution in favor of capital, or what is called "downsizing" of enterprises. Their aim is to increase company profitability through intensifying of labor exploitation and curtailment of their less profitable activities.

The era of financial undervaluation of enterprise assets which enabled some speculators to buy out companies cheaply only in order to demolish them (to break them up) and sell them piece by piece, has been over since the early nineties. Tension between companies and financial markets has now eased. Share values everywhere have reached levels that are clearly higher than the actual market value of the companies' assets, and managers now have every reason to co-operate with those who take a proprietary interest in the shareholder value of their companies. Financial takeovers of companies are now organized in a less counterproductive way, with managers and banks also participating, as we will illustrate below, citing the Krupp-Thyssen case.

The downsizing process is represented by the various hegemonic capitalist forces – economic and intellectual alike – as "modernization" of the economy. Its concomitant of increased unemployment is depicted as an inevitable by-product of modernization. In reality it represents nothing more than a strategy of reshuffling power relations to the benefit of capital and to the detriment of employees. It may perhaps be a different strategy from the one deployed during the sixties and seventies (in response to the different relationship of forces prevailing at that time) when high (and rising) rates of profit were related to rapid increases in output, stable or even increasing wage incomes and low unemployment. Nevertheless the defining characteristic of the strategy, now as then, is that it serves to link the interests of managers and shareholders, i.e. the different fractions of capital.

Before closing this section, let me illustrate how the German "social market" operates in the nineties by citing some specific (albeit characteristic) examples. This, by the way, is a method very much favored by Hutton. The number of Volkswagen employees has fallen from 261,000 in 1990 to 241,000 in 1996. At BASF during the same period numbers have fallen from 135,000 to 107,000. At Thyssen from 149,000 to 123,000. At Daimler-Benz from 377,000 to 299,000. The downward trend in employment was followed by a steep increase in the share value of all these companies. From January 1996 to March 1997 the share value of VW increased by 95%, of BASF by 98%, of Thyssen by 30%, of Daimler-Benz by 75% (Stamatis 1997).

The comparatively low increase in the share value of Thyssen is related to the secret plans of Krupp (who had for this purpose paid more than 200 million DM to market analysts) to take over Thyssen by purchasing 66% of the company's shares (80% of which had already been dispersed) for a sum of 9 billion DM. In order to implement its plan Krupp did a deal with two major German banks (Deutsche Bank and Dresdner Bank) to borrow the entire amount of 9 billion DM from them, and in return to sell, immediately on takeover, seventeen of its own subsidiaries and four of Thyssen's subsidiaries, for the purposes of paying back part of the loan. It is worth noting at this point that from the viewpoint of the market value of its assets, the Thyssen group is nearly twice the size of the Krupp group.

The takeover of Thyssen by Krupp and the subsequent downsizing of the conglomerate was expected to push its shareholder value rapidly upwards, to the benefit of all "stakeholders" in the plan (Krupp, the two major banks, shareholders of Krupp and Thyssen). After an upheaval of workers in both enterprises in March 1977 (the manager of Krupp could not enter or leave the company premises without police protection), the takeover plan was abandoned. Instead the two companies agreed to merge their steelworks (with 60% of the shares held by Thyssen and 40% by Krupp). Under the terms of this agreement there was an immediate reduction in the workforce at the new steelworks from 66,800 to 58,900 workers.

Speculation, downsizing, raising shareholder values, increasing unemployment, all of these flow from the logic of capital, not from national "cultures." The poverty of the "stakeholder capitalism" analysis is glaringly evident in the sterility and ineffectuality of all reform programs of actually existent capitalist relations, at least wherever they lock themselves inside the ideological and strategic straitjacket of capitalist economic indices.

The Inherent Conservatism of the Plan for European Monetary Union

Hutton's methodological approach is not new. While advancing an ostensibly radical critique of domestic conditions, of the "form of capitalism" prevailing at a particular location, he postulates a supposedly humane, decent and socially responsive nucleus of capitalism, a putative "successful capitalism" which remains only to be identified and brought to the attention of the public.[12] It does seem worth asking, however, why Hutton and the supporters of "stakeholder capitalism" should choose such a banal model for humane capitalism as Kohl's Germany.

The answer to this question may be found in Hutton's latest book, *The State to Come*, published just a month before the May 1, 1997 British general elections. In this book Hutton presents a summary of his major ideas, reviews critiques of his previous book,[13] in some cases modifying his position in response to them, advocates an electoral victory for the Labor Party, and presents for the first time his ideas on European unification. In the final section of the book Hutton identifies "stakeholder capitalism" with European monetary union and the Maastricht criteria. He writes: "The stakeholder economy and society are related to if not identical with the European economic and social model, and it is easier to build and sustain them in a wider European context than acting alone (...) The euro could be the trigger for moving Europe into a virtuous economic cycle of rising investment, consumption and employment – a millenial boom. (...) The single currency, in short, could be a potential master stroke" (Hutton 1997, 92, 97, 99). In the final analysis "stakeholder capitalism" is conceived as being the Maastricht Treaty agenda for a European Economic and Monetary Union (EMU).

It is not by chance, then, that Hutton grounds his pro-euro stance in argumentation derived from financial considerations:

> The world's investment and financial community holds too many dollars and wants to diversify, but neither the mark nor the yen can take the strain (...) By contrast the euro is backed by a European economy that runs a trade surplus and is self-sufficient; moreover, it will be launched (...) against a background of low inflation, high unemployment and output well below potential. There will be a clamour to buy it, and it will appreciate against both the yen and the dollar. (...) The low interest-rate regime will lead to an increase in asset values from houses to shares. (...) That increase in wealth will help create a Continent-wide feel-good factor, helped by the hard euro making imports cheaper and thus real income higher (Hutton 1997, 96-97).[14]

Hutton therefore becomes a supporter of the same speculative increase in shareholder values that he had previously regarded as the cause of "short-termism" and all the other evils that prevented British capitalism from being successful.

The disintegration of Hutton's progressivism illustrates the inability of the EMU perspective (which has been adopted by all European center-left parties, in or out of office) to promise the European peoples anything other than increasing profits or share prices, or the creation of a European financial market that will be able to compete with or even outflank the American and East Asian financial markets. The only way to integrate this prospect with the vision of a humane, decent "stakeholder" capitalism is to adopt the conservative view that increase in profits or in shareholder value is the motor for the provision of welfare and the distribution of wealth to all of society. But center-left parties and center-left intellectuals have differentiated themselves from such conservative ideas, haven't they?

Over-accumulation, Profitability and the Capitalist Offensive

The decay of center-left reform plans testifies to the continuing conservative hegemony, at least in the field of economic and social policies. A slight moderation of increases in taxation and an even more moderate and less significant increase in public spending on education and social security do not suffice to distinguish a policy from the one that would be implemented by a conservative government.[15]

How then are we to comprehend this conservative hegemony, which appears to prevail irrespective of which party happens to be in power? I think that to answer this question we must give serious consideration to Marx's analysis of the immanent regularities that govern the evolution of capitalism – what may be called, using the theoretical conceptions that he introduced, the expanded reproduction of capitalist relations. This means bearing in mind that capitalism is an exploitative class power, the motive force of which is *"the valorization of capital, i.e. appropriation of surplus labor, production of surplus value, of profit"* (Marx 1981, 360), and not the production and distribution of wealth in general.

Having re-established these general preliminaries, one can now explore the "specific difference" that characterizes capitalist development since the early seventies. This is a period in the post-war history of all developed Western capitalist economies marked by diminishing or low growth rates. Statistical analyses confirm that poor economic performance during this period is correlated with a fall in the profit rate of overall capitalist production. This era can be comprehended in Marxian terms as one of "over-accumulation of capital," as I have argued elsewhere (Ioakimoglou-Milios 1993, Milios 1994, 1996). Accordingly, following Marx's logic, we may reiterate that any period of decreased profitability points to an inability on the part of capital *"to exploit labor at the level of exploitation* required by the 'healthy' and 'normal' functioning of the capitalist production process" (Marx 1981, 364, emphasis added).

A declining ability of capital to exploit labor should not be attributed, however, primarily to increasing wages or other forms of labor income, as if the capitalist economy did not differ from the economy of societies of antediluvian crop-picking tribespeople, working without means of production. As evidenced by many empirical analyses, falling rates of profit are almost invariably linked to decreasing "capital efficiency," which very simply means that the value of the fixed capital stock is increasing at a higher rate than the value of the product gained by means of that capital stock (Busch 1978, 1992, Ioakimoglou 1994, Milios 1996).[16] From the capitalist viewpoint there is only one way to deal with this problem of declining profit-rate levels: *economize on constant capital (means of production), at the same time reducing labor's share of the net product* (the percentage of net product going on wages).

Having examined this trend, have we then arrived at an explanation for the capitalist offensive against wages and against the labor movement? Not yet, for as can be shown both theoretically and empirically, the most effective way to reduce labor's share of the net product is not to cut real wages but to increase labor productivity (see Milios 1996, for a detailed analysis). Many people would argue at this point that since an increase in labor productivity presupposes a restructuring of the productive apparatus, investment in new technologies and the introduction of innovation, it is also dependent on a supportive workplace environment that will enable workers to make effective use of the means of production, to the advantage of capitalist production itself. Such approaches appear to me to miss the whole point of Marx's scientific analysis of the exploitative and inherently contradictory character of capitalist production. It is no accident that they fail to understand why the capitalist class insists on its own offensive against labor, or why governments insist on restrictive policies (favoring downsizing of enterprises, financial speculation and increasing unemployment). After all, is there actually a "lack of consensus" in contemporary capitalist societies?

Marx's analysis shows that the ability of the capitalist class to reorganize production, to modernize the means of production and to economize on constant capital (as the only way out of crises of over-accumulation) is not a technical aspect of the economy but an outcome of the social relation of forces, anchored in class struggle. Restructuring the enterprise, above all, means restructuring a set of social (class) relations and aims at increasing the rate of exploitation. It is thus a process which presupposes on the one *hand an increasing power of the capitalist class over the production process itself,* and on the other *a devalorization of all inadequately valorized capital* (downsizing or liquidating enterprises) and thus economizing on the utilization of constant capital. It therefore presupposes not only increasing despotism of managers over workers (the suppression of all trade union or institutional barriers to "enterprise culture" and the vested interests of capital) but also increasing unemployment. Consequently, *economic restructuring is synonymous with the capitalist offensive against labor.*

So far the capitalist offensive against labor has been resoundingly successful. It has succeeded in depressing wages and increasing labor productivity, thus reducing labor's share of the net product. In other words it has dramatically changed the relation of forces in favor of capital. As a result a specific type of social consensus has indeed been created, for the first time in the post-war period, based on the acceptance by the laboring class of capitalist ideas and objectives. It is a consensus not only among the "secure" fractions laboring in large and profitable enterprises (who generally receive above average wages), and their employers, but also among trade unions and employers' organizations, which have almost everywhere become "social partners." Isn't it consensus when trade unions accept that a key issue in social dialogue is how to increase profitability, or how to secure the national economy's competitive position in the global economy? It is consensus: consensus between the winners and the defeated.

Yet profitability in most capitalist economies has remained low, due to decreasing or at best stagnant capital efficiency. There are many parameters to this problem, and a variety of social factors underlying it. They have to do not only with the way technology is created and applied to the production process. They also have to do with resistance by labor, which has never ceased, despite the reshuffling of power relations to the benefit of capital. What is decisive, however, is the vicious circle created by curtailment of demand (a by-product of reduced working class income and increasing unemployment) which in turn leads to decreasing rates of utilization of capacity, i.e. to decreasing capital efficiency in the economy.

Center-left parties (and their "organic intellectuals" like Hutton) are part of the capitalist offensive, as I tried to illustrate in previous sections of this paper. They acknowledge "the abandonment of (...) corporatism, the lowering of trade union power and the assault on the nationalized industries" (Hutton 1997, 104, also see footnote 12). But they also realize that the problem of capitalist profit levels has not been solved and also that diminishing social cohesion and rising social distress may in the long run undermine the successfully accomplished "consensus of the defeated."

The case of Hutton is in my opinion worth discussing because he tries to tackle the problem from the viewpoint of "social capital" (as Marx called it), i.e. in relation to the interests of the capitalist class as a whole. So he talks about co-operation and "stakeholding," calling for increased commitment of workers to profit maximization, in exchange for more employment and an increasing wage income (which is then expected to boost demand). But who is the "auctioneer" who will make such a deal? Who could ensure that the thousands of workers fired after this year's mergers might remain at work? Who would re-employ the millions of unemployed Germans, Spaniards or Americans?

Given the low rates of capital accumulation and the existing social relation of forces, enterprises ("individual capital" in Marx's terminology) "choose" to cope with the profitability problem not by expanding production and demand but by further depressing the labor share on the one hand, and on the other by collaborating with financial capital to increase shareholder value. *Financial hegemony is embedded in over-accumulation and diminished profitability. It is not their cause.* Without a radically different balance in the relation of social forces (as established through class struggle), no "auctioneer" and no reformer can foster an expansionary and socially decent capitalism.

The End of the Welfare State?

From the above analysis it becomes clear that in the present conjuncture and the with the present social balance of forces, it is impossible to re-establish the institutional framework of the welfare state as it existed in Western capitalist societies during the sixties and seventies. The reason for this is that *the main prerequisite for the welfare state is a collectively organized working class, capable of imposing its demands on the state, i.e. capable of bargaining with the capitalist class from a position of relative strength.*

Gunnar Myrdal explicitly defended the above argument nearly forty years ago in his lectures delivered at Yale University in 1958, i.e. before the fully-fledged welfare state had come into existence. Myrdal correctly regarded "the reshaping of the labor market in the workers' interest" as a key element in the building of the welfare state (Myrdal 1960, 32), and he further clarified his views as follows:

> The inherited liberal ideal of fair play has more and more generally and definitely been translated into a demand that wages, prices, incomes and profits should be settled by various sorts of *collective bargaining*. It has become the responsibility of the state to provide such conditions by legislation and administration. (...) The workers in all the Western countries have succeeded in getting the state to lay down a great number of rules and to create institutions which very much strengthen their bargaining position in the labor market against the employers. (...) Gradually the state has been moved to enter the la-

bor market more directly, by undertaking to increase the demand for labor in times of rising unemployment by means of public works and in other ways (Myrdal 1960, 32, emphasis added).

The welfare state is incompatible with "labor market flexibility" and the replacement of collective bargaining at the national level by "social partnership at the level of the firm" that deprives labor of its combativeness in the face of the capitalist offensive.

Does the above thesis mean that we are now witnessing the final retreat of the welfare state? I don't think that such a conclusion would be warranted. Capitalism has proven to be a very flexible social system, capable of undertaking a variety of transformations, so long as the inner structural element of the whole social edifice, i.e. the capital-labor relation, remains untouched.

However, in order to establish a new distribution of the social balance of forces, the working class must once again elaborate its own autonomous class objectives, independently of the capitalist imperative of labor discipline and profit maximization. For this to be possible, labor must recreate its strategy of socialist transformation, i.e. of overthrowing capitalism.

Notes

1. "A diminished propensity to consume today can only be accommodated to the public advantage if an increased propensity to consume is expected to exist someday" (Keynes 1973, 105).
2. The case of L. Jospin and the French Socialist Party may differ in some respects as it incorporated some of the demands of the radical demonstrations and mass strikes of workers in Paris in December 1995. However, it did not constitute an alternative political strategy to the other center-left European governments.
3. "At odds with conservative and pro-market ideologies, markets will never replace governments in making strategic choices, organizing solidarity over a given territory and still more in institutionalizing markets (...) The state remains the most powerful institution to channel and tame the power of markets" (Boyer 1996, 110, 108).
4. Some date from as far back as Carey and Bastiat's mid-19th century treatises on Political Economy.
5. "Successful capitalism and socially cohesive societies at bottom incorporate the idea of membership; that workers are members of firms and that individuals are citizens of the state. The two conceptions go hand in hand – but not in Britain" (Hutton 1996, 287). "We should see workers as members of a social organization – the firm" (Hutton in Kelly et al 1997, 6). For a Marxist critique of this idea of "social partnership" see Balibar 1984.

6. "Stakeholding has a strong strand of individualism running through it (...) This tension between individual autonomy and the need for a common public culture runs through the heart of the stakeholder agenda, as it does in other political philosophies such as communitarianism, social democracy and civic conservatism." (Kelly et al, 1997, 244). From a methodological point of view, the "stakeholder capitalism" approach resembles therefore "analytical Marxism," which "focuses on the importance of methodological individualism" (Roemer 1986, 7).

7. "Stakeholding is not an attempt to supplant capitalism with socialism. Rather, the project of the moderate left – namely, making the free market system socially bearable – has been around for about a century, inventing and reinventing a social market economy, which after all is an oxymoron" (Robert Kuttner, in Kelly et al 1997, 30). "A company's profitability depends on its relationships with a variety of groups – consumers, investors, workers and suppliers being the most obvious ones. (...) There is no reason why the interests of these groups should all coincide" (David Willetts, Conservative MP, in Kelly et al 1997, 23).

8. The same author quotes the following citation from a Report written back in the years of "full employment", i.e. long before the era of "unmanaged capitalism": "Once it becomes easier for people to make money faster by buying du Pont stock than the du Pont corporation can make money by producing nylon, dacron, and chemicals, then it is time to watch out" The Senate Banking Committee's Report on its Stock Market Survey, *The New York Times*, May 27, 1955.

9. The only developed capitalist economy where this frenzied rise in the value of shares has not taken place (for institutional and other reasons) is Japan. Thus, while the Tokyo Nikkei index has never reached long-term levels significantly higher than those registered at the time of the international stock market crash of October 1987, the Frankfurt DAX index and the London FTSE index in July 1997 were respectively 4.1 times and 3.2 times higher than their corresponding October 1987 values. The rise in the value of shares is in fact even more frenzied in Germany than in Britain (*Der Spiegel*, 21.07.97, 64-66). Recent developments have shown that the rise in share values in Europe and the USA is temporarily stoped by acute stock market crises, resulting from major international economic events such as the mid-1997 turmoil in Asian financial markets and the August-September 1998 Russian crisis. However, such events do not reverse the long-run increasing trend of Western stock market indices, although they slow it down (IMF 1997).

10. "The similarities disguises *vast differences* between the social and economic purposes of apparently similar institutions, so that each capitalist structure ends up with very different specific capacities and cultures" (Hutton 1996, 257-58).

11. The number of employed in Germany fell from 36.6 million in 1991 to 34.2 million in 1997. The number of unemployed in July 1997 (4.396 million) sets a post-war record (*Financial Times*, August 7, 1997). Wage deductions have been increased from 30.5% of wage incomes in 1990 to 35.3% in 1996 (*Der Spiegel*, 4.8.97, 65). Germany's jobless rate further surged in the first months of 1998, but declined to 11.4% in April 1998 from March's 12.1%. (*Wall Street Journal*, May 8, 1998).

12. "It has long been a pragmatic and legitimate practice of Britain's center-left to borrow policies from abroad: in the 1950s and 1960s we looked to French planning; in the 1970s and 1980s to the Scandinavian social democracy; in the 1990s we look to Germany and stakeholding" (Soskice, in Kelly et al 1997, 220).

13. It is worth presenting the following example. Hutton was criticized by the Labor peer in the House of Lords Professor M. Desai for being extremely anti-Thatcherist:: "It is a blind spot of Hutton's that he is so upset by the effects of the Thatcher revolution that he sees it in purely negative terms. (...) He fails to see that the reform of trade unions (...) was tackled by Thatcher" (Desai, in Kelly et al 1997, 206). In his *The State to Come*, Hutton writes of the Conservative Party: "Its mission – the abandonment of British corporatism, the lowering of trade union power and the assault on nationalised industries – is complete. It is time to move on" (Hutton 1997, 104).
14. Hutton forgets to add that if his scenario actually eventuates, then "cheaper imports" will turn Europe's trade surpluses into trade deficits, a process which, given the "low interest-rate regime," will lead to a depreciation of the euro. But before that happens, "the world's investment and financial community" will rush to sell euros in order to buy dollars, speculating on the euro's depreciation.
15. The share markets have responded very positively to all recent cases of center-left governments coming to power, further boosting share prices. For the first time in its history, the London FTSE 100 index broke the so-called "psychological barrier" of 5,000 points on August 6, 1997, just as the Labor government was preparing to celebrate its first 100 days in power. Neither the Labor electoral victory nor the abolition by the new government of the tax credit on dividends did anything to dampen the frenzied rises in share values.
16. This quantitative decline can also be seen as the outcome of a faster increase in capital intensity (capital stock per worker) than in labor productivity (output per worker).

References

Balibar, Itienne. 1984. "Marx et l'entreprise," *Politique Aujourd'hui*, July-September.
Boyer, Robert. 1996. "State and Market. A new engagement for the twenty-first century?". in Boyer, Robert and Drache, Daniel (eds.). *States against Markets. The Limits of Globalzation*. London: Routledge.
Busch, Klaus. 1978. *Die Krise der Europäischen Gemeinschaft*, Frankfurt/M.: EVA.
_____. 1992. *Umbruch in Europa*, Köln: Bund-Verlag.
EU. 1997. *The Community Economy 1996-98 - Spring 1997 Economic Forecasts. Main Economic Indicators 1961-1998*. Internet edition.
Hutton, Will. 1994. "Back by Popular Demand," *The American Prospect* no. 16. 50-57.
_____. 1996. *The State We're In*. 2nd ed., London: Vintage.
_____. 1997. *The State to Come*. London: Vintage.
International Monetary Fund (IMF). 1997. *World Economic Outlook. Interim Assessment*. Washington, D.C.: IMF.
Ioakimoglou, Elias. 1994 *Hegemony and Integration. The International Economy in the Nineties*, Thessaloniki: Iamos (in Gr.).
Ioakimoglou, Elias and Milios, John. 1993. "Capital Accumulation and Over-accumulation Crisis: The Case of Greece (1960-1989)," *Review of Radical Political Economics*, Vol. 25(2), 81-107.
Kelly, Gavin/ Kelly, Dominic/ Gamble Andrew (eds.) 1997. *Stakeholder Capitalism*. London: Macmillan.

Keynes, John Maynard. 1993. *The General Theory of Employment, Interest and Money*, London: Macmillan.
Marx, Karl. 1990. *Capital, Volume One*. London: Penguin Books.
Marx, Karl. 1981. *Capital, Volume Three*. London: Penguin Books.
Mattick, Paul. *Marx and Keynes*. Boston: Porter Sargent.
Milios, John. 1994. "Marx's Theory and the Historic Marxist Controversy (1900-1937) on Economic Crisis," *Science and Society*, Vol. 58, No 2, 175-194.
_____. 1996. "'Crisis of Capital' and Wages: Recovery through Austerity?," in Milios, J. (ed.) 1996. *Social Policy and Social Dialogue in the Perspective of the Economic and Monetary Union and of the "Europe of Citizens"*, Athens: Kritiki.
Myrdal, Gunnar. 1960. *Beyond the Welfare State*, London: Duckworth.
Roemer, John (ed.). 1986. *Analytical Marxism*. Cambridge: Cambridge University Press.
Stamatis, Giorgos. 1997. "We do it for value." *Epohi*: 20.06.97 (in Gr.).
TUC. 1996. *Your Stake at Work - TUC Proposals for a Stakeholder Economy*. London.

12 From Competition to Confrontation: The Role of European Economic and Monetary Union in the Triad

JÖRG HUFFSCHMID

Introduction

When on Jan. 1, 1999 the European Economic and Monetary Union (EMU) enters its third and final stage by starting the monetary union (MU) between a majority of member countries the relations between the European Union and the rest of the world will also be severely affected. The structure of monetary and economic relations between the main capitalist countries will probably enter into a third large phase after the end of World War II. The *first phase* was that of economic reconstruction with economic policy priority on domestic growth and full employment within a framework of international monetary co-operation, the Bretton Woods system. In this system, the USA played the leading role and the US dollar served as national and world currency at the same time. The internal systemic contradictions of such a construction and the policy of the USA undermined this system and lead to its collapse in the first half of the 1970s. The *second phase* was that of fluctuating exchange rates, greater financial instability as a consequence of the deregulation and liberalization of financial markets, to a slow-down of growth and a rise in unemployment in all OECD countries. Increasing internationalization took mainly the form of regionalization and regional block building while the US dollar remained – though contested several times – the dominant reserve medium for the world. In the EC, the European Monetary System (EMS) was introduced with the intent to form a counterweight against the American monetary predominance, but it was quickly transformed into an instrument of German predominance in Europe. The *third phase* will be marked by the introduction of the *euro* as a potentially strong challenger to the US $ in the world-wide currency competition. While it will by definition bring more stability into the monetary relations between the participating countries, by replacing their national currencies by one common currency, the effects upon the relations between the *euro* and third country currencies are very uncertain. This is true with regard to the other European currencies as well as with regard to the US $ and the Japanese Yen.

The following remarks are based on two assumptions: Firstly I assume that the development of the international monetary relations will depend essentially on the economic policy course of the main OECD countries and particularly upon the line which they adopt for their domestic policy. The basic question is whether economic policy is willing and able to structure the proportions of domestic demand in a way which makes the development of the economy as a whole not dependent on the achievement of permanent current account surpluses. If this is the case there is room for balanced international trade and investment relations and for sustainable international cooperation. If not, international economic relations will drift into uninhibited competitive structures which will impede cooperation and give rise to increasingly severe conflicts.

Secondly I assume that the pattern of economic policy in Europe has during the last 15 years been greatly formed by the enforcement of a particular concept of economic stability by Germany (and more specifically the German Bundesbank). This concept restricts the task for economic policy to keeping (or making) markets open and inflation low. The political implementation of this very narrow concept of economic stability leads to slow domestic growth and therefore to a necessity to generate high current account surpluses in order to stimulate economic activity and profits. If this rather aggressive strategy will be adopted by the EU in the next decade, this would considerably enhance the fight for market shares in the world and transform economic competition to forms and levels of confrontation which can well go beyond political control.

In order to substantiate the implications of the second assumption I will in the following firstly analyze the way in which Germany gained economic predominance and economic policy hegemony in the European Community (EC) (sect. 2). Secondly I will discuss the risks of such a policy if it were adopted as European strategy with regard to the rest of the world (sect. 3). The conclusion is of course that in order to avoid these risks a new cooperative pattern of international economic relations is required, which must go beyond crisis management and in the long run be based on a new domestic economic policy course (sect. 4).

Austerity-Based Competition: The German Way to European Hegemony

Germany had from the end of the 1950s been the strongest economy in Western Europe. German economic policy conceptions had a great influence on the structure and strategy of European integration from the start of the European Economic Community. But it was only in the 1980s that the German economy and economic policy rose to a clearly hegemonic position in the EC. This position was only slightly weakened when the severe problems of the new Bundesländer affected the overall performance of the German economy.

The rise of German economic hegemony in Europe is essentially not the result of the size and productivity of the country. It was established and consolidated since the mid 1970s through a neomercantilistic economic strategy of strong export promotion and conquest of international markets, particularly at the expense of other EU members. The domestic basis for this policy was the victory of the Bundesbank conception of economic policy, with exclusive priority for price stability as a springboard for international competitiveness.

Strong export orientation is not new for the German economy, and it is essentially based on its specific sectoral structure, with a high share and a broad range of manufacturing industries.[1] One of the great pushes for German reconstruction in the early 1950s was the export boom induced by the Korean war. In the 1960 and 1970s Germany already had the second highest export share in GNP of all big industrial nations (after the UK, cf. table 1).

The most decisive development, however, occurred in the 1980s: whereas the export share in the other large countries rose only modestly or remained constant, that of West Germany made a big leap forward: from a quarter of GDP in the 1970s to 30 per cent in the 1980s and a third in the first half of the 1990s. German unification and a complete collapse of eastern German exports brought a sharp fall in overall German export share in the last seven years. But even so Germany is today the second largest export nation in the world (after the USA), with the world's highest per capita export, a world market share of around ten per cent and a trade surplus of about 121 bn DM in 1997.

TABLE 1   Export shares in GDP of four leading EC members, the USA and Japan

	1961-70	1971-80**	1981-90**	1990-97**
West-Germany	19,3	24,2	30,3	33,0
Germany*	-	-	-	24,0
France	13,5	19,5	22,3	23,2
Italy	14,6	20,8	21,4	23,9
United Kingdom	20,5	26,5	25,9	26,4
USA	5,3	8,0	8,6	11,0
Japan	9,9	12,2	12,6	9,9

* including former GDR
** average of yearly shares

Source: European Economy, Nr. 64, 1997, Statistical Annex, Table 36.

The different export development of Germany and the other G7 countries during the 1980s suggests that German success occurred at the expense of the latter. This is indeed reflected in the development of the trade balances of the four big EC members (cf. table 2):

TABLE 2   Trade balances of the four leading EC members in the 1970s, 1980s and 1990s; cumulated bn $

	1970s*	1980s*	1990s*
Germany**	142,7	399,0	271,4
France	-9,3	-83,35	4,8
Italy	-12,6	-44,46	116,7
UK	-48,4	-112,2	-129,8

*cumulated trade surpluses or deficits (-) in bn $, 1970-1979,
1980-1989, 1990-1995
** 1990s including former GDR
Source: OECD: Economic Outlook.

As can be seen in table 2, Germany had already realized a considerable trade surplus during the 1970s, whereas France and Italy had a moderate and Great Britain had a considerable deficit. In the subsequent decade – when the European Monetary System (EMS) was already in place – the disparities in the development of international trade exploded, leading to an enormous surplus in Germany and very problematic deficits in the other three countries.

This absolute and relative improvement of the German trade position with regard to her European partners was to a large extent the result of an economic strategy, which the German government and especially the German Bundesbank could enforce domestically and impose upon the rest of Europe. It has rightly been called a neomercantilistic strategy of permanent undervaluation of the increasingly stronger DM, which at the same time became the second important reserve medium of the world.[2] The main elements of this strategy can be described as follows.[3]

After the economic crises of 1975 and 1981 and even more so after the take-over of the government by the conservative coalition in 1982 the era of the Bundesbank arrived. From then on economic policy meant mostly restrictive money supply and reduction of government expenditures primarily in the welfare sector of the economy. The multi-objective, multi-level and multi-tool approach of the social democratic government, which had – not in theory but in practice – also been the general guide-line for conservative governments during the 1950s and 1960s, was more and more abandoned and replaced by the exclusive fixation on price stability, austerity and deregulation. Economic stability was increasingly defined as price stability, disregarding the alarming increase in unemployment, and the income and social instability.

The monetarist fixation on internal price stability led to conflicts with the task of external currency stabilization in a regime of fixed exchange rates. The Bundesbank, which could not openly oppose the Bretton Woods System, welcomed its abandonment in the first half of the 1970s and was from the beginning skeptical or even hostile to the introduction of a regional exchange rate regime like the European Monetary System (EMS), which was introduced in 1978.[4] One might think that if, in case of parity imbalances between two countries, the central banks of *both* countries are obliged to intervene in the currency market in order to restore equilibrium this would force the Bundesbank to compromise between internal price stabilization and external exchange rate stabilization, thus accepting a part of the adjustment burden. This was – or could have been – the spirit of solidarity behind the EMS.[5] But this was not the understanding of the Bundesbank, nor that of the majority of the German scientific community at the time. The Bundesbank made it quite clear from the beginning of the EMS that it was not willing to follow the obligation of unlimited intervention if that would endanger its primary concern about price stability. What is more, if the report of Emminger is correct, the Bundesbank obtained the assurance by the German government that it would be released from the obligation of intervention if necessary and that it could even decide whether it was necessary or not (cf. Emminger 1986, 362). When it did intervene in exchange markets or took measures to the like effect, the Bundesbank regularly accompanied these measures by sterilising measures on the German money market, usually through restrictive open market operations.

This policy did not only generate sharply falling inflation rates in Germany. It also maintained the competitive advantage over the weaker countries and thus the superior German trade position. Persistent inflation differentials made the DM a permanently undervalued currency – in spite of more than a dozen realignments with appreciation of the DM against one, several or all EMS currencies.

German unification in 1990 brought a dramatic change in the German economic situation without a corresponding change in economic policy. For the first time in more than two decades the German export boom stopped, the trade surplus fell sharply from 75 bn $ in 1989 to 18 bn DM in 1991[6] and the current account balance showed a deficit. After unification imports into the new Länder from West Germany exploded, mainly financed through transfers from the West, which in turn were financed through a sharp rise in public deficits. Thus the government involuntarily triggered off a unification boom with growth rates for West Germany of 5.7 per cent in 1990 and 5.0 per cent in 1991; similar rates had the last time been reached in the 1970s. This boom, which generated spill-over effects for the relevant trading partners of Germany (cf. DIW 1991) was brought to an abrupt end by the obsessive policy of the Bundesbank which raised the discount rate five times in 18 months from 6.0 per cent to 8.75 per cent between November 1990 and June 1992 as a preventive strike against supposed inflation dangers. This contractionary policy (together with the complete liberalization of capital movements achieved in the EU by July 1, 1990) generated devastating consequences for the EC, exacerbating recession tendencies and exposing partner currencies to speculative pressures which led to the currency crisis in 1992 and in the last instance to the factual abolition of the ERM in 1993. Thus shortly before the introduction of the single currency in the EU we have the strange situation that Europe has returned to a floating rate regime instead of – as one would expect in the run-up to monetary union – consolidating a system with ever narrower fluctuation bands.

The German government and the Bundesbank seem determined to continue the twin strategies of domestic austerity and external mercantilism. This strategy has imposed slow growth, high unemployment and severe cuts in the domestic welfare system in Germany long before Maastricht. On the other hand it has not been and is not devastating for all: it has generated increased profits for German business and a remarkable redistribution of income and wealth towards the rich: from 1980 to 1993 gross profits rose by 185 per cent against a 63 per cent rise in gross wages. Tax policy exacerbated the disparity: the increase in net profits was 251 per cent, five times the rise in net wages (52 per cent) (cf. Schäfer 1996, 598-9).

The "Strong Euro" – a Risky Strategy

It can safely be assumed that in the third stage of EMU the European Central Bank (ECB) will try to continue the course of a very restrictive interpretation of the already restrictive rules which have been written into the TM under the pressure of the Bundesbank: monetary policy will concentrate exclusively on disinflationary measures and it will exert strong pressure upon member states' fiscal policy to focus primarily on the reduction of public deficits via expenditure cuts. Under these circumstances employment policy will remain confined to deregulation and the "loosening" of labor market rigidities. This is essentially the direction of activity which the summit on employment in November 1997 has recommended. The overall consequences of this policy are obvious and have already been felt during the years after the signing of the TM. Under the austerity regime of Maastricht the economy of the EU will remain trapped in a downward spiral with low growth or stagnation, high and rising levels of unemployment, increasing inequality of income distribution and an erosion of the financial basis for all social security and welfare systems. The European domestic components of final effective demand – private consumption and government expenditure – will develop only sluggishly, stagnate or even fall because of low wages and a further erosion of the tax base which is underway in Germany, France and in other EC countries in a wave of competitive tax reductions. Therefore the prospects for private investment as intermediate demand are not brilliant either.

What, then, are the prospects for external expansion of a domestically stagnant monetary union? In public statements we often find the reassuring assertion that the monetary union will be a *strong* union with a *strong euro* at its heart. Mostly it remains unclear what is meant by that. What is a strong euro? Is it a euro which everybody wants to have and to invest money in? In this case the exchange rate of the euro would more or less continuously move up with damaging effects for export oriented countries like for instance Germany and France which have strong export links to third countries – primarily the USA and the UK. The strong euro would weaken the export prospects of strong sectors of the economy like cars, chemicals and mechanical engineering. That may be desirable in a conception for an ecologically sustainable development but is certainly not intended by those advocating a strong euro. Or is a strong euro a currency with a very low inflation rate, lower than other currencies? That would of course be favorable for exports and lead to further trade surpluses and additional employment in the benefiting sectors. But in the next phase it would also lead to a tendency of the euro to appreciate and to affect exports to third countries.

The solution of this problem is expected to come from the Central Bank and European monetary policy: They could restore the price advantages lost by appreciation through a still more austerity prone policy, putting domestic prices all over the monetary union under increased pressure, thus at least containing the appreciation effect or even keeping the "domestic" European currency, the euro, externally undervalued in spite of nominal appreciation. As I have shown in some detail in the preceding section, this is exactly what the Bundesbank did with regard to Germany's neighbors, and this policy of artificially generated undervaluation resulted in the "strong DM" and in permanent trade and current account surpluses of Germany and equally permanent current account deficits of the main European countries (cf. Herr 1991, 236-239). My assumption is that the policy of the strong euro is aiming at a new edition of this rather aggressive strategy as European policy. The MU will – under the leadership of Germany and France – try as a whole during the next decade or two to play the same role with regard to the rest of the world – mainly the two other capitalist centers – which Germany had played towards the rest of the EC during the 1980s: to accomplish through a policy of strict austerity competitive price advantages on world markets and thus expand the share in MU-GDP going to exports into third countries (which is at present about the same size as that of the USA and Japan, around eleven per cent). If this strategy is successful, it would still not or only marginally contribute to the creation of new jobs in the MU, but it would create positive profit perspectives for the leading firms of the MU – who happen to be to a large extent German and French firms.

The strong euro will therefore be a – in real terms – undervalued euro, on the basis of which the MU seeks to conquer additional shares of the world market. This looks very elegant and tricky, and it has worked for Germany for two decades. But as a strategy for Europe is a very risky and in my opinion not viable conception for three reasons (cf. Huffschmid 1998):

Firstly the *price differentials* (and the differentials in productivity fundamentals) between the EU and the US (or NAFTA) and Japan in the 1990s are not so large as they were between the members of the EC in the 1970s and 1980s.

Secondly, the *economic policy differentials* have almost been eliminated: most countries are following the neoliberal course and would follow a deflationary course: artificial depreciation would be answered by artificial devaluations, leading to a wave of competitive devaluations.

Thirdly, the power relations between the EU on the one hand and the US and Japan on the other in the years to come will be significantly different from the ones prevailing between Germany and most other countries in the EEC during the last two decades. For the success of Germany in the 1980s was not only based on an undervalued DM but also on German political power to enforce such a mercantilistic policy against the rest of Europe without triggering off retaliations from the most affected countries. This will not be possible for the MU as a whole against the other two centers of the capitalist world. An attempt to sterilize the pressure to appreciate the euro resulting from gains of world market shares via restrictive monetary policy would undoubtedly – and correctly – be regarded as an element of economic warfare provoking retaliation which could easily escalate into dimensions beyond political control.

In any case, if the MU adopts a strategy of expansion via a strong – i.e. undervalued – euro, the intensity of confrontation between the three centers will increase with an uncertain outcome. It is improbable that the EU as a whole is capable of reaching such considerable and persistent competitive advantages over the rest of the world as would be sufficient to compensate for a chronic weakness of domestic demand in the EU. On the other hand, the weak performance of the European economy will work as a powerful brake against growth elsewhere in the world. Furthermore intensified competition will enhance economic insecurity and risks in the world economy. This could lead to a further increase in the level of interest rates, impeding real and promoting financial investment. Unless a new form of international economic cooperation is developed during the next years – including managed trade, FDI rules and mechanisms of international monetary balancing and control – the result will be increasingly hot economic wars, including competitive austerity and devaluation strategies.

The abandonment of a – however imperfect and hegemonic – political framework of international cooperation and its replacement by uninhibited international competition, the replacement of growth and employment by international competitiveness and world market superiority as primary economic policy goals is therefore a very risky strategy: Domestically it requires cost cutting and subordination of all social claims and aspirations under the imperative of competitiveness creating permanent unemployment, social polarization and political instability. Externally it creates exclusion of most countries from the potential benefits of international division of labor and increasing confrontation emanating from economic competition. In short the neoliberal pattern of capitalist development is internally and externally inconsistent and generates severe contradictions and severe social polarization.

Perspectives for an Alternative European Strategy

The inconsistent, polarizing and destabilizing perspective of an aggressive economic warfare strategy does not mean that it is bound to break down at a certain point more or less automatically. The risk management capability of capitalism has always been considerable and has even been enhanced during the last decade. The aggressive pattern of development is not able to achieve a path of sustainable development, but it seems to be capable to survive by muddling through. Therefore criticism of this pattern cannot rely on its inevitable collapse.

Criticism can however contribute to the counter-movement and resistance which have begun to develop during the last few years. The theoretical foundations of neoliberalism as theoretical basis of aggressive internationalization are increasingly criticized in economics and social science which particularly turn against its individualistic and ahistorical character and propose alternative strategies for full employment, social cohesion and equity in the EU (cf. European Economists 1997). Economic and social policy in the EU is increasingly met by social protest and rejection. This has not remained without impact on some governments. In France even a whole government was ousted as a consequence of social movements against austerity in the name of Europe. The new government has started to implement a decisively different policy, putting employment at the top of the agenda and taking energetic measures to implement this objective: raising purchasing power, creating jobs by public expenditure and passing a law for reduction of weekly working time to 35 hours. In other countries like Sweden and Italy, the replacement of austerity by efficient employment measures is also seriously discussed.

These movements are severe challenges to the aggressive course of the strong euro which the leading forces in the EU are still pursuing. If these forces remain as strong as they were during the last 15 years, it will be extremely difficult to accomplish an economic policy change in the above direction, and France will encounter big problems in Europe which may eventually lead to the failure of the whole attempt – an experience which she had already made in the early 1980s. Therefore it is extremely important to strengthen the demands for an economic policy change in other countries, too, specifically in Germany. A large number of participants in the MU could improve the chances for a less rigid and monetarist policy, for a broad interpretation of the narrow rules – and eventually for an amendment of the treaty provisions altogether. But all this will not come as a result of theoretical criticism but on the basis of social movements.

With regard to external economic relations an alternative to the aggressive expansionist course has to concentrate on two issues:

Firstly it has to take *protective measures against attacks*. Such attacks will mainly come in the form of capital flight or short-term speculative capital movements against the euro (or before 1999 one of the currencies of the participating countries). To protect the chances of an economic policy reform against these attacks, the unlimited mobility of capital has to be restricted in one way or the other. That can be done by a variety of measures: enhanced bank surveillance restricting short-term loans for speculative purposes, a tax on foreign exchange turnover which prevents short-term arbitrage and impedes speculation; or, if serious attacks through fundamental speculation or massive capital flight have to be averted, there is the instrument of capital controls, which the EU has – in article 73f – reserved as an instrument which can under exceptional circumstances be applied for a limited time. The matter of protection is not a question of instruments and technical capability to use them, it is a question of political willingness and determination to do so.

Secondly an new economic policy should also undertake a *new attempt toward comprehensive international cooperation.* It should on the one hand focus on monetary cooperation, but on the other hand also aim at a common regulation of the connected problems of current account balances and international development strategies. Essential elements of such a new cooperation system would have to be the reintroduction of a system of quasi-fixed exchange rates with mandatory central bank interventions. With regard to the old Bretton Woods arrangements there should, however be two differences: The anchor for such a system cannot be a national currency but must be a collectively created artificial currency or fiat money (like the existing special drawing rights). And the cooperation has to be designed in a symmetrical way in the sense, that weaker deficit countries are urged and empowered to catch-up and the stronger surplus countries must be prevented from endlessly extending their position of superiority (for instance by transferring an increasing part of their surpluses to a common fund which lends them to favorable conditions to the deficit countries).

Notes

1. Germany is the country with the highest share of employment in manufacturing in the EU. In 1983-85 it was 33.6 per cent for Germany against 27.3 per cent for the EU average and until 1990-1992 this share had only decreased marginally to 32.4 per cent against a much stronger reduction of the EU average to 24.9 per cent, see European Commission, 1996, 52-3
2. The share of the DM in world currency reserves rose from 10.2 per cent in 1981 to 20.8 per cent in 1990, see Deutsche Bundesbank, *Annual Reports* 1982, 69 and 1990, 67. In 1996 it had fallen to 14.1 per cent, still remaining the second largest reserve medium behind the US $ (62.7 per cent) and before the Yen (7.0 per cent), see Deutsche Bundesbank 1997, 29
3. cf Herr, 1991. Huffschmid, 1996, vol. 2, chap. 2.
4. See the memoirs of the former president of the Bundesbank Otmar Emminger, 1986, 228-251, where he describes very frankly and even proudly the decisive role of the Bundesbank in the abolition of the fixed parity system of Bretton Woods.
5. "The intervention rules and credit arrangements of the EMS had been designed to guarantee that countries with weak and strong currencies would bear joint and symmetric responsibility for the defense of the system. Whenever a country's currency reached the edge of its band vis-à-vis one of its partners currencies, the partner was supposed to intervene unstintingly to keep the exchange rate from leaving the band (...) In effect the

system was meant to protect a weak-currency country from exhausting its reserves and being forced to devalue." Kenen, 1995, 162.
6. Measured in DM the fall was even steeper, from 135 bn. DM to 22 bn DM; see Sachverständigenrat 1996/7, 418.

References

Committee for the Study of Economic and Monetary Union (ed.) 1989. *Report on economic and monetary union in the European Community (Delors-Report)*. Brussels: Office for Official Publications of the European Communities.

Deutsche Bundesbank. 1996. *Kapitalverflechtung mit dem Ausland*. Statistische Sonderveröffentlichung 10. Frankfurt/M.

Deutsche Bundesbank. 1997. "Die Rolle der D-Mark als internationale Anlage- und Reservewährung," *Monatsberichte*, April, 17-30.

Deutsches Institut für Wirtschaftsforschung. 1991. "Vereinigung wirkt positiv auf Weltwirtschaft", *Wochenbericht*, 32, 447-456.

Eichengreen, B. and Ch. Wyplosz. 1993. "The Unstable EMS," *Brookings Papers on Economic Activity*, 51-124.

Emminger, Otmar. 1986. D-Mark, Dollar, Währungskrisen. Erinnerungen eines ehemaligen Bundesbankpräsidenten. Stuttgart: Deutsche Verlags-Anstalt.

European Commission. 1996. *Economic Evaluation of the Internal Market*, Reports and Studies, No.4. Luxembourg: Office for Official Publications of the European Communities.

European Economists. 1997. *Full Employment, Social Cohesion and Equity for Europe - Alternatives to Competitive Austerity. A Declaration and a Memorandum of European Economists*. Bremen: Manuscript.

Herr, Hansjörg. 1991. "Der Merkantilismus der Bundesrepublik in der Weltwirtschaft." in: Voy, Polster and Thomasberger, *Marktwirtschaft*, 227-61.

Huffschmid, Jörg. 1994. *Wem gehört Europa? Wirtschaftspolitik und Kapitalstrategien*, vol 1: *Wirtschaftspolitik in der EG*. Heilbronn: Distel-Verlag.

_____. 1998. "Hoist with its Own Petard - Consequences of the Single Currency for Germany," in: Jonathan Michie and Bernard Moss (eds.) *Domestic Consequences of the Single Currency*. Houndmills: MacMillan (forthcoming).

Kenen, Peter B. 1995. *Economic and Monetary Union in Europe. Moving Beyond Maastricht*. Cambridge: Cambridge University Press.

Lamfalussy, Alexandre. 1989. "Macro-coordination of fiscal policies in an economic and monetary union in Europe," in: Committee for the Study of Economic and Monetary Union (ed.) *Report on economic and monetary union in the European Community*. Brussels: Office for Official Publications of the European Communities.

Polster, W. and K. Voy. 1993. "Von der politischen Regulierung zur Selbstregulierung der Märkte – Die Entwicklung von Wirtschafts- und Ordnungspolitik in der Bundesrepublik," in: Voy, Polster and Thomasberger. *Marktwirtschaft*, 169-226.

Sachverständigenrat zur Begutchtung der gesamtwirtschaftlichen Entwicklung. 1997. *Jahresgutachten 1996/97*. Bonn: Bundes-tagsdrucksache 13/6200.

Schäfer, Claus. 1996. "Mit falschen Verteilungs-'Götzen' zu echten Standortproblemen – Zur Entwicklung der Verteilung in 1995 und den Vorjahren." *WSI-Mitteilungen*, 597-616.

Voy, K.laus, Werner Polster and Claus Thomasberger (eds.). 1991. *Marktwirtschaft und politische Regulierung. Beiträge zur Wirtschafts- und Gesellschaftgeschichte der Bundesrepublik Deutschland (1949-1989)*. Marburg: Metropolis.

United Nations Conference on Trade and Development. 1996. *World Investment Report 1996. Investment, Trade and International Policy Arrangements*. New York and Geneva: United Nations.

13 Unemployment and the Welfare State in Western Europe

FRANK DEPPE

Introduction

A recent publication by the Marburg FEG-group[1] is our starting point: We begin from the following thesis: the crisis of employment in the developed capitalist countries since the 70s is a primary condition of the crisis of the welfare states as they were constructed in the "Golden Age" of Fordism after the Second World War. This crisis is closely related to neoliberal strategies, aiming at the reconstruction or "renovation" of state interventionism. We have been asking if there exists a convergence of national policy patterns in the field of labor markets and welfare regimes. Obviously, general problems – like mass unemployment, socio-economic change, world-market pressure, the impact of European integration – exist everywhere. Do the different welfare regimes in Western Europe move into the same direction, and what strategies are applied – what are the constellations of political and social forces which decide upon this direction?

The second part mainly refers to the EU-level. Is there any reaction confronting the crisis of employment and welfare regimes at the national level? Discussing the results of the Amsterdam EU-summit (June 1997) seems to be of special interest. Before the summit, in two of the major member states of the EU (Britain and France), government changed in favor of social-democratic parties. Especially the French socialists – during the electoral campaign – criticized the dominance of neoliberalism as well as the "Maastricht" concept of integration policies (primacy of monetary union and austerity policy). Moreover, they announced their own initiatives

191

to combat unemployment in France. Obviously, these transformations are embedded into a more general change of the political climate in France which was shaped by the mass strikes at the end of 1995.

The Neoliberal Triumph

The employment crisis in the developed capitalist countries begins in the middle of the 70s (cf. Table 1). It is a consequence of the crisis of the fordist mode of socialization. Already in 1979, Nicos Poulantzas, had characterized the crisis of the social democratic parties as a consequence of the crisis of the "model" that Social Democracy had been representing: Keynesianism plus capitalist welfare state. "Social Democracy did not succeed to prevent the economic crisis and the increase in mass unemployment. Since it failed to do this, the material conditions of its political attractiveness and of its political strategy are eroded" (Poulantzas 1979, 134).

However, the retreat from policies of full employment and universalistic socio-political inclusion was not accomplished evenly. National strategies of crisis management varied considerably, because of different national constellations of social and political forces. The social democratic regimes (in Scandinavia and Austria) at least followed their own path of employment policy by enlarging the public sector. Only at the end of the 80s they had to adapt to the neoliberal model. By this time even in these countries full employment could be no longer sustained at the cost of a rising public deficit, high inflation rates and relatively strict controls of trade and currency. Preparations for EU-membership as well as the competitive dynamics of the Common Market enforced willingness to accept neoliberal forms of regulation.

Neoliberal criticism to the welfare state now seemed to be supported everywhere: The welfare state did not only fail to solve the social problems and the labor-market crisis of the 70s, but it had rather caused these problems because it blocked economic efficiency, competitiveness and the capacity for innovation. The welfare state simply has become too expensive – it has become the main obstacle for social reforms as well as for the solution of the employment crisis. The central task of politics therefore does not consist in a redistribution of wealth, but in improving flexibility and efficiency of labor markets and social security systems. Deregulation, privatization and a general reduction of public services became the strategies to realize these politics.

The Crisis of Employment

The continuous crisis of employment is characterized by the following features:

- In the 80s the base of unemployment has been widen from recession to recession quite, independently from economic growth rates. The EFTA-countries remained below the average, while at the periphery (Spain, Ireland) exceptionally high rates of unemployment persisted.
- Flexible and deregulated labor markets have produced, especially in the services sector, an increase in so-called "bad jobs" or "precarious employment." "Normal employment" (unrestricted full-time employment with full access to social security services) – a characteristic of "Fordism" – erodes.
- The number of long-term unemployed as well as of these who are permanently excluded from the official labor market, is continuously rising. The formation of a so-called "underclass" (Kronauer 1995) is immediately related to this process.
- The pattern of labor market segmentation has hardened. Women with low qualification (bringing up children on their own), young people, old workers and migrants are foremost hit by exclusion.

These tendencies – increase in mass unemployment accompanied by polarization of incomes and wealth (pushed forward by the dominant neoliberal and conservative politics) – now carry on for more than two decades. They provoke rising criticism and social protest. Jeremy Rifkin (1995, 216) speaks of the danger of a new "barbarism" at the outcome of modernity. Ethan B. Kapstein demands political intervention in order to prevent a global social catastrophe with far reaching consequences for the international system:

> The world may be moving inexorably toward one of those tragic moments that will lead future historians to ask, why was nothing done in time? Were the economic and policy elites unaware of the profound disruption that economic and technological change were causing working men and women? What pre-

vented them from taking the steps necessary to prevent a global social crisis? Kapstein (1996, 17-18).

The French writer Viviane Forrester published in 1996 a book with the title "L' horreur économique," (The economic horror). This book sold more than 300 000 copies in a few months. The author sharply condemns the tendency of present capitalism to exclude an ever growing part of the population from employment.

European Welfare Regimes

In our research project we have been asking the following questions: How do political institutions react to the pressure exerted by the crisis of the labor market? What are the transformations enforced within the structures of different labor market regimes? These questions were examined by a comparative analysis of 9 member countries of the EU. We used the typology of three welfare regimes developed by Göran Esping-Anderson (1990), adding a fourth type of "post-authoritarian welfare regime" in the southern periphery of Europe (Lessenich 1994).

Let us briefly summarize the key features of these four regimes:

- The *liberal* welfare state – represented in Western Europe by Great Britain – is organized as a residual regime. The institutions of the welfare state are secondary to institutions of social care, regulated by the market. The principle of individual responsibility guides the "philosophy" of welfare politics. Public welfare follows the principle of subsidiarity. Claims are granted after rather restrictive checks of needs.
- The *corporatist* regime – besides Germany and France the Austrian "model" – is based upon rather conservative or paternalistic and traditional values. Welfare institutions normally care for professional and material safety of status. Corporative ties are reproduced by the organization of the virtually state managed system of social services integrating institutionally trade unions, churches and welfare associations.
- The prototype of the *social democratic* regime is Sweden. Its orientation is universalistic and egalitarian (obviously it is the model which Esping-Anderson regards as the best one). Emancipation from market dependency and decommodification of social relations are its main objectives. Social problems should not be solved post-festum, but by pre-

ventive labor market and social policies. The labor market regime is explicitly oriented towards full employment.

• The *post-authoritarian* regime – especially in Spain, Portugal, Greece and the Italian mezzogiorno accepts the model of western modernity. Traditional structures however persist – such as the interplay of productivism, paternalism and repression. Still the social security systems are characterized by clientilist fragmentation and a low rate of social services. The welfare state still has a lot to catch up.

National and European Institutions, "Negative" and "Positive" Integration

Before discussing transformations within these regimes as a reaction towards mass unemployment we should sketch the institutional frame of the European Union in relation to national and supranational regulation of social policy.

In the field of social and employment politicies there still exists a clear primacy of the national state and of national politics. EU-regulation and intervention – for instance by the social funds – does of course influence employment (especially in the periphery). Yet, in spite of all processes of transnationalization, the nation state is still the core institution of collective political identity. Questions of justice, solidarity, cultural autonomy and political participation are still treated as national issues. Social policies at community level mainly have the function to support the common market formation. The processes of market integration and of social integration obey to different logics. Market integration follows the logic of transnational competition which impose "objective constraints" ("Sachzwänge"). It seems to be highly de-politicized and constitutes a mechanism of "negative integration," which means removing obstacles to market liberties. "Positive integration", however, in the field of social politics – connected to redistributive measures – is highly politicized. It refers to all agreements on enlarged competence and financial resources of the EU in the field of social policy.

Blockades in respect to a European regulation of labor relations do not result alone from insufficient competences, procedures and resources, but also – as K. Armigeon has remarked – from "sectoral and national coalitions (concerning unions, employers and governmental institutions), who prevent the implementation of European-wide regulations of industrial relations. These national coalitions defend material interests – and are often guided by the common interest to improve national competitiveness. At the same time associations as well as organizations have a marked interest in the preservation of national institutions. Developing a European system of industrial relations might be realized by extraordinary social, economic or political events – or by a supranational government based upon a programmatic consensus. Neither of them is actually in sight within the European Union" (Armigeon 1994, 220).

Wolfgang Streeck – in his recent publications – has supported the positions of the so-called "Euro-skeptics." He favors the "defense of the welfare state at the national level." It is necessary, "to accept that the moment has been missed when the process of integration might have led to a re-edition of the national welfare state at supranational level (...) Trade unions and others who depend upon the ability to act in the national state are forced – voluntarily or not – to concentrate upon the question how this capacity could be preserved within the European Union. If there will be no European (supranational) system of industrial relations which generalizes the German post-war achievements of co-determination and (territorial) collective agreements (Flächen-tarifvertrag), then they have to look for strategies, aimed at – in spite of internationalization and political integration – preventing these national institutions of social balance decay within any compensation at the supranational level" (Streeck 1996, 13).

The "euro-sceptics" support the opinion of Fritz W. Scharpf, because of its intergovermental structure of power and decision-making – with the council of ministers as its center. The EU can manage "negative integration" (removing obstacles to market integration), but not "positive integration," which means "harmonization of regulations related to production and location (...) especially in the field of social politics." In the 90s – since Maastricht – this corresponds to the primacy of realizing the Common Market, removing controls at the borders as well as national monetary sovereignty. The strategic option which follows from this, is quite clear:

> Europe will fall behind if negative integration paralyzes national and subnational politics, whereas at the European level insufficient agreements could only be achieved by lengthy negotiations. Successful European multi-level policies must concede a wider scope of action to the member states. It must not only critically check – in every case – the necessity of positive integration according to the criteria of subsidiarity , but also reduce the claims of negative integration (Scharpf 1996, 116, 136).

Forms of Deregulation

The most interesting results of our research project may be presented in the following very brief summary:

Transformations in the labor market regime are – in the first place – characterized by the growing importance of flexibility. The guiding motive of pushing forward this issue is – of course – not the expansion of employment, but flexible adaptation of the labor force to the new structures of production and accumulation with the result of minimizing labor costs. Especially in Southern Europe the so-called "precarious" or "informal" forms of employment have increased (temporary employment, seasonal and hired work, pretended self-employment). The Netherlands lead in the flexibilization of working time in the form of part-time employment – followed by Great Britain and Sweden. There exist two patterns of expansion: in Britain for instance, the market-induced expansion of private services are dominant; in Sweden (and in some part of the Netherlands too) the part-time offensive concentrates upon the public sector. It is therefore part of a conscious employment policy which guarantees protection by means of social policy and legal claims. In some countries, the age-limit for retirement has been reduced – either by law or by collective bargaining. Under the condition of high unemployment rates such measures additionally burden the budget of the government or of the social insurance institutions.

Besides working time, the wage systems have come under the pressure of flexibility, creating a low wage sector. Measures in this field have been the abolition of wage subsidies (GB) and of agreed minimum wages (NL), also wage-levels below wage contracts (E, D). Especially in countries with national, regional or sectoral systems of collective agreements – with generally obligatory regulations for wages, working time and working conditions – the pressure from employers' associations and neoliberal governments in favor of flexible regulations has become dominant.

In the field of welfare regimes the range of government action is of course much wider than in the case of working time and wage regimes. Financing of the social systems is regulated quite differently. In the 80s, however, changes in the rules of financing were evident: on the one side contributions and/or taxes were increased, on the other side charges on enterprises were reduced.

In as far as the benefits from social systems are concerned, we must distinguish between the "older" welfare states, where social services and benefits have been frozen or reduced, and the Southern European countries where – from a rather low level – social services and benefits have been improved. Nearly everywhere additional revenues have been mobilized (by higher taxes or contributions); public service have been privatized or "opened" to market orientation: the access to social services and benefits was defined more restrictively.

The transformation of welfare state regulations follow a rather general pattern which enforces social differentiation and segregation. The former claim for solidary inclusion is replaced by the practice of an exclusive (particularistic-selective, in some cases even repressive and disciplinary) supply with social services. The dualism of social policy illustrates the class dimension of these politics: the rather prosperous parts of the population (core segments of the industrial working class; new and old middle classes) do not suffer serious trouble when the social security systems require more individual responsibility and contribution. They even may gain some advantages. They may buy further social security from private insurance companies. For those at the bottom of society cuts in basic social services produce growing deficits of social protection.

The proportion of unemployed receiving benefits has been drastically reduced between 1975 and 1990: in Germany from 66 to 42 percent, in Japan from 79 to 36 percent, in the USA from 75 to 37 percent. This reflects – mediated by politics – the neoliberal answer to intensified transnational competition. Its objective is the "re-commodification" of the labor force – the neoliberal answer to the fordist welfare state which was oriented towards the "de-commodification" of the services enjoyed by a growing part of the labor force. "It is obvious that the period of increasing de-commodifiation for prime-age workers has ended and we are currently witnessing a process of increased re-commodification of the workforce as a result of economic globalization. This process (...) can to a large degree be defined as policy responses that force workers into the labor market independently of the wage they can achieve. These responses, in combination with the market forces set free in this era of increased globalization resemble a vicious circle through which the segmentation of the labor market is deepened" (Seeleib-Kaiser 1997, 59).

The results of our research show at the same time that in nearly all Western European countries there exist so-called "taboo-zones" which still possess a strong symbolic force in public debates and which are not yet fundamentally attacked by transformations in the social systems – in Britain for instance the public health service; in France the educational system;

in the Netherlands and Germany the system of pensions, in Ireland family subsidies and in the Scandinavian countries active labor market policies enlarging the public sector.

What are the changes going on within the structures of the before mentioned regime-types? Obviously these exists a tendency towards a convergence of problems to be solved, exerting pressure upon these structures. However the divergence of national paths still persists. Differences still exist in the level of social benefits as well as in the institutional structures of the regimes. Finally, the specific national strategies for neoliberal "reforms" reflect different traditions, power structures and different attitudes of the population towards the welfare state.

- In the 80s the *social democratic regime* pursued its own strategy of labor market and social policy. Reacting to the crisis of the welfare state, universalistic claims had to be reduced. Labor market and social policies are increasingly characterized by market-liberal and selective-corporatist tendencies (for Sweden cf. Michelsen 1997). However, in the Scandinavian countries – including Norway – strategies of an active labor market policy are still pursued. In Denmark, for instance, where the rate of unemployment has been significantly reduced since the early 90s, the state plays an important role in organizing workplace and qualification programs – and these policies (combined with the defense of the Danish welfare state) are supported by a large consensus within the population (Fuhrmann 1997, 109). Also in Norway, there exists a stable interest in the preservation of the welfare state as well as a large support to the labor market policy of the government – and this has influenced the EU-referendum of 1992 when the majority had refused the Norwegian entry into the European Union.
- In the *corporatist regimes* transformations go on rather slowly; policies of "muddling through" prevail, though many achievements of social democracy and trade unions during the period of Fordism have been revised. The strength of national trade unions as well as the stability of corporatist integration of trade unions are important factors influencing the speed and content of political and institutional change. In some countries – for instance in Austria – the welfare state is renovated within the existing regime structures.
- The *liberal regime* of Great Britain in the Thatcher era made a radical break with the tradition of the Keynesian welfare state – dated since the "Beveridge Plan" in the Second World War. Privatization and deregu-

lation have been achieved systematically. However, the social obligations of governments have not been diminished in as much as the ideology of "Thatcherism" proclaimed. Poverty, unemployment and marginalization produced enormous costs. On the other hand, the infrastructure of a modern economy and society as well as the institutions of education and qualification could not be let entirely to the forces of free markets.

• *Post-authoritarian regimes* tried – mainly by becoming member of the EU – to approach social democratic and corporatist regimes. Due to economic restrictions and the crisis-prone character of modernization processes they failed largely to attain this goal. Most of them have deregulated and flexibilized the labor markets. The systems of social insurance however cannot compensate for growing unemployment, precarious employment and life-conditions. At a quite low level we find a policy-mix of market-oriented and clientilistic-fragmented social care.

A European Employment Policy?

The EU-summit of Amsterdam (June 1997) passed a declaration on growth and employment which confirmed the schedule for the introduction of the European currency (the Euro) in 1999 as well as the "Stability-Pact"-Agreement of Dublin. As a result of tough negotiations a new chapter on "employment" has been added to the European Treaty. The initiative, which originally has been started by Jacques Delors and the Commission's *White Book on Growth, Competition and Employment* (1993), seems to have been extremely successful: acknowledgment of a European responsibility in respect to employment and unemployment *and* an enhanced status of social and employment policy of the EU. Of course the results of the general elections in Great Britain and France (with the shift of governmental responsibility to the Labor Party and the Socialist Party) have been a decisive factor determining the results of the Amsterdam negotiations.

A more precise analysis of the political process (starting with the publication of the *White Book* in 1993) reveals however, that the dominant mode of integration has not been questioned at all – due primarily to the tough resistance of the German government. In the preparing works of the so-called "Reflection Group" some governments (nearly all led by the social democrats) demanded a revision of the European Treaty giving more importance to the aim of full employment and to employment policies.

Some even proposed to fix a criterion for reducing (national) unemployment according to the stability pact which obliges national governments to keep the state deficit below 3 percent. These governments held that the legitimization of market liberalization was seriously challenged by growing unemployment and marginalization within the EU. It was first of all the conservative British government (backed by the conservative-liberal German government) which rejected such demands without any compromise. In the course of these negotiations, the protagonists of a more active EU-employment-policy sacrificed step by step their original proposals (though it was not clear what could be compensated by "package-deals"). As the French elections were decided – creating a big surprise – only one week before the Amsterdam summit, the new socialist Prime Minister Lionel Jospin (who additionally has to manage his government's "co-habitation" with the conservative president, Jacques Chirac) could not achieve positive results in the field of a new employment and social policy of the EU, which was intensely and controversially discussed during the French electoral campaign. Also the new French government is so far not interested to question the Franco-German alliance as the power axis of the integration process. This implies to recognize the primacy of the monetary union and of the "stability pact" (confirming the preservation of convergence criteria for the period after the introduction of the Euro).

The new Employment Chapter of Amsterdam seems to be a concession to the French government. Yet, in reality it does not go beyond the already existing agreements on the basis of the *White Book* (Essen 1994, Madrid 1995). The new Article 109c is the central passage of a new title on "Employment." It introduces a method of reporting, consultation and co-ordination. On the basis of an annual report of the Commission and the Council the situation of employment in the Community will be observed. The Council – by proposal of the Commission – adopts guidelines which should be taken into account by the member states. On the other hand, national employment policies have to be evaluated annually. The member states send a report to the Commission and the Council. The new procedure is restricted to co-ordination. There is no procedure which implies sanctions (comparable to the control of government deficit-spending); this proposal was explicitly rejected, especially by the German delegation.

Article 109r contains the second core element of the new title. It mentions: "The Council can – according to the procedure of Article 189b and after hearing the Economic and Social Committee and the Committee of the Regions – decide upon incentives in order to support co-operation between member states and in order to support initiatives in the field of employment which aim at the exchange of information and which develop procedures to support comparative analysis and expertise and innovative approaches, to evaluate experience, especially by pilot projects. These measures do not include a harmonization of law and other regulations in the member states." This Article was – until the end of the conference – intensely disputed; it offers at least the opportunity for some European initiatives. These will depend from the Commission's ability and willingness to take advantage of political actions aiming at an enlarged competence in the field of employment policy. The German government however enforced its position that no additional financial resources would be mobilized for these projects.

At first sight the new Employment Chapter might be interpreted as a – rather modest or symbolic – victory of those forces which plead for a new orientation of integration politics. Yet, Jörg Huffschmid is right to argue that the economic concept of the EU remains hostile towards employment. Therefore, in Amsterdam "old thinking" prevailed (Huffschmid 1997).

A Growing Resistance to Neoliberalism

The development from Maastricht (1991) to Amsterdam (1997) has shown that within the EU a tendency towards re-nationalization of politics – and this means an enforcement of intergovernmental negotiation systems and power relations. Thus the concept of a step-by-step emergence of a supranational EU-sovereignty, which replaces national sovereignty, should be abandoned. More productive seems to be an analytical and strategic perspective which concentrates upon single policy fields and upon bargaining system within the multi-level-system of the EU. This enables a more realistic conception of the scope of political action and of the political actors.

Eventually, progressive transformation of EU-policies could only be achieved by the dynamics of social and political movements and struggles. The dominance of neoliberalism has been the expression of a specific constellation of class forces – it has been the consequence of a heavy defeat of the political Left and the European trade unions from the end of the 70s – a period which Donald Sasson (1996, 645 ff.) has described as the "great crisis of Socialism." The collapse of soviet communism and its allies only aggravated the crisis and the disorientation of the Western Labor movement.

In reaction to the crisis many trade unions have accepted the ideology of a "new social partnership." This strategy of survival accepts the subordinate role of unions and – even more important – of workers' councils (in enterprises) within international competition ("Standortkonkurrenz") – the rules of which are dictated by the market, by the management and by neoliberalism.[2] The "modernization of unions in Europe," propagated especially by the German DGB within the ETUF (cf. Transit 1/1995), underestimates the resistance of organized capital interests and of neoliberal politics against the achievements of the "European social model", and also it underestimates the negative impact of the monetary union under the leadership of the German Bundesbank ("Model Tietmeyer") for the national and sectoral bargaining power of the unions.

Even minor democratic and social progress within the EU have been the result of political pressure emerging from the national and the European level by trade union and political forces, but also from spontaneous social protest movements. Progress in Amsterdam (from the point of view of trade unions and left wing parties) resulted from a change in the political majorities in France and Britain. Though the new governments in these countries differ significantly in their political orientation, the defeat of conservative forces is an expression of the crisis of legitimacy of the neoliberal project. It is a result of an erosion of hegemony "from above" *and* of the pressure by social movements "from below."

Protest against neoliberalism has not only shaped the resistance against the Berlusconi government in Italy, but, even more, the great social movement in France at the end of 1995. During 1996 there have been mass strikes or union demonstrations in Belgium, Spain, Portugal, Greece and even in the rather socially peaceful "islands" of Switzerland and Germany. In the USA and other countries of America strike activity has increased (Moody 1997). The political dimensions of these movements consisted in a common attack and criticism of dominant (neoliberal) politics and ideologies. Solutions to the social and ecological problems at the end of the 20th century cannot be achieved by further radicalization of market liberties, my more deregulation and privatization, by more speculation in the global financial markets – they could only be achieved by successful struggles for a limitation and social control of these "liberties" (which always reflect a certain structure and constellation of class relations). Society – which is threatened by fragmentation and decay – must regain its capacity to control the dynamics of the market forces (in the first half of the 20th century this problem – the core problem of the *Age of Catastrophe* (Hobsbawm) – has been reflected by Karl Polanyi, 1978). The solution to the global crisis of employment – according to standards which have been set by the modern welfare state and by the needs for ecological reconstruction – could only be realized by regulative interventions (by law, redistributive measures in order to increase employment outside the private sector, political control of transnational capital movements). In the European Union the question of how to concretize the "social dimension" of the Common Market – against the resistance of conservative governments and organized capitalist interests – is still of utmost importance for the progressive forces.

Trade unions play a significant role in these movements for a progressive change. On the one hand trade union programs imply central elements of an alternative economic and employment policy. They demand a correction in the present distribution of wealth and income, and a reduction of the working time; they defend the basic principle of qualified public services in education, social security and infrastructure as a constitutive element of Western civilization. On the other hand only the dynamics of social movements and struggles will be able to achieve a substantial change in the political and ideological relations of forces, which might give new strength to a project of modernity committed to the traditions of Enlightenment, Human Rights and Socialism.

The recent interventions of the French sociologist Pierre Bourdieu (Bourdieu et al. 1997) throw a new light upon the eminently important function of the intellectuals in reflecting and analyzing the present situation of confusion, but also of an emerging struggle against the hegemony of neoliberalism. The demand of the American philosopher Richard Rorty "Back to class politics"[3] obviously strengthens the (international) choir of voices which demand a more critical engagement of intellectuals (especially of social scientists) in the analysis and criticism of present capitalist developments. To such voices we should pay more attention, at our European universities.

Notes

1. *Forschungsgruppe Europäische Gemeinschaften.* Cf. Bieling and Deppe (1997). In October 1996 this group organized a conference on "Labor Markets and Employment Policy in the European Union". Cf. Alain Lipietz et al. (1997).
2. The crisis of the trade-unionism which was oriented to class struggle, a general depolitization of trade union activities – a new type of co-operative politics – tries to defend the privileges of qualified workers in big corporations (for instance in the automobile sector) by offering co-operation and compromise. J. Kelly (1996, 101-12) summarizes the

results of an empirical comparison between "militant" and "moderate" unionism: "Reliance on employer sponsorship and co-operation with consultive and advisory institutions can weaken or inhibit the growth of workplace union organization and of any capacity to mobilize the union's membership for action against the employer. Advocates of moderate unionism have seriously underestimated the antagonism of employers to union presence, to union organization at the place of work and to collective bargaining (...) Militant unionism (...) embodies a recognition of the antagonism of interests between workers and employers (...) Consequently, militant trade unionism quite rightly seeks to defend the right to strike and to maintain the willingness and capacity of the membership to take collective action. Trade unionism without these attributes depends on employers and the state for its survival, whereas militant trade unionism builds on the only reliable foundation, namely its membership and their willingness to act".

3. "The best that could happen to the American Left, would be a return of the academics to class struggle", R. Rorty, in: *Die Zeit*, 18th july 1998.

References

Armigeon, K. 1994. "Die Regulierung kollektiver Arbeitsbeziehungen in der Europäischen Union," in: Streeck, W. (ed.). *Staat und Verbände*. 207 ff. Opladen.

Bieling, H. J. / Deppe, F. (eds.). 1997. *Arbeitslosigkeit und Wohlfahrtsstaat in Westeuropa. Neun Länder im Vergleich*. Opladen.

Bourdieu, P. et al. 1997. *Perspektiven des Protests. Initiativen für einen europäischen Wohlfahrtsstaat*. Hamburg.

Deppe, F. and Weiner, K. P. (eds.). 1991. *Binnenmarkt '92. Zur Entwicklung der Arbeitsbeziehungen in Europa*. Hamburg.

Esping-Andersen, G. 1990. *The Three Worlds of Welfare Capitalism*. New Jersey.

Forrester, V. 1996. *L'Horreur Économique*. Paris.

Fuhrmann, N. 1997. *Zur Entwicklung des Wohlfahrtsstaates in Dänemark. Magistraarbeit*. Marburg (unpublished).

Huffschmid, J. 1997. "Altes Denken in Amsterdam. Ohne Kurskorrektur kommt die europäische Einigung nicht voran." *Blätter für deutsche und internationale Poilitik*. 9/1997. 1083 - 1093.

Kapstein, E. B. 1996. "Workers and the World Economy." *Foreign Affairs*, Vol. 75. No. 3. May/June, 16 - 37.

Kelly, J. 1996. "Union militancy and social partnership," in: P. Ackers et al. *The New Workplace and Trade Unionism*. London.

Kronauer, M. 1995. "Massenarbeitslosigkeit in Westeuropa: Die Entstehung einer neuen 'Underclass'?" in: Soziologisches Forschungsinstitut Göttingen (ed.). *Im Zeichen des Umbruchs*. Opladen. 197 - 214.

Lessenich, S. 1994. "'Three Worlds of Welfare Capitalism' - oder vier? Strukturwandel arbeits- und sozialpolitischer Regulierungsmuster in Spanien." *Politische Vierteljahresschrift*. 35. Jg., Heft 2, 224-244.

Lipietz, A., et al. 1997. *Labor Markets and Employment Policy in the European Union*. Marburg: Studien der Forschungsgruppe Europäische Gemeinschaften (FEG), No. 10.

Michelsen, K. 1997. *Die gescheiterte Transformation des Schwedischen Modells*. Marburg: FEG-Studie No. 9.

Moody, K. 1997. *Workers in a Lean World. Unions in the International Economy.* London / New York.

Polanyi, K. 1987. *The Great Transformation* (1944). Frankfurt/Main.

Poulantzas, N. 1979. Interview, in: *Prokla,* no 77, 131 ff.

Rifkin, J. 1995. *Das Ende der Arbeit und ihre Zukunft.* Frankfurt/New York.

Sassoon, D. 1996. *One Hundred Years of Socialism. The West European Left in the Twentieth Century.* London.

Scharpf, F. W. 1996. "Politische Optionen im erweiterten Binnenmarkt," in: M. Jachtenfuchs / B. Kohler-Koch (ed.), *Europäische Intgeration,* 109 ff. Opladen.

Seeleib-Kaiser, M. 1997. "Globalization and the Re-Commodification of the Workforce," in: A. Lipietz et al, *Labor Markets and Employment Policy in the European Union,* 49 - 63.

Streeck, W. 1996. *Gewerkschaften zwischen Nationalstaat und Europäischer Union.* Unpublished man., Frankfurt/Main.

Transfer. European Review of Labor and Research. 1995. ed. by the European Trade Union Institute, Brussels, 1/ 1995.

PART E
LEGAL AND POLITICAL
ASPECTS
OF EUROPEAN
INTEGRATION:
A DEMOCRATIC DEFICIT

14 The Peculiar Tripolarity of the European Model of Legal Integration and the Deficiencies of European Legal Theory

DIMITRIS CHRISTOPOULOS
DIMITRIS DIMOULIS

A Triumph of Decisionism

Legal theory has for centuries constituted *de facto* an important *source of law*. Through the interaction of conflicting opinions on various legal problems, jurists formulate what becomes the "prevailing view," which then exerts decisive influence over the practical outcome of doctrinal disputes.[1]

Anyone reading the writings of jurists on the legal aspects of European unification will discover that one particular "style" is absolutely predominant. It is only too apparent that writings of the type in question –which are proliferating at a vertiginous rate along with the progress of European unification and are spawning European research centers, universities, professorial chairs, periodicals etc.— are in most cases quite *uncritical*. They summarize the legislative or even purely political decisions of European institutional bodies, cite judgments by European Courts and provide information on how these bodies see the future in the different fields of legal integration. The result is that in all countries of Western Europe, identical articles are being written on the same subjects with the same official bodies as their more or less exclusive sources of reference.

If we were to devise an index of *self-referentiality* of legal theory to indicate the frequency and density of an author's recourse to the views of other writers for the purposes of arriving at a satisfactory interpretation, a comparison of the coefficients for texts on European legal issues with those on other legal topics would reveal a great disparity.

In European law, legal theory tends to a zero point. There is a tendency to dispense with traditional legal methodology and reasoning. European courts in a similar spirit issue "free" interpretations in total indifference to the opinions of legal theory and to the need to follow specific interpretative procedures. So for instance the European Court of Human Rights of Strasbourg explicitly claims the "freedom" to make rulings on the basis of what it itself judges to be "present-day needs," interpreting "the terms of the Treaty on the assumption that it is not bound by the conventional meaning of the terms or more generally by the laws of semantics" (Cohen-Jonathan 1989: 195, 197 ff.).

If a national court dared to do any such thing, there would be a political scandal and jurists would be denouncing the anti-democratic magistrate who would presume to be a legislator. In the European Union context this stance on the part of the courts does not meet with any comparable resistance. The question therefore arises: are the lawyers who occupy themselves so injudiciously and so tediously with European law the same as those who created the legislative framework of the European States and continue to create it in ever new fields, functioning de facto as a source of law?

In fact they are not, and we shall see why. If you ask a jurist what is marriage, or even something more difficult such as, for example, what "is" France, he will give you a comprehensive and precise answer, producing thousands of quotations from laws and lawyers to support his view. To the question what is France, he will reply with an exact description of its borders, the legal way it was founded, the type of constitution it has and anything else that interests you. Legal definitions are of course poor, one-sided things but they constitute data of tremendous practical importance: they provide information as to what is the case on the basis of law.[2]

So as to be in a position to make this information available, jurists have developed a strict interpretative procedure (notwithstanding the fact that they have never been in complete agreement about it), and the specialized legal debate which has resulted therefrom has led, as indicated, to the formulation of the "prevailing views." This has provoked jealousy among other scholars, e.g. historians, who are unable to define exactly what, for example France "is" or how it was brought into existence, since they do not possess "sacred" texts that they might consult or authoritative methods for defining what is "correct."

Ask a jurist what is Europe. He will not be able to answer you. He finds himself in a worse predicament even than the historian, because he possesses neither methodology nor criteria that would enable him to reply. There are numerous institutions which describe themselves as European, each with different member countries. The competences of these institutions are indeterminate, as are the relations between them. European bodies include countries which not even the broadest geographical definition could include as part of Europe, and the opposite case is even more prevalent.

Of course there remains the promise (or perhaps the utopia) that in future a juridical and political integration of all the institutions of Europe will in fact take place and there will exist something called "Citizens' Europe" or even "Peoples' Europe," which will be the realm of peace, democracy and freedom under the rule of law. But in the meantime jurists find themselves in the utmost confusion. Some acknowledge that their situation is one of total perplexity,[3] others have elaborated the theoretical conceit that the law is a "chameleon" and argue that we have made the transition to a post-modern juridical culture where everything is mired in the quicksands of "interlegality" (Sousa Santos 1987: 298 f.). Even specialists in European Law have neither the time nor the means to articulate a coherent legal discourse in relation to the decisions of European juridical bodies.

So what is new? The answer is that the European legal system does not share the traditional characteristics of a legal order. A state legal order is founded on four elements:[4]

a) Undivided sovereignty, implying the absolute and exclusive control of a certain territory (the monopoly of power).
b) Legal regulations which the sovereign power also imposes on itself (the rule of law).
c) Stability of the legal order, with sufficient time available to jurists to elaborate it into a system.
d) Democratic legitimization of sovereignty by the people. Decisions of state firstly issue from bodies that have been elected by the citizens and secondly are seen as implementing the will of the people as laid down in the Constitution.[5]

Nothing of these elements exists in the procedures of legal integration in Europe. There is a normative multiplicity of doubtful applicability, located in a field of contested sovereignty and jurisdiction between member states and European institutions. There can be no question of stability in the legal system when institutions and organizations are being reshuffled, with the entry of new members bringing with them different legal systems which pose great problems of harmonization, of transitional stages and compromises over which laws are to be applied; when maximalistic projects like the common currency are constantly on the European agenda, meeting with the most bitter disappointments only to come back again as projects – that is to say when the terms of sovereignty have not crystallized.[6]

In today's Europe, councils, commissions and courts make policy on the basis of very fluid conceptions of legality, having recourse to a number of subterfuges so as to impose their will amidst a maze of deadlines, negotiations, buck-passing from one body to another and political compromises.[7] Unstable polycentrism with constant reallocation of the spheres of influence and the bearers of sovereignty results in a European Law which is at the mercy of politics. And this situation arises because no political force exists which is capable of exercising centralized control. The reference points from which jurists formerly took their bearings are no longer there. Yet most continue to regard this situation as something natural.[8] They ignore the rift entailed in the Western European states' post-war decision to create a legal order without clearly defined bearers, limits and directions.

"European" jurists are witnessing *the end of legal theory as a source of law* and this is attributable to a radical change in the object of their labors. The traditional function of establishing "order" and so removing arbitrariness and secrecy from the practice of government (certainty and security of law) is not objectively possible under European law. And obviously, the non-existence of the rule of law in Europe also implies the *non-existence of democracy*.

Questions of Democracy

The concept of democracy is often given a procedural connotation. Democracy is seen as the safeguarding of certain decision-making procedures for political matters (universal participation – chiefly in relation to the right to vote – the rule of the majority, conditions of the dialogue, means of implementing decisions, etc.).[9] This definition is formally agnostic but actually biased. Its purpose is to exclude from the concept of democracy (and thus to delegitimize) all radical questioning of the present-day social system which has to do with (representative) democracy. Democracy needs to be defined substantially: as its name implies, it is the sovereignty of the people.[10]

There is another problem. Often those who write about democracy "forget" the purpose of the sovereignty of the people.[11] It is not an end in itself; it serves the purpose of averting rule *over* the people by a third party. Its aim is to prevent power from being used as a means of oppression and exploitation. Democracy can therefore exist only as the sovereignty of the people *in practice*.

We do not seek to advocate that which has been disparaged as "the political fantasy of the One" (Rancière 1990: 59) – a "fantasy" which was decisive for the ideological construction of nation states as "communities" of those who are said to have the same interests. And we are not unaware that the concept of democracy "joins the unassignable quantity of the *demos* to the indefinable action of *kratein*" (ibid. 94). But even if the content of democracy is not susceptible of positive definition and can be defined only as the ideological program of a movement, it can also be employed "negatively" as a means for analyzing political reality. When people are unable effectively to control their conditions of life, that is to say when it is ascertained in practice that there exists a certain inequality in the distribution of political power and that this may be attributed to the structures of a society, then it is safe to say that there is no sovereignty of the people even if democratic procedures are religiously observed. Partial or formal or procedural democracy is a contradiction in terms, because sovereignty cannot be shared. If democracy is merely formal, this means that the demos is an "icon" (Müller 1996: 33 ff.). And to recognize this it is not necessary to possess a positive definition of the quantity of the demos or of the dimensions of *kratein*.

To move beyond this proceduralist outlook what is necessary is a history (and a theory) of the relations between the different models of democracy and the structures of society.[12] Only in this way can the limits of what is today called "democracy" be made visible and its functions clarified. And on the subject of this undertaking, the ideological terror that has accompanied the overthrow of East European socialism and the collapse of the working class movement should not lead intellectuals to ignore a very basic point. Private ownership of production signifies control over the lives of the majority of people and determination – direct or indirect – of culture and of political decision-making. Private ownership of a company is not an individual matter like private ownership of a pair of trousers. It is a matter for society as a whole, which nevertheless today is decided by *individuals*, who exercise *private-structural violence* in order to obtain submission to their decisions. As long as private ownership of this kind persists, the majority in society cannot determine the conditions of their common existence.

Bourgeois states – under the pressure of the popular masses – attempted to control private violence, at least in its more extreme manifestations. The "promise" inherent in the contemporary nation-state was *not* one of democracy or government *by* the people; it did however entail a certain *democratizing tendency* which could be called government *for* the people,[13] whose basis was the popular participation in defining the principles of social regulation.

Government *for* the people is on the way to being abolished in present-day Europe. The multiplicity and confusion of power centers put these beyond the citizens control. Thus, for example nowadays the standard riposte to citizens' protests at unemployment is the inability to act, both on the part of states ("community policy," the need to meet "convergence criteria") and on the part of the central administrative bodies of the European Union (subsidiarity, flexibility, lack of competence over social policy owing to shortage of Community resources).

In the course of this return to the "state of nature," the private power of the owners of the means of production is greatly strengthened. European administrative bodies exempted from popular pressures implement policies which more and more favor the holders of real power, that is to say the social classes and groups which can exert material influence on European policy-making. The results are only too visible: a removal of barriers for capital, reduction in social protection, repressive policies for the defense of the powerful from internal and external "dangers."

In united Europe *invisible private violence* triumphs under the cover of "deregulation" and the inability of political mechanisms to react to it. At the very time that Europe is paraded as a synonym for democracy and human rights, and even constructs its own institutional identity on the basis of that equation,[14] the traditional legal safeguards and the democratizing tendencies are demolished.

Without clear and undivided sovereignty there can be no clear framework of protective laws and legal uncertainty always functions to the detriment of the weaker party. Secrecy and the democratic deficit in Europe bring us back to the mediaeval maxim *quod principis placuit legis habet vigorem*, to a framework of laws without the rule of law.

Crises in International Law - Emergence of European Law

The year 1989 has already become a historical milestone. It has been invoked by commentators to indicate the end of history, the post-war era, the division of Europe, etc. In our days it is more evident than ever that the division is still there. The post-cold-war gap between the East and the West of Europe is social. For many years to come arguments will persist about what determined the collapse of the old post-war order and shaped the contours of the new one. Among the diverse theoretical traditions there exists a shared vocabulary for describing the world that has become fluid and is being remade: in its simplest terms, it is the world of *strategic bipolarity*.

The same cannot be said of another world that may also be fluid and in the process of being remade: the modern system of states. This world exists at a deeper level and on a temporally more extended plane. Its remaking involves a shift not in the play of power politics but rather of the stage on which that play is performed (Ruggie 1993: 139). Here no shared vocabulary exists in the literature to depict change and continuity. As a case in point we might take efforts to express the emerging architecture of the EU.

The Marxist theorist Etienne Balibar stresses that: "it is a negative characteristic that first imposes itself. The State today in Europe is neither national nor supranational, and this ambiguity does not slacken but only grows deeper over time" (1991: 16). From the other side of the political spectrum, the *Economist* agrees: in the place of the old federate visions that gave birth to the concept of the European construction after the Second World War, it sees "a Europe of many spires".[15]

It has been some years since Europeans starting questioning themselves about their "identity" (Fenet 1994: 397 ff.; Stolleis 1995: 279 ff.; Lock 1996: 38 ff.).The theme of European identity is one of the most fashionable questions in contemporary social and legal theory on this continent. But it is also a sign of vulnerability, related to the loss of the European hegemony in international relations after the Second World War (Kunz 1955; Académie de Droit International de la Haye 1984). This replacement of hegemony has caused a structural crisis of international law, which until that time had been exclusively European, at least insofar as its origins and its references were concerned. However, after World War II its "transatlantic" qualifications are what count. This is the explanation for its territorially far more limited and politically far less ambitious profile.

The emergence of a distinctive model of legal integration with the establishment of the Council of Europe in 1949 and the signing of the Treaty of Rome in 1957 marks the gradual establishment of a new legal order, a new *ius commune* for the European states. This regime reflects the necessities, the contradictions, the conflicts and the coalitions among the states in question. The western European states had hitherto considered themselves safe enough to govern their colonies without any particular legal support. Yet, the decolonization process proved that this was no longer the case for the European powers. At the end of World War II decolonization and serious competition from the USA and Japan, not to mention a host of other less important factors, all contributed to the emergence of a new unificatory legal framework: "European law." But, to pose the question again: *What is Europe?*

In our day every political body has a different answer to this question. Every academic discipline also has a different answer, depending on the criteria employed.[16] There may be difficulties with the prevailing perspectives, not to mention disagreements as to how the process of European construction should be accounted for or described. But at least there is a common reference point: everyone acknowledges that the process is occurring.

Two Models for Understanding European Integration

We wish to argue in this paper that neither of the prevalent modern conceptualizations of political reality provides adequate intellectual means for a global comprehension of this reality on the European continent. The two present-day models for conceptualizing international relations, both deeply implicated in the political project of modernity, are the following: realist balance-of-power thinking and idealist institutionalism, both of which have their origins in the eighteenth century.

From the realist viewpoint, the Treaty of Utrecht (1713) enshrined the notion of a self-regulated equilibrium as a central regulating principle of European society, along with the idea that the defence of this equilibrium should be of concern to one and all (Osianter 1994). For realist theories "the sovereign States followed their orderly paths in a harmony of mutual attractions and repulsions" (Wight 1973: 98). On the idealist side, the eighteenth century opened with the Abbé de Saint Pierre's institutionalist plan to secure a "perpetual peace" and closed with the in many ways similar Kantian project (Hinsley 1978: ch. 2, 4). Post World War II realism and liberal institutionalism are the latest incarnations of realist and idealist thought, but neither has much to say about the fundamental transformation occurring today in the process of European construction.

The Fluid Validity of the Three Pivots of European Integration

Take first the EU, in which the process of unbundling territoriality and transferring sovereignty has gone further than anywhere else. Neorealism ascribes its origins to strategic bipolarity. Institutionalism examines how the national interests and policy preferences of the major European states are reflected in patterns of EU collaboration (Ruggie 1993: 171).

The Council of Europe offers a very convenient field for liberal institutional analysis. The fundamental common values of human rights and the rule of law constitute the basic instrument of legal integration inside the organization. More than 150 conventions and treaties have been signed within the framework of the Council of Europe, a figure that could be interpreted as evidence of a high level of mutual understanding and collaboration. Yet, a realist analysis would stress instead the social inefficacy of all this legal material, thereby minimizing the contribution of the institution as international judge or legislator.

Finally take the Organization for Security and Co-operation in Europe (OSCE). Roughly similar considerations in terms of neorealism and liberal institutionalism would serve to confirm their less than total validity in the wider geographical context (and the more fluid institutional context) of the Organization.

However, from the vantage point of this study, there comes into view a very different aspect of the inter-institutional relations between the international bodies in question and the relationship between states and international organizations in Europe: political Europe as what one might call a *multiperspectival* entity, in the sense of being comprised of inconstant pivots of decision-making, ruled by fluid internal coalitions, contradictions or conflicts, and as such constituting a peculiar legal system which seemingly does not share the fundamental attributes of "modern" legal systems.

Within the framework of domestic law, whether public or private, the three crucial axes determining validity of legal norms are: *legal formality*, in the sense that norms originate from a pre-established formal procedure. (As might be expected, this criterion is highly esteemed by the positivist approach to legal theory.) The second criterion for validity is *social effectivity*. A norm is valid if and only if it is respected and followed by those it designates. This criterion is more or less applied by several schools of legal sociology and law-in-context-theories. Last but not least, the third prerequisite for validity is the *moral legitimacy* of norms. Natural law theories would derive such a criterion from ethical arguments (legal moralism).[17] Considered from these three identification points, the validity of European law is at best debatable and in many ways quite problematic.

Formality

Legal formality is the strongest element in European law, in the sense that this law is founded on certain administrative procedures that at least guarantee its existence. This is the case with EU-law and the human rights norms of the Council of Europe: decisions of the Courts of Luxembourg and Strasbourg, directives of the European Council or the European Commission, resolutions of the European Parliament, etc. However, clearly defined pre-established techniques are entirely absent when it comes to the OSCE. Here the rule of power seems to dominate the decision making process, since everything depends on international bargaining.

Since the Helsinki Final Act, international and European legal doctrine have entered into endless discussions about the legal or political nature of the OSCE Concluding Documents. The question has been whether these documents implement legal obligations or political commitments.[18] Without wishing to enter into this discussion, it has been proven that whatever the nature of the documents, some of them contain certain provisions that have been implemented and some (the majority) have been completely neglected. After a succession of failed attempts to establish a judicial mechanism, the OSCE recently established a Court of Conciliation and Arbitration in Geneva. Nevertheless, it is not the first time in its history that the OSCE has taken the initiative of establishing such a mechanism.[19]

The previous failures underline the structural impossibility of establishing an OSCE Court and the immobility of the Court of Geneva offers no promise of a better future.

Effectivity

Even if social effectivity as such is a highly disputed concept in international law, it could easily be claimed that European law is by far more "effective" than international law in general. However, this is true of practically all regional international systems when compared with universal ones. In that sense, the social effectivity of European law does not represent a very original element. What is original in European law is the fact that formal variability of normative categories (directives, resolutions, decisions, etc.) does not correspond to their degree of social implementation in the legal orders of the member states. In other words, social effectivity does not depend on the formal character of norms.

The different *a priori* levels of applicability of European rules (conventions, recommendations, resolutions, etc.) are to a great extent overturned in practice. For example, it is quite commonplace for some of the Strasbourg Court decisions to be implemented in the internal legal order of the member states and some not to be. This is also true of the decisions of the Luxembourg Court and the directives, regulations etc. of the EU.

This brings us to very peculiar *normative duality* within European law. Within every normative category there is always a proportion that is in fact implemented by national authorities and another that remains in a proclamatory stage.[20] This vertical cleavage, which traverses every formal normative category of European law, renders extremely fluid and unstable the element of social effectivity.

Legitimacy

Legitimacy is by far the weakest element in European law. It has become a commonplace in our day to speak of the "democratic deficit." However, the democratic deficit in the strict sense of the weakness of the European Parliament's role in the legislative process is nothing other than a symptom of the *structural deficit problem of the European order* and its formation as such. And that is a product of the uncertain *a posteriori* ratification of current legal developments by Europeans, due to the aforementioned fundamental "irregularity" or innate impossibility of European law: the non-existence of popular legitimization of a "European sovereignty."

The legitimacy of European law is thus dependent on a very unstable factor: European public opinion. The volatility of public opinion makes it anything but a reliable source for the authority of European legislative bodies. Legitimization of power is not something which should be dependent on statistical research. And of course the problem becomes serious when this public opinion appears reserved, negative or even hostile to the whole project of European integration. In our days the referendum, the most suitable democratic method for confirming the sovereignty of the people in a modern liberal state, is regarded with suspicion by the architects of European integration. The results of referendums on the Maastricht Treaty, which were in manifest contradiction to the favorable stance of Europe's political leadership, provided evidence of a far more substantial democratic deficit.

Legal Integration and Tripolarity

If we were to attempt to get a global view of Europe from an institutional view-point, the image would be more fluid than one would expect. Institutions are supposed to offer a minimum of stability and legality as a reference point for identification. This requirement is not satisfied by any of the European institutional bodies. The coexistence in Europe of multiple normative and political orders confirms what we have called the *peculiar tripolarity* of the European model of legal integration. The poles in question are firstly the EU of the 15 member states; secondly the Council of Europe, embracing 40 states and including since 1989 all the states of Eastern and Central Europe; and the OSCE of 55 states. This last-mentioned entity covers virtually the entire northern hemisphere from Alaska to Siberia, including the mainland United States and Canada.

The European model of legal integration – if we can call it a model, since it can be codified as such only *a posteriori* – appears to be a most singular case when compared with all the other models for federations that have been conceptualized in the modern world. The term "integration," very widespread in our day in the field of legal theory, is mathematical in origin and was only later extended to apply to the social sciences as well. There it denotes the process that permits one entity to absorb another, generally distinct from and weaker than the first. This is the case, for example, with integration of migrant workers. However, a quite different sense is assigned to the term when we are speaking of European integration. Here we refer to a *sui generis* model which involves the incorporation of European states into a more comprehensive institutional ensemble, within which they are nevertheless supposed to retain their specificity. From a legal point of view, the European states have voluntarily agreed to surrender to some collective entity – the supranational bodies – the exercise of certain competencies, undertaking moreover to refrain from active in a manner incompatible with their international obligations. This is the meaning of the term "integration" in the sense in which it is employed in the field of European law (and international law generally).

The European model of integration possesses the following peculiarities when compared with the typical federal constitutional model from the viewpoint of its *formal sources* and its *legal reference of subject and object.*

The Formal Sources of the Integration

There is a considerable difference between the formation of a federal state and a multinational ensemble such as the EU. Whereas the federal constitution is a normative act of internal law, the instruments of European integration are international treaties founded on the general principle of international law: *pacta sunt servanda.* Even if federal constitutions contain imperative rules providing for a very strict review procedure, there is no mechanism that could prevent a radical – even revolutionary – constitutional change. By contrast, the mechanisms of European integration are governed by an absolute *contractualism* among member states.[21]

The Legal Reference of Integration

At this point we are obliged to focus on the exclusively judicial order, an order that has at its disposal a mechanism of jurisdictional control. From this perspective, one pivot of this peculiar tripolarity, the OSCE, can be regarded as, indicated, as a political system, *in extremis* an institutional order, but not a judicial one. In this strictly judicial aspect, the European integration model is characterized by *bipolarity*. On the one hand is the legal order of the EU, on the other the order established by the European Court at Strasbourg. Each system for integration serves a different purpose. The first aims at the transfer of competencies mainly of an economic nature, but in fact aspires to much more than establishment of the common market: it seeks gradually to develop different legal articulations between economics and politics, economics and social policy, economics and culture, at the same time fostering sound economic relations with third states, and more recently external policy and security.

What we must stress at this point is that the exclusive link between persons and the judicial authorities of the EU is the link of *citizenship*. Until the signing of the Maastricht Treaty the only form of citizenship recognized was that of the member states. The Maastricht Treaty has institutionalizes a new (?) category of citizenship, European citizenship (art. 8). One may well ask wherein lies the innovative element in European citizenship. The answer is disappointing. Nothing apart from a common passport, the right of EU citizens to diplomatic protection by the authorities of every member state, the right of petition before the European Parliament – as well as before the European Ombudsman – and the right to vote and stand as a candidate at local and European elections (Kovar / Simon 1993; Closa 1995). If one excepts the last item, the modifications are evidently of minor importance. The really important point about the link of European citizenship boils down to one strikingly negative characteristic: the final institutionalization of the distinction between "Europeans" and "Foreigners," i.e. *the reproduction of the nation-state model at the European level* (Giannoulis 1992: 154 ff.).

The European Convention of Human Rights (ECHR) serves broader objectives, but its practical efficacy is far more limited. As far as objectives are concerned, the European Convention has jurisdiction over all issues of fundamental individual rights. As for efficacy, the decisions of the Court of Strasbourg do not possess executive force under the legal order of the member states. Only by political means could the Council of Europe coerce the states to respect the Court's decisions.

The Division of the Legal Subject in European Law as a Symptom of the Contradictions Between Political and Economic Liberalism

Hence, a radical discrepancy appears when it comes to the subjects legitimized to exercise their rights according to the letter of the Convention. Article 1 of the ECHR states that "The High Contracting Parties shall secure for *everyone within their jurisdiction* the rights and freedoms defined in the Section 1 of this Convention."[22] Every person who deals with the judicial authorities of a member-state of the Council of Europe has the right of recourse to the Court of Strasbourg. In other terms the European citizen cedes his place to "every person."

At this stage we are witnessing a fundamental displacement of the legal subject. *Every person* denotes the ahistorical, asocial, ageographical, abstract individual entity on which the modern, liberal, legal tradition of human rights, briefly the heritage of European political liberalism and democracy, is founded. A number of objections might be raised to this Kantian, abstract variety of human rights subject. Can we conceive of an actual individual who is not situated in a certain social, historical and geographical context?[23]

However, our object is to focus on the fundamental contradiction between "every person," the beneficiary of human rights thanks to his innate human dignity, and the far more limited category of the "European citizen" who enjoys the protection of the judicial mechanisms of the EU. These mechanisms cover the *sui generis* model of legal integration which prevails within the framework of what we call the "little Europe" of 15 member states. Why should it be so difficult for jurists dealing with European law to admit this? Why is it that all kinds of jurists, realists, functionalists, idealists, positivists, (along with their "neo-" heirs) do not simply focus on this radical limitation of the legal subject, in order to reveal the real mechanisms of European integration?

In answer to this we may quote Wittgenstein, according to whom "the aspects of things that are most important for us are hidden because of their simplicity and familiarity. One is unable to notice something – because it is always before one's eyes" (1969: § 129, 50). We could add, and this seems to be more appropriate for our case, that one is *unwilling* to notice something, *even though* it is always before one's eyes. This evident fact of the *division of the legal subject in Europe* is entirely neglected by the contemporary legal theory.

This division reflects the innate contradiction between political and economic liberalism in contemporary Europe. It reveals the essence of what has been named the "European liberal utopia": the historically impossible identification or articulation between the abstract philosophical premises of political liberalism and the concrete social segregation of capitalism, emanating from the neoliberal economic policy of the EU. How far would it be from the contemporary European reality to say that in the end *liberalism is not liberal*, in the sense that the fundamental premise of liberal theory: the inalienable dignity of the human being, the transcendental human values of Kant, along with the related principle of non-discrimination, is territorialized through the dichotomy between Europeans and non Europeans, through the division of the human legal subject, and finally through its own violation.

The demonstration of this contradiction and the "misunderstandings" it causes for contemporary European legal theory highlights two basic intellectual assumptions: First, that the discipline of European law is governed by a particular, historically conditioned discourse which is, in fact, quite simply the transference into the European domain of some basic tenets of liberal political theory, dictated by the strategic – or even tactical – choices of capital forces. This implies for the jurist an intellectual work of *translation,* of decodification, a demystificative discourse on the sacred axioms of European law. A theory of legal translation must begin with the realization of the very partial, multilayered and fragmented nature of international society, and in our specific case of Europe.[24]

Secondly, it could be that the potential task of legal doctrine in Europe is to reconstruct conflict situations in accordance with basic principles of social understanding.[25] What is needed is a interdisciplinary theory of knowledge[26] based on exposure of ruling doctrines in Europe, rather than a summary of the decisions of the European judicial authorities. Within the framework of this intellectual experience, we have tried to highlight the impossible articulation, otherwise stated the contradiction between the economic and the political aspects of liberal thought.

The Uncertain Future of the European Legal Order

Liberal jurists rejoice at nation-states' loss of sovereignty and believe in international law as a world religion which will bring eternal peace and the triumph of human rights. The new panacea is called "global constitutionalism" and makes its appearance as a consequence of (and an answer to) the crisis of sovereignty of nation states, which was made irreversible with the creation of the United Nations and the international declarations of human rights, that is to say with the creation of a global legal order not grounded on a *status naturalis* (hostility between sovereign nation states) but – potentially – on a *status civilis* (outlawing of war and integration of states into an international human-rights-based legal order) which must be extended in the direction of a "global civil society."[27]

This approach does not answer the question of who it is that is to impose this "global" legal order, i.e. does not examine the identity of the bearers of sovereignty. It doubtless takes it for granted that this all-powerful subject is to be denoted Reason or Justice. Nowhere is it acknowledged that the present world order comprises conflicting interests. The twofold illusion is propagated that present-day states are becoming steadily more democratic and that there is a simple cause-effect relationship between (representative) democracy and world peace. But those who regard "national sovereignty" as juridically obsolete and politically improper are in the final analysis merely echoing the ideological discourse of today's world order, portraying it as a triumph of legality and attempting to delegitimize the resistance of weaker countries struggling for their self-determination.[28]

We see now that the abolition of "national sovereignty" in Europe leads to a situation which is the exact opposite of what is promised: a situation of unemployment, repression and lawlessness. If the crisis of sovereignty is examined in the light of the protective elements of the rule of law, the question is raised of where Europe is going, what evolution we can expect in this unacceptable situation of a volatile European law at the mercy of neoliberal politics. We can distinguish four possible lines of development, which we will correlate with the factors inherent in the present state of legal integration in Europe.

Law in a European State

The first is the official prospect. The creation of an integrated European polity with all the hallmarks of "national" sovereignty (central government, army, bureaucracy and judiciary, fiscal sovereignty, foreign policy). Important steps have already been taken in this direction. Nevertheless, this process has been carried out under the exclusive hegemony of capital.[29] The creation of a European "nation-state" would doubtless favor the consolidation of the legal system. Be that as it may, there are no political forces which could impose a legal regime that would favor the consolidation of democracy.

National Law in Europe

The second – diametrically opposite – scenario is that of the collapse of the ambitious model of European integration amidst economic and political crises. Numerous institutions for collaboration and facilitation of capital and labor movements remain trapped in its ruins. The nation-states reinforce their sovereignty and their rule of law.

From a legal viewpoint, this prognosis is strengthened by the fact that in European countries today the legal system continues *de facto* to operate within a closed national framework. The administrative machinery and the national courts only exceptionally cite European law. This is often stigmatized as provincialism. Nevertheless, it represents an effective strategy for averting the delegitimizing consequences that would ensue from the direct importation of the volatile European rules.[30] As a result, citizens do not experience directly the crisis of sovereignty described in the first part of this paper. This will however boomerang against the future imposition of a uniform European legal order.

Europe without the Rule of Law

The third model is based on "free market" rules, which means the autonomous arbitration of conflicts through negotiation. This is the neoliberal/libertarian model involving the predominance of magistrates and solicitors as intermediaries, using not legal but "functional" decision criteria. A prospect of this kind represents an adaptation of medieval legal casuistry to the "needs of the market." It is a model which fulfills every jurist's dream of becoming a legislator. It will lead to abolition of social protection and entails the risk of provoking mass revolts. It is therefore not only reactionary but also improbable.

Rule of Citizens in Europe

The fourth model could be called the Europe "of" citizens, a model that exposes the innate paradoxes of the very concept of democracy in Europe. What modern liberal theory has proclaimed in relation to democracy and human rights can only become reality in a post-liberal, actual and *empirically "demonstrable" democracy*. The contemporary challenge is not so much the proclamation as the realization of human rights *by* the citizens *for* the citizens. This is a human rights policy as an object of collective decision-making by the interested parties to a specific issue.[31]

The crisis in Europe's model of legal integration manifests itself in fluctuation between an inadequate political liberalism and an economic liberalism which underwrites private violence. This crisis also presents an opportunity for showing up the real function of law, i. e. for getting across the point that legal order, like every "order," is the opposite of democracy. To contribute to this task, legal theory should investigate the mechanisms of *multiple* – and in many ways invisible – *domination*. Through the juridical contrivances of democracy and peace which have held sway in our age, this type of political power has converted the loftiest ideals into ideologies of subjugation. "Sed si servitium, barbaries, et solitudo pax appellanda sit, nihil hominibus pace miserius."[32]

Notes

1. On the "prevailing view" in questions of law and the historical configuration of legal theory as a source of law, cf. Wesel (1979: 88 ff.); Larenz (1975: 215 ff., 350 ff.); Paladin (1996: 97 ff.).
2. Thus, for example, a legal analysis of marriage would be advantageous for a person thinking of marrying or divorcing, even though it would provide no insights at all into such eminently interesting topics as the relations between the genders as social relations of domination in part created and in part reflected by the institution of heterosexual marriage.
3. Cf. the conclusions of Eleftheriadis (1996: 42).
4. These elements reflect the conventional definition of sovereignty as supreme power based on law. For a historical perspective see Rigaudière (1993: 5 ff.).
5. The fourth element has not always been there, but it exists today in all the European states.
6. See for instance Stolleis (1995: 277 ff.); Baratta / Giannoulis (1996: 240 ff.).
7. To cite the example of two issues that cropped up during the summer of 1997. When in France certain mayors banned children under the age of twelve from walking unaccompanied in the streets after midnight, the constitutional courts overruled these decisions and not a single mayor thought of "resisting," invoking, for example, his own sovereignty or arguing that the Court was ignoring local conditions. (*Le Monde*, 22 July 1997 and 9 August 1997). While under the Maastricht Treaty the EU States are obliged to permit "citizens of the Union" permanently resident in another member-state to participate in municipal elections (Article 8b), five years after the signing of the Treaty Belgium, France, Germany, Portugal and Greece have, for domestic political reasons, still not passed the relevant legislation. The EU is not in possession of any procedure which might secure the prompt and unobstructed observance of this obligation. The European Commission tried for months to exert pressure on the states in question and finally decided to lodge an appeal with the Court of Justice of the European Communities only against Belgium because it considers that in the light of the exceptions specifically provided for in the case of Belgium (i.e. conditions which inhibit the exercise of the right by certain EU citizens) it is particularly unacceptable for Belgium not to pass the law (see La Belgique sanctionée, *La Lettre de la citoyenneté*, 29, 1997, p. 3). Meanwhile "European" jurists never tire of pointing out that primary Community law has unconditional supremacy even over the various national constitutions.

8. Nevertheless the embarrassment of certain European jurists at the state of their "discipline" is obvious when they refer to the question of whether there exists a common European legal culture and if so whether it should be strengthened and what the consequences will be for that culture of the multilingualism, both literal and figurative, of European law, including the many points at which it conflicts with the corresponding national law. See for instance Ress (1995: 82 ff.), where among other things it is pointed out that European law "is mired down in language" (86).
9. Bobbio (1991: XVIII-XIX, 4-7, 83).
10. This definition conceals a fundamental paradox. If the people are sovereign, i.e. if "all" rule, then what is the "object" of their rule? Do they rule over the wicked elements in their own natures (violence, injustice etc.)? Or do they rule over others (foreigners, the "immature," those otherwise excluded from the various levels in the hierarchical game of democratic participation)? Or are they in fact incapable of actual sovereignty? The problematic nature of any answers that might be given to these questions is a testimony to the divisiveness of the concept of democracy and to the ideological elements which are concealed in it. For some significant observations see Balibar (1997: 19 ff., 101 ff., 397 ff.).
11. This occurs when the self-determination of the people is portrayed as the key element in democracy and made the starting point of an analysis not of the actual content of the people's sovereignty but of the different constituent elements of "the people" themselves. So Müller (1996: 24 and passim).
12. See for instance C.B. MacPherson 1977.
13. For these terms see Müller (1996: 39). The distinction dates back to the work of Aristotle. See Rancière (1990: 15 f.).
14. Title I, art. F Maastricht Treaty. This equation is accepted uncritically by all those who refuse to examine the reality of Europe and simply ask themselves which philosophical theory can be best adapted to define "European identity" so as to find "a satisfactory way" to the "unified constitutional foundation" of a Federal European Republic on the basis of "common European rights and principles" (de Moor 1993: 71 ff.). For a critique of these contrivances for manufacturing a "European identity" see Lock (1996: 48 ff.).
15. "Many-spired Europe" *The Economist,* 18 May 1991.
16. As Saussure (1968: 23) puts it, "c'est le point de vue qui crée l'objet."
17. Bobbio (1967: 47 ff.); Ost (1987: 257 ff.; 1993: 638); Dreier (1991: 95 ff.).
18. For a brief overview of this often wordy doctrinal discussion, cf. Buergental (1990, especially ch. VIII: The Character of the CSCE Commitments).
19. Reference is made, *inter alia, to* the European Court of Conciliation and Arbitration, a very ambitious project that was the brainchild of Robert Badinter, ex-president of the French Constitutional Council, but never got off the ground, and also to the successive mechanisms for the peaceful settlement of disputes that have been periodically initiated since 1989 but have never appeared realistic projects given the actual capacities of the OCSE. Cf. Badinter (1993: 15 ff.); for more general information on the OSCE method for conflict resolution, cf. several studies in the periodical publication *Helsinki Monitor.*
20. This duality has been further analysed by the French jurist M. Chemillier-Gendreau (1987) in the wider context of international law. In this approach, the distinction between proclamatory and executory international law is made pertinent by traversing all the generally admitted distinctions between norms: a) norms of internal and external origin; b) international acts of statutory or conventional origin; c) conventional, custom-

ary and imperative law; d) simple obligations or obligations accompanied with sanctions, etc.

21. Cf. the original analysis offered by F. Rigaux (1995).
22. One might also quote Article 25 of the Convention: "The Commission may receive petitions addressed to the Secretary General of the Council of Europe from any person, non-governmental organisation or group of individuals claiming to be the victim of a violation by one of the High Contracting Parties...".
23. A very interesting review of these critiques is presented by Binoche (1989).
24. Such a "translative" approach is followed in the domain of international law by critical jurists. An overview of these approaches is given by Carty (1991: 66 ff.).
25. Cf. also Carty (1986).
26. Interdisciplinarity is used here in the sense proposed by Piaget (1970: 70 ff.).
27. For a fully-elaborated presentation of this ideological viewpoint see Ferrajoli (1995: 39 ff.); a critique of various proposals and perspectives of "institutional cosmopolitanism" is to be found in Zolo (1995).
28. This observation should not be interpreted as advocacy of a nationalistic outlook, nostalgic for the sovereignty of nation states and structurally associated with exclusion, racism and violence. We would simply like to point out that present day internationalism (expressed through the "centralist model of legal cosmopolitanism" - Zolo 1995: 146) is based on an unstable convergence of the interests of certain countries. Its material basis is the antagonistic model of unfettered accumulation of capital and the drive for subjugation of the weaker. An authentic internationalism "from below" is by contrast founded on the ideal of brotherhood. For the two types of internationalism see Sousa Santos (1997: 29 ff.).
29. Money is the real European passport. Under EU regulations there are two kinds of freedom of movement. Firstly, for those who work. Their mobility obviously introduces pressure for curtailment of social protection. Secondly, for those who can purchase services in other countries (e.g. tourists, pensioners). Everyone else is unwelcome in this Europe "without borders."
30. If for example, in a member-state, disputes break out in everyday practice between the administration, the courts and the citizens as to whether European rules should override the national legal norms, the uncertainty of law will reach crisis point and state institutions will lose their legitimisation as guarantors of law and order.
31. See certain comments in Baratta / Giannoulis (1996: 253 ff.).
32. "But if slavery, barbarism, and desolation are to be called peace, peace is the greatest misfortune that men can suffer."

References

Académie de Droit International de la Haye, Université des Nations Unies. 1984. *L'avenir du droit international dans un monde multiculturel,* Colloque. La Haye 17-19.11.1983, Martinus Nijhof Publishers.
Badinter, R. 1993. "L'Europe du droit," *European Journal of International Law,* 4, 1993, 15 ff.
Balibar E. 1991. *"Es gibt keinen Staat in Europa:* Racism and Politics in Europe Today," *New Left Review* 186, 7 ff.

Balibar, E. 1997. *La crainte des masses. Politique et philosophie avant et après Marx*, Paris: Galilée.

Baratta A. and Giannoulis, Ch. 1996. "Vom Europarecht zum Europa der Rechte," *Kritische Vierteljahresschrift für Gesetzgebung und Rechtswissenschaft*, 3, 237 ff.

Binoche, B. 1989. *Critiques des droits de l'homme*, Paris: PUF.

Bobbio, N. 1967. "Sur le principe de légitimité," in *L'idée de la légitimité*, Annales de philosophie politique, 7.

Bobbio, N. 1991. *Il futuro della democrazia*, Torino: Einaudi.

Buergental, T. 1990. "CSCE Human Dimension: The Birth of a System," *Collected Courses of the Academy of European Law 1990*, Vol. I-II, Martinus Nijhof Publishers.

Carty, A. 1986. *The Decay of International Law*, Manchester: Manchester University Press.

Carty, A. 1991. "Critical International Law: Recent Trends in the Theory of International Law," *European Journal of International Law*, 2, 1991, 66 ff.

Chemillier-Gendreau, M. 1987. "Le droit international," in *Réalités du droit international contemporain 2, La relation du droit international avec la structure économique et sociale*, Reims: Publications du Center d'Etudes des Relations Internationales, 25 ff.

Closa, C. 1995. "Citizenship of the Union and Nationality of Member States," *Common Market Law Review*, 487 ff.

Cohen-Jonathan, G. 1989. *La Convention européenne des droits de l'homme*, Paris: Economica.

Dreier, R. 1991. *Recht – Staat – Vernunft*, Frankfurt/M.: Suhrkamp.

Eleftheriadis, P. 1996. "Aspects of European Constitutionalism," *European Law Review*, 21, 32 ff.

Fenet, A. 1994. "L'identité Européenne: Variations contemporaines sur une interrogation ancienne," in CURAPP, *L'identité politique*, Paris: PUF, 365 ff.

Ferrajoli, L. 1995. *La sovranità nel mondo moderno*, Milano: Anabasi.

Giannoulis, Ch. 1992. *Die Idee des "Europa der Bürger" und ihre Bedeutung für den Grundrechtsschutz*, Saarbrücken: Vorträge, Reden und Berichte aus dem Europa-Institut.

Hinsley, F. H. 1978. *Power and the Pursuit of Peace*, London: Cambridge University Press.

Kovar, R./ Simon, D. 1993. "La citoyenneté européenne," *Cahiers du droit européen*, 285 ff.

Kunz, J. 1955. "La crise et les transformations du droit des gens," in *Recueil de Cours de l'Académie de Droit International*, II.

Larenz, K. 1975. *Methodenlehre der Rechtswissenschaft*, Berlin: Springer.

Lock, G. 1996. "Philosophies of Europe: a brief Survey of the Prehistory and History of the European Idea," *Scienza & Politica*, 14, 37 ff.

MacPherson, C. B. 1977. *The Life and Times of Liberal Democracy*, London: Oxford University Press.

Moor, de A. 1993. "Contract, Justice and Diversity in the Remaking of Europe," *Rechtstheorie*, Beiheft 15, 71 ff.

Müller, F. 1996. *Was ist das Volk?*, Berlin: Duncker & Humblot.

Osianter, A. 1994. *The State System of Europe, 1640-1990, Peacemaking and the conditions of International Stability*, London, Oxford: Clarendon Press.

Ost, F. 1987. *Jalons pour une théorie critique du droit*, Bruxelles: Publications de Facultés Saint-Louis

––––––. 1993. "Validité," in *Dictionnaire encyclopédique de théorie et de sociologie du droit*, Paris: LGDJ, 638 ff.

Paladin, L. 1996. *Le fonti del diritto italiano*, Bologna: Il Mulino.
Piaget, J. 1970. *Epistémologie des sciences de l'homme*, Paris: Gallimard.
Rancière, J. 1990. *On the Shores of Politics*, London: Sage.
Ress, G. 1995. "Die Anforderungen an die Rechtswissenschaft in Deutschland im Zuge der europäischen Einigung," *Commentationes Scientiarum Socialum*, 49, 80 ff.
Rigaudière, A. 1993. "L'invention de la souveraineté," *Pouvoirs*, 67, 5 ff.
Rigaux, F. 1995. "Huitième leçon, Analyse et comparaison des systèmes d'intégration juridique étudiés" in: *Théorie de l'intégration européenne*, Syllabus de l'Académie Européenne de Théorie de Droit 1994-1995.
Ruggie, J. G. 1993. "Territoriality and Beyond: Problematizing Modernity in International Relations," *International Organisation* 47, 1, 130 ff.
Saussure, de F. 1968. *Cours de linguistique générale*, Paris: Payot.
Sousa Santos, de B. 1987. "Law: A Map of Misreading," *Journal of Law and Society*, 14, 279 ff.
_____. 1997. "Towards a Multicultural Conception of Human Rights," *Sociologia del diritto*, 1, 27 ff.
Spinoza, de B. 1958. *Tractatus politicus*, VI, 4, in: *The Political Works*, edited and translated by A. G. Wernham, Oxford: Oxford University Press.
Stolleis, M. 1995. "Das 'europäische Haus' und seine Verfassung," *Kritische Vierteljahresschrift für Gesetzgebung und Rechtswissenschaft*, 3, 275 ff.
Wesel, U. 1979. "hM," *Kursbuch*, 56, 88 ff.
Wight, M. 1973. "The Balance of Power and International Order," in *The Bases of International Order*, A. James, (ed.) London: Oxford University Press, 87 ff.
Wittgenstein, L. 1969. *Philosophical Investigations*, Oxford: Blackwell.
Zolo, D. 1995. *Cosmopolis. La prospettiva del governo mondiale*, Milano: Feltrinelli.

15 The European Citizens' Right to Free Movement in its Democratic Dimension. The Socio-political Meaning of a Social Right

KLAUS SIEVEKING

Introduction

The topic of my paper is part of the pan-European discussion about democracy and constitution, especially about the democratic deficit of the European Union. The shaping of the Western idea of democracy derives from a specific link between Freedom and Right and is based on the democratic legitimization of political power on the grounds of general, equal and free elections, the elaboration of institutional guarantees as well as social guarantees of physical existence and human rights. The current discussion about the democratic deficits within the European Union focuses on institutional mechanisms and decision-making in EU institutions. In this paper I will, however, emphasize the socio-legal dimension of democracy, i.e. aspects of substantive instead of merely formal democracy.

Looking at the European Union since 1957, there has been an enormous push towards increased freedom of movement for goods, services, capital and persons within the area of the single market. The free market as the aim of the Community is indeed the basis of the European Union in its present status. According to the theory of democracy we distinguish between political, economic and social rights.[1] They refer to the citizens' political participation in the process of the political legitimization of power, to their free use of property and the guarantee of their social security (at least a minimum standard of physical existence).

The European Parliament has made various proposals in an attempt to establish a catalogue of civil and social rights,[2] but up to now they have not resulted in any contractual commitment. There had been hope that during the so-called Maastricht II Negotiations and the Amsterdam Resolution of July 1997, further steps would be taken to deepen the democratic substance of the Union. However, the present draft of the contract contains little that is tangible in this respect. At the end of July 1997, the European Commission submitted a proposal for a regulation "On the further development and strengthening of democracy and constitutionality as well as the protection of human rights and civil liberties,"[3] which is supposed to introduce measures for the protection of human rights and the strengthening of democracy as well as for their financing.

Against this background it makes sense to identify attempts to open up the EU for more democratic legitimization. This will be done hereafter for the example of the right to free movement. First, I shall give a short survey of the concrete contents of the right to free movement for Union citizens according to the EC Treaty and secondary Union legislation as interpreted by the European Court of Justice (ECJ). Then I shall look into the democratic dimensions of the right to free movement: the dimensions of political participation, of private law and the right to freedom, and the dimension relating to social security. Finally, I shall reflect on democracy-theoretical hiatuses in the EU concept of free movement as well as perspectives to overcome these.

The Right to Free Movement as a Fundamental Right for EU Citizens

Art. 8a ECT stipulates that every Union citizen has the right "to freely move around and reside within the territory of the Member States, subject to the restrictions and conditions provided in this treaty..." Any citizen of any Member State is considered a Union citizen. Art. 8a does not regulate questions of free movement and residence. In this respect, it refers to Art. 48ff ECT which grants Union citizens freedom of movement within the Union if they move to another Member State as employees or self-employed (Art. 52ff), also as providers or recipients of services (Art. 59ff). Spouses and children fall under this provision even if they themselves are not Union citizens. This right to free movement can only be curtailed on the grounds of public policy, security policy and/or health policy. According to the ECJ, this only applies in the case of a real and sufficiently serious danger which touches upon a fundamental interest of society.

In its many years of judicial decisions the ECJ has defined the term "employee" more clearly. It includes, e.g., part-time employees and public servants, provided the latter do not hold positions connected with sovereignty or with the safeguarding of general concerns of the state (e.g. in the areas of military or judiciary). Unemployed persons, too, have the right to free movement, at least for a limited period of time, provided they are registered as unemployed at a labor exchange in their home country or in their country of residence. Thus the term "employee" has become more inclusive over the years, and after three Council Directives for students, for persons who have retired from gainful employment, and for other citizens were passed in 1990, the right to free movement and residency today includes practically all Union citizens and their families, provided they have health insurance cover and sufficient means to live. Connected with this right is in particular the law against discrimination on the grounds of nationality. The principle of equal national treatment permeates the entire field of free movement regulation. The equal treatment proviso refers to all conditions of work and employment and is not only directed at the individual countries, but also at employers and trade unions. Social and tax benefits also apply to migrant employees, as do social security rights, such as health insurance or pension payments, on migration to another Member State.

These legal positions are enforced within the framework of the implementation of EU law on Member State level, where European law has paramount and immediate effect. When there are doubts about the interpretation of EU law, national courts have to refer the case to the ECJ for decision. A look at ECJ rulings to date reveals the enormous importance of questions of free movement and social security.

Political Rights

Since the founding of the European Community, its democratic deficit has been lamented, in particular with regard to the lack of rights of political participation. Nevertheless over the past few years there have been small steps towards further democratization of the Community: the introduction of general and direct elections to the European Parliament in 1976, the expansion of the majority principle in various sectors of politics by the Single European Act of 1986, the extension of the so-called approval procedure which leaves the final say for certain decisions with the European Parliament, and the introduction of the right to a vote of approval by the European Parliament on the appointment of the Commission, as stipulated in the Maastricht Treaty on the European Union in 1992.

Until recently, the use of the right to free movement has meant the loss of political participation in the country of residence. This democratic deficit was alleviated in 1992 with the EC-wide introduction of the right to vote and to be elected on community level (Art. 8b par. 1 ECT). After all Member States have incorporated a respective Council Directive into national law, Union citizens have the same right to participation in communal elections as the citizens of that country.

Thus now the Market citizen as a European citizen has, in connection with the freedom of movement, the opportunity to participate in politics. However, in many countries of the Community an essential component of electoral participation is lacking: the right of political activities and the right of assembly and freedom of association for foreigners in general. Political parties, a major element in the formation of political intent, are open to the migrants; however, they are not entitled to found their own parties. This means that there are no equal terms for political participation of EU citizens and citizens of the respective country, and it also means that the social conditions which are necessary for such a right to take effect, are lacking. A further deficit is the lack of political participation at the national level.

Union citizens who are entitled to free movement within the EU are also given the right of participation in the European elections (Art. 8b par. 2 ECT) in their country of residence on the same terms as the citizens of that country. Further political rights, such as the right to diplomatic protection on the territory of a third country, the right to petition and the right to apply to a citizens' representative, are legal positions which are available regardless of the right to free movement. Such rights are therefore not considered in this context. It remains to be stated that from the viewpoint of free movement the understanding of democracy is essentially oriented on the functioning of market structures: Throughout the Community, non-market-related liberties, such as the political freedom rights, are only regarded as an annex of the status of the market citizen.

Private Legal Positions

The influence of the right to free movement on the shaping of the private law system, which deals with juristic and natural persons taking up legal relationships with one another, has so far not been at the center of reflections on the Community law system. The verdict in the court case of the Belgian football-player Bosman has added a new dimension to this issue. Already in 1974, the ECJ had declared that football was of economic importance and the practice of this sport therefore subject to Community law: Freedom of movement also applies to professional football-players who are employed or who provide a service against payment. We are here concerned with the aspect of democracy, and in this context the question arises whether and to what extent football clubs (as juristic persons in private law) are restricted by the guarantee of free movement according to Art. 48 ECT in their private autonomy to issue sports regulations which may in turn restrict the free movement of citizens. To what extent may the autonomous action of a private person vis-à-vis another private person be curtailed by Community law?

This was the central question in the Bosman judgment of the ECJ of 15.12.1995.[4] The Belgian football-player had wanted to change from his Belgian football club to a French club, and had found his plan thwarted by his club. He sued his former Belgian employer for compensation. The Belgian court passed the case on to the ECJ with the request to clarify whether the football associations' transfer regulations and foreigners clause (limitation of the number of foreign players in league games) were in accordance with Community law. The ECJ decided that the obligatory payment of a transfer sum in the case of a professional football-player changing to a club in another Member State as well as the limitation of the number of players from other Member States are in conflict with Art. 48 ECT.

According to the ECJ these regulations impede the right to free movement of the employees, as they stop a professional football-player from changing to a club in another Member State if that club has not paid his former club the transfer compensation which was agreed between both clubs or was set according to the sports association's regulations. The transfer regulations represent an infringement of the right to free movement of employees, and are as such illegal according to Art. 48 ECT. The ECJ could not discern any compelling reasons of general interest that would justify such regulations. Also in violation of Art. 48 ECT is the sports association regulation which stipulates that only a limited number of professional players who are citizens of other Member States are allowed to play at any one match organized by these associations. According to the ECJ, there is no proof that the transfer regulations are an appropriate means of maintaining financial and athletic equilibrium in the world of football. These, as well as further purposes (compensation payments for transfer, training and qualification) could just as well be achieved by other means which do no impede the right to free movement of the employees.

The special significance of this decision in our context is that Community law restricts the autonomous shaping of laws within what is perceived as private society. The relevant factor is, again, the functional view of the Market citizen, not the autonomous right of freedom of a European citizen. As far as the private autonomous rights of the football clubs are concerned, they derive from the rationality of the economic functioning of the Market, not from, e.g., the economic monopoly power of pan-European associations. Consequently the right of ownership which constitutes European societies is not subject to the limitations of a general welfare proviso the contents of which follow, e.g., certain principles of justice, but instead falls under the limitations of an obstacle to the right to free movement. Criteria of general welfare are measured in terms of a Market-relevant rationality of free movement, not in terms of democratic criteria of rationality. What matters is the political and even more so the democratic character of private and/or civil rights which characterizes the new democratic dimension of the understanding of the fundamental right to free movement.[5]

Social Security Positions

The right to free movement bears upon social positions in two respects: First, acquired positions of social protection, e.g. pension claims, are upheld when exercising the right to free movement, e.g. by an export guarantee. To this end, the regulation on social security for migrant employees and their families (Regulation EEC No. 1408/71) was issued, based on Art. 51. It has in the meantime been more clearly defined by over 300 ECJ decisions. Second, migrant employees are also eligible to social and tax benefits in their country of residence. Over the past few years, there have been a number of ECJ decisions in favor of an extensive export of the right to benefits, which has, however, resulted in open criticism by some Member States. What was the issue?

In the cases Ghatto[6] and Bronzino[7] it had to be decided whether an Italian employed in Germany is entitled to child benefit for his unemployed children living in Italy. According to § 2 par. 4 German Child Benefits Act (previous version), unemployed children between the ages of 18 and 21 could only be considered if they were unemployed in Germany. The ECJ decided, contrary to the wording of the German Child Benefits Act, that youths could also be unemployed in another Member State for their parents to be entitled to child benefit. If these children were not considered, the use of the right to free movement would result in social disadvantages. In the case of this state benefit, the principle of equal treatment of migrant employees and resident employees requires that German child benefit is also paid for children who are unemployed in another Member State.

The Paletta case,[8] which has gained a certain notoriety, was concerned with the Italian family Paletta (parents and two children), living in Germany, who spent their holidays in Italy. At the end of their holidays, all family members sent their German employer a sick note, issued by a resident doctor in their place of holiday. This note was not accepted by their employer, however, on the grounds of its lack of probative value, and he refused to continue the wage payments. The ECJ decided that the continuation of wage payments during sickness represents a social benefit in case of illness according to Art. 4 Regulation EEC 1408/71 and that according to Art. 18 par. 1-4 Regulation EEC 574/72 the employer (as responsible party) is committed in the real and in the legal sense to accept the facts ascertained by the physician regarding commencement and duration of the illness, unless he has the person in question examined by a physician of his choice. This decision has been widely criticized in Germany, and the Federal Labor Court referred the case to the ECJ for renewed decision, but the ECJ upheld its former position.[9] From an integrational point of view, this decision may be an indication of the abuse discussion that has been institutionalized on EC level.[10]

A similar issue was at the root of the ECJ's judgment of 10.10.1996 in connection with benefits under the German Child-Rearing Benefits Law.[11] According to the ECJ, it was the declared aim of Art. 73 of said Regulation to ensure that family members living in a Member State other than the competent Member State be granted the family benefits provided for under the applicable legal provisions. The ECJ goes on: Hence it follows that the distinction between rights of one's own and derived rights basically does not apply to family benefits. The consequence is that family members of migrant workers working in the Federal Republic of Germany must be granted family benefits even if they have remained in their home State.

These court decisions exemplify the socio-political conflict: On the one hand welfare-related consequences from the right to free movement must be taken into account, on the other hand benefit-related decisions and procedures in the welfare sector have to be reciprocally accepted throughout the EC. And neither aspect is easy to enforce. Possibly, the tendency of the Member States to cut back their benefit systems is party a result of the fact that the ECJ interpretation of social welfare law promotes free movement. After all, even in the social sector the issue of free movement is subject to market factors rather than conditions of social freedom. Democracy-related aspects remain tied to an economy-oriented principle of freedom of movement as long as there are no further factual criteria which bear upon a European society of citizens. The funds for structural improvement supported by the EC tend to follow along the lines of regional assistance (regions such as the Mediterranean or industrial locations, problem groups within the labor market, the agrarian sector). The EC still has a long way to go to a pan-European social order that is citizen-related. This would not only require an EC nationality, but also a system of social solidarity. The lack of both represents the Achilles heel of the democratization process within the EC.

The Changing Concept of Free Movement

The concept of free movement within the EC is based on the idea of the citizens as "Market citizens." The step towards the *citoyen* has not yet been taken. Nevertheless, the Community as a political multi-layer system is in a changed position vis-à-vis its citizens. Free movement has become a tangible chance for many citizens. The market orientation of the concept of free movement has been extended by a further component: the concept of a "European citizenship."[12] However, we are still only at the beginning of our "way towards a Europe of citizens." It is no coincidence that now as before the main obstacle to free movement is the socio-economic barrier. Wealthy citizens can cross Member State borders regardless of labor markets, while poverty is being nationally administered. Social solidarity exists on a national level rather than on EC level. German history presents a vivid example of how relations of citizenship can, by the process of national integration, lead to changed bonds of solidarity. The specific

political organization of the EU has already lead to the development of
new forms of citizenship: Nationality stands next to a European citizenship
– The freedom of movement shows a tendency of freeing itself from its
nationality-oriented and exclusively market-oriented function. However,
some typical shortcomings remain.

Exclusion of Non-EU Nationals

As already mentioned, the marginalized groups within the Member States
cannot benefit from the right to free movement. Another group which is
practically entirely excluded are non-EU nationals, unless they are relatives
of eligible persons. This is a vulnerable point of the democratic structure of
the Community, the aim of which is a European integrated community of
citizens. It is, however, an indication of a changed understanding that the
integrational concept, which has so far been dominated by the traditional
principle of nationality, has been amended by a supplementary Union
citizenship, which is not equivalent to full citizenship, but is meant to
convey a certain affiliation with the Community. This is in line with the
fact that the EC itself is not a sovereign state, but a supranational organization – the German Constitutional Court refers to the EC as a *Staatenver-
bund* (union/confederation of states) – with a law-making competence that
is autonomous, but only recognized in isolated instances.

The Community excludes non-EU nationals from the right to free
movement, even if these citizens were born in or have taken permanent
residence in a Member State.[13] Evidently, this signifies a democratic deficit, with regard to human rights as well as with regard to aspects of democratic theory. This democratic deficit in the concept of free movement has
its analogies in the political, the private and the social security dimension
on the national level. Non-EU nationals – with few exceptions also in the
other Member States – do not enjoy political equality, i.e. instead of the
right to vote and be elected they only qualify for advisory participation in
various forms. Also in the private law sector they are denied full equality,
even if they possess a permanent residence permit. Consider, for example,
discrimination in vocational training, restriction of the right to information
(parabolic reflector aerials in high-rise flats) or occupational freedom (e.g.
license to practice for foreign physicians).

These democratic deficits result from a peculiarity of Community law:
the regulation of access and residency, the shaping of political, civil and

social status rights of non-EU nationals are still the responsibility of the individual Member States. The national competence of law-making is partly eclipsed by coordination procedures on the Community level, in particular for questions regarding non-EU nationals. The Amsterdam Treaty stipulates in a new Article A to the ECT that the Council is to issue measures relating to "the protection of the rights of non-EU nationals according to Article C." Art. C stipulates that the Council will issue "within a period of five years after entry into force of this Treaty .....4. measures for the stipulation of rights and conditions according to which non-EU nationals who are legally resident in one Member State may stay in other Member States."

Perspectives

At present we are witnessing a continuing process of Europeanization in EU law-making competence for matters of personal law: The areas of political asylum and immigration increasingly come under Community responsibility. In the course of this process new forms of burden-sharing are developing within the EU. At present, the tendency is to allocate welfare-related status rights in a national context/nationally, this being an expression of the political structure of a multi-layer system in which, on the one hand, political responsibility is assigned to different levels and legitimized in different ways, while on the other hand public solidarity only takes place on a very limited scale. Whether and to what extent a Community-wide welfare sector will play a role in the economic and currency union – this is one question which the democratic substance of the Community will be measured on in future.

Notes

1. Cf. Th. H. Marshall (1964).
2. For further discussions see the fundamental contribution of: B.-O. Bryde (1984), 305. E. g. Resolution on the Declaration of Fundamental Rights and Freedoms (12 April 1989). EP Doc. A 2-3/89. For the rulings of the ECJ in this field cf. M. Zuleeg (1992), 329 et seq.; S. Peers (1997), 342 et seq.; K. Sieveking, in: Y. Jorens (ed.) (forthcoming 1998).
3. Cf. COM (97) 357 final. See also the Commission's "Report on the implementation of actions to promote human rights and democracy," COM (97) 672 final.
4. ECJ Cs C-415/93, ECR 1995, I-4921 - Bosman. Cf. L. Gramlich (1996), 801.

5. This idea refers to the ECJ's conceptualization of European subjective rights and reflects the applicability of Art. 48 ECT in the private sphere, see also C. Joerges (1997), 378 et seq. (405) with more references; N. Reich (1977), 131 et seq.
6. ECJ Cs C-12/88, ECR 1990, I-557 - Gatto.
7. ECJ Cs 228/88, ECR 1990, I-531 - Bronzino.
8. ECJ Decision of 3.6.1992, Cs C-45/90, ECR 1992, I-3423 - Paletta. See also the preceding decision of 12.3.1987 in Cs 22/86, ECR 1987, 1339 - Rindone. In the meantime, the ECJ has again affirmed its position, cf. ECJ decision of 2.5.1996, Cs C-206/94, ECR 1996, I-2357- Paletta II.
9. BAG (Federal Labor Court), Ruling of 27.4.1994., *Europäische Zeitschrift für Wirtschaftsrecht* 1994, 574.
10. See, e.g. P. Altmeier, Territorialitätsprinzip. in: M.Zuleeg/E.Eichenhofer (1995). In in text 3.
11. ECJ ECR 1996, I-4895 - Cases C-245/94 - Hoever and C-312/94 - Zachow; for a fundamental criticism of these judgments see E. Eichenhofer (1997), 449 et seq.
12. For the meaning of the notion of European Citizenship see the Second Report of the European Commission on European Union Citizenship, COM (97) 230 final. See also S. O'Leary (1996).
13. See M. Hedemann-Robinson (1996, 1997), 321 et seq.; S. Peers (1996), 7 et seq.; the same (1997), 342 et seq.

References

Altmeier, Peter. 1995 "Territorialitätsprinzip," in: Zuleeg, D. and E. Eicenhofer. *Die Rechtsprechung des Europäischen Gerichtshofs im Streit*, 71-91. Bonn.

Bryde. Brun - Otto. 1984. "Die bundesrepublikanische Volksdemokratie als Irrweg der Demokratietheorie," in: *Staatswissenschaft und Staatspraxis*, 305-330.

Eichenhofer, Eberhard. 1997. "Deutsches Erziehungsgeld und Eropäisches Sozialrecht." *Die Sozialgerichtsbarkeit*, 449-455.

Gramlich, Ludwig. 1996. "Grundfreiheiten contra Grundrechte im Gemeinschaftsrecht?." *Die Öffentliche Verwaltung*, 801-811.

Hedemann-Robinson, Martin. 1996-97. "Third-Country Nationals, European Union Citizenship, and Free Movement of Persons: a Time for Bridges rather than Divisions" in: *Yearbook of European Law* 16/1996, 1997, 321-362.

Joerges, Christian. 1997. "The Impact of European Integration on Private Law: Reductionist Perceptions, True Conflicts and a New Constitutional Perspective." *European Law Journal (ELJ)*, Vol. 3 No. 4, 378-406.

Marshall, Thomas H. 1964. *Class, Citizenship and Social Development, Essays by T.H. Marshall*, Chicago - London.

O'Leary, Siofra. 1996. *European Union Citizenship. The Options for Reform.* London.

Peers, Steve. 1996. "Towards Equality: Actual and potential rights of third-country nationals in the European Union" *CMLR* 33, 7-50.

———. 1997. "Equality, Free Movement and Social Security." *E.L.Rev.*, Aug., 342-351.

Reich, Norbert. 1977. "A European Constitution for Citizens. Reflections on the Rethinking of Union and Community Law," *ELJ* 3 No. 3, 131-164.

Sieveking, Klaus. "The Rulings of the European Court of Justice on the legal position of non-European Union nationals under labor law and social security law," in: Yves Jorens (ed.), *The European Union and the Associated States. Non-European Union Nationals and the Coordination of European Social Security Law: Relations with Third States* (forthcoming 1998).

Zuleeg Manfred. 1992. "Der Schutz sozialer Rechte in der Rechts-ordnung der Europäischen Gemeinschaft." *Zeitschrift für Europäische Grundrechte.* 329-334.

16 "Citizens' Europe" as a Transitional Concept

CHRISTINA GIANNOULIS

"Reden wir eine Zeitlang nicht mehr vom Volk.
Reden wir von der Bevölkerung"

B. Brecht[1]

Concepts of a Transition

"Citizens' Europe" can be seen as a transitional idea.[2] Its connotations are in the first instance positive: a Europe of citizens is a powerful political and social demand, in the sense of a concrete utopia or a program for emancipation involving the perennial promise of transition to an ideal society. But it is transitional in the negative sense also, insofar as it proclaims transition to a state of institutionalized compromise. What is more, it is often employed for purely cosmetic purposes, in the context of ideological endeavors to sanction the existent. The boundaries between the various invocations of "Citizens' Europe" are fluid, particularly in official discourse on Europe.

In terms of space, the concept of "Citizens' Europe" is equally transitional, since it promises an area "without internal borders," within which there will be guarantees on freedom of movement and equal treatment of citizens. But this does not mean that border controls, border crossings, discrimination, restrictions and exclusions will all be done away with: they will simply be transposed onto another plane.[3]

"Citizens' Europe" is also transitional from a chronological viewpoint: the concept acquired increasing currency after 1974 in the course of the EC unification process and was formulated as a political goal, a development to be curtailed only in 1992 with the signing of the Treaty of Maastricht.[4] Mention is no longer made of Citizens' Europe but of "Union Citizenship" (Article 8 of the EC Treaty), which admittedly possesses the advantage of being legally binding. With its enactment in the European Community Treaty, the corresponding citizens' rights implied by it are incorporated into the primary law of the Community, i.e. they have become legally binding and judicially underwritten: the Court of Justice of the European Communities has the power to enforce them. They are in fact quasi-constitutional rights, which should be interpreted as broadly as possible.[5] But at the same time Union citizenship has defined the borders and limits of Citizens' Europe in a clearly restrictive way and drastically diminished the promise which it seemed in so many ways to offer.

The Legal Battlements of Fortress Europe

Although some progress has been made in elaborating a system for protecting fundamental rights in the EC/EU (Baratta/Giannoulis 1996, 242 ff.), European juridical discourse continues to be marked by contradictions, paradoxes and ambiguities. We could cite two legal paradoxes, which have been very much sharpened since the enactment of Union citizenship.

Are all Italians European Citizens?

Union citizenship is linked to nationality of a Member State and necessarily mediated through it (Article 8 of the EC Treaty). National states objecting to the weakening of their own sovereignty requested that this point be particularly emphasized: European law is not permitted to involve itself in questions of nationality in the Member States of the Union: such decisions remain the exclusive preserve of each Member State. Thus no harmonization of state legislation on nationality is sought – at least for the moment – at the European level (Closa 1995, 509 ff., Sauerwald 1996, 87 ff., 120 ff., 156 ff.).

Nationality is a legal construct which creates problems for both national and international law. It has now also become a problem at the level of EC law, simply because reality throws up situations which cannot be subsumed under the categories of Article 8 of the EC Treaty. This became clear with the decision of 7.7.1992 of the Court of Justice of the European Communities concerning the Micheletti case (D'Oliveira 1993, Ruzié 1993,

Zimmermann 1995, 65 f., Hall 1996, 133 ff.). This case is a characteristic example of the conflicting jurisdictions between the European Union and the national states, of the problematic relationship between nationality, citizenship and Union citizenship, and also more generally of the exclusionary practices so prevalent in present-day Europe (Balibar 1993 and 1994, Preuss/Everson 1996, Wiener 1996, Menegazzi Munari 1996, 21 ff.).

Micheletti had double nationality: born in Argentina of Italian parents, he automatically acquired both Argentinean and Italian nationality. After many years' residence in Argentina he moved to Spain, intending to settle there and work as a dentist. He applied for a residence permit and a work permit invoking the relevant rights afforded to him in Spain under the Treaty on European Union on account of his status as an Italian national.

The Spanish state would not recognize his Italian nationality, considering him an Argentinean, with the result that he was excluded from the rights of Union citizenship. The legal basis of this decision was a provision in the Spanish Civil Code which is included in the civil law of many states and derives from the theory of "effective nationality." According to this, in a case of multiple nationality, the nationality which recognized as effective or active is the one which is based on a genuine link, on an "authentic" or actual tie to the state of which the person is a national (e.g. permanent residence – Mansel 1988, 85 ff., 125 ff.). The Spanish authorities contended that Micheletti habitually resided in Argentina before his arrival in Spain, and was therefore to be regarded as an Argentinean and not as an Italian citizen of the Union.

The case was judged by the Court of Justice of the European Communities, in accordance with the procedure provided by Article 177 of the EC Treaty, which therefore de facto involved itself in a question of nationality. It was ruled that the definition of the conditions of acquisition and loss of nationality is, in conformity with international law, within the competence of each Member State, which competence must be exercised with due regard to Community law: thus no Member State has the right, on the basis of the theory – in any case disputed – of effective nationality, to draw into question the nationality provisions of another Member State.

The legal controversies, the arguments and counter-arguments put forward on this question in the field of tension between national, international and supranational law are as interesting as they are complex.[6] We shall confine ourselves here to a critical remark on the invocation of the principle of "effectiveness" on the part of the national state: effectiveness is linked to the urge to curtail multiple nationality – which is frequently seen as a legal anomaly – with a view to recognizing only one, the "effective," nationality. In other words what is involved is a kind of "filter" which serves to exclude (e.g. Mansel 1988, 159, 174 ff., 497, Ruzié 1993, 107 ff.). In the present instance the criterion of effectiveness on the basis of place of residence was used in Spain so that the Italian Micheletti could be treated as an "extracommunitarian".

The absurdity of the legal construct becomes even more glaring if one takes into account the fact that the criterion of residence in fact constitutes a democratic claim for admission on the part of the resident foreigner, e.g. the recognition of political rights for all immigrants in a country or the facilitation of their acquisition of nationality in the country of their residence, because a real ("effective") relationship with that state has been created. Precisely because of that democratic function of facilitating admission, the prevailing legal theory, or rather ideology, does not recognize the principle of the effective relationship.[7] So it is on the one hand paradoxical but on the other completely in accordance with the ambiguous logic of juridical theory that the argument of the real or "effective" link is in the present instance employed to exclude a resident of a Member State of the Union from citizenship rights in the Union.

Are "Local Issues" of Equal Concern to all Residents of a Locality?

This leads us straight into the next paradox: the granting of voting rights in municipal elections in the state of residence (Article 8 b of the EC Treaty). Here we have to do with a political right which is seen as constituting the core of Union citizenship.

The outlook which seeks to ascribe a "European," supra-national character to a vote in local elections is incompatible with the character of local government as a vehicle for the management of local issues and/or the expression of local interests. The "common interest" at the local level can be embodied only in the residents (all of the residents) of a particular territorial unit, the municipality or the local community.

In any case, ever since it was first formulated, the demand for a vote for resident aliens in local elections has been linked to the criterion of place of residence, on the basis of the thinking that representation on matters concerning a particular area is the right of all residents of that area, irrespective of nationality.[8]

No logical, social, political or constitutional argument exists which can justify the exclusion of immigrants from "third countries." The right to vote in local elections, which had formerly been the exclusive privilege of citizens of the state in question and should have been transformed into a general right for the members of every local community – something which would have been in keeping with the criterion of "locality," the principle of equality and the demand for actualization of democracy – was transformed into a special right for citizens of the Union, by means an amalgam of the criteria of nationality and place of residence. This is but one expression of a broader "European" nationalism, which does not challenge the nationalistic criteria for the right of participation in local elections.[9]

Of course from the viewpoint of legal theory nothing prevents each member state from passing a law or revising its constitution so as to extend the right of participation in local elections to all "non-Community" nationals residing (and usually working) on its territory, as has already occurred in Sweden, Denmark and Holland, and (selective) extension of the franchise for local elections is also under consideration in Italy. This in any case would be consistent with the relevant Council of Europe initiative which – two days before the ratification of the Maastricht Treaty! – called upon all members of that body to take measures for the participation of foreigners in public life at local level (e.g. D'Oliveira 1993-a, 101, Silvestro 1994, 72). But it is very probable that legal codification of Union Citizenship, which has led to revision of the Constitution of many Member States so as to make possible the participation of Union citizens in local elections,[10] will operate primarily as an inhibiting factor and will be used by many Member States as a criterion for deeming "anti-constitutional" any further extension of this right to the benefit of the great majority of foreign citizens, who are therefore once again deprived even of this minimal entitlement.

Prerequisites for a Transition (or for a Break)

What is the meaning of these observations for the claim of democracy and emancipation in Europe?

What is the meaning of this utopia called "Citizens' Europe"? We have seen that Union citizenship bestows a common status on those that possess it by excluding "non-Community" aliens[11] and also that it reproduces at the European level certain dubious features of the nation state. The legal construct of Union citizenship institutionalized a formal and static categorization which contributes nothing to the struggle against nationalism and racism at the European level. Of course an institutional structure cannot be expected in and of itself to solve social problems associated with state policies and directly linked to class antagonisms. Nevertheless it is certain that if the millions of Turks in Germany and Africans in France or the hundreds of thousands of Albanians in Greece could acquire the – albeit symbolic – status of European citizens in the context of a radical democratization of the European Union, the institutional racism against them, along with its violent "private" manifestations, would be swiftly and drastically curtailed.

Official European Community discourse has taken into account the claims of "Citizens' Europe" and, in a partial and contradictory way, assimilated them, in the process largely eliminating the emancipatory prospects evoked by the idea.

Looking at this development pessimistically and critically, one is obliged to admit that it was to be expected. For the same can be said of Citizens' Europe as can be said of all other utopias: that they refer to ideals, representing "the polar opposite of the origins which scientific thought is searching for."[12] Yet the transition or passage to the ideal world cannot take place "really...."

Usually, in the final analysis the ideals we evoke merely serve to reproduce the existent. The present instance this means that European citizenship – as enacted in the Maastricht Treaty – does not mark a break or rupture but provides legal codification of an ongoing situation. It indicates, indeed prescribes, the course which European unification much follow. This means that the "weak" unificatory dynamic of Union citizenship is subordinated to the "strong" dynamic of exclusion which develops at the same time. Thus, for example, we learn from the official information bulletin entitled *The European Union – What's in it for Me?:* "... common immigration, visa and asylum controls must be agreed so that internal borders *really can be passport-free*"![13]

Does this mean that there isn't any way to ascending to Citizens' Europe? We believe that there may be one, provided that we perceive the utopian, i.e. "biased," quality of "Citizens' Europe," as a type of committed discourse[14] which struggles for the rights of citizens while at the same time maintaining a critical perspective on the rigid legalistic forms in which at times this claim may be expressed. We persist therefore in speaking of the Europe of Citizens' in the plural, something which is not seen when the idea is put forward in the organizational framework of constitutionalism, which turns it into something individualistic. Constitutionalism does not imply citizens and their active participation in various types of collaborative endeavor, but to the citizen, who is said to exercise as an individual the "fundamental rights" that are granted to him. This individualization, which is characteristic of construction of "subjects" in civic constitutionalism, undermines the prospects for a Citizens' Europe, that is to say the potential for citizens' self-determination and the ascription of a new actuality to the exercise of rights.

Our aim should be neither to compare European citizenship with citizenship in a nation state nor to embark on endless discussions as to how an "authentic" European political identity might be constituted.[15] Equally sterile seems to be the discussion about whether there is such a thing as a "European people" and the controversy over the form that a "European federal state" might take.[16]

Attempts to deal with the present reality of large-scale migration to the European states with projects for "turning back the tide," clamping down on immigration or even simply turning a blind eye to it – should be abandoned. Facilitation of the acquisition of multiple nationality by immigrants is just a small step in a progressive direction (Marx 1997). But even here we should not be content simply to introduce legal reforms. The association of certain people with certain places and problems – the bond having as its basis a social fact of attachment – should be an undisputed criterion for recognizing their real rights of participation in decision-making.

Each kind of politics has its own language. Let us therefore cease referring to "the people" (the state). Let us refer to the population (the residents). Let us no longer speak of the citizens of the Union but of the citizens in Europe. Let us leave aside the nationality rules and talk about the entitlement of all fellow-citizens to equal rights. Let us speak of Citizens' Europe as a transitional concept.

Notes

1. "Gespräche mit jungen Intellektuellen," *Werke*, Bd. 23, Berlin/Frankfurt 1993, 101.
2. For ways of "thinking through" this transition, see Messner (1997, 119 ff. with a reference to answers given by Kant, 179, n. 282).
3. For the comprehensiveness and multiplicity of the (visible and invisible) borders within Fortress Europe see Pastore (1993, 19 ff.); Baratta/Giannoulis (1996, 237 ff., 249 ff.); Wiener (1996, 504 f.).
4. For the different stages of this development see Giannoulis (1992).
5. D'Oliveira (1993-a); Marias (1994); Menegazzi Munari (1996, 161 ff.); Sauerwald (1996, 54 ff.); Sepi (1997).

6. Zimmermann (1995, 54 ff.); Sauerwald (1996, 94 ff.); Hall (1996, 129 ff.). The decision by the Court of Justice of the European Communities on the Micheletti case is an interesting example of the margins for manoeuvre which the fluid legal structures of the European Union place at the disposal of individuals and groups of citizens seeking as "citizens of Europe" to acquire certain controversial rights and influence the evolution of the law on both the national and the supranational level. See Pollmann (1993); Menegazzi Munari (1996, 80 ff.).
7. The relevant discussion in Germany is critically reviewed by Marx (1997).
8. See the analysis and the bibliography in Giannoulis (1992, 105 ff.); D'Oliveira (1993-a, 101 ff.).
9. For the profile of "European" nationalism see Balibar (1994, 551 f.).
10. For the relevant constitutional issues in each Member State see, for example, Battis/Tsatsos/Stephanou (1995).
11. The Federal Constitutional Court of Germany defined European citizenship as a "long-term legal bond between the nationals of the Member States" (Entscheidungen des Bundesverfassungsgerichts, vol. 89, 184).
12. Messner (1997, 130). This means that an inverse reading of Althusser's phrase "the end of history is already inscribed in its origins" (cited by Messner, 133) is also possible: the origins of history are inscribed in its end. For the relationship of projection between genealogical narratives (original position, social contract) and utopian narratives and its implications for political theory and legal thought see Messner (1997, 130 ff., 149 ff.).
13. European Commission 1996, 7 (my emphasis). Interesting is here the function of the word "really." For the central philosophical issue of the "reality of the real" and for the "stance which refuses to consider the reality which bursts upon us as "the" reality" see Messner (1997, 22, 35, 127).
14. Utopian narrative possesses an enlightened, liberating dynamic because on the one hand it "demonstrates," it "brings up" the way that there can be no transition or passage to an ideal world and on the other it "lays bare the manner of functioning of this rejection" (Messner, 1997, 130, 149, 154).
15. "The point is not to propose a refashioning of the equation of citizenship with nationality or to transpose it to a supernational level. nor is it simply to proclaim that this equation is obsolete. The point is to dissolve its imposing self-evidence. to expose it as a problem and not as a mere given. or as the rule." (Balibar, 1994, 551).
16. For this discussion see on the one hand Balibar (1994, 551 ff.), Hobsbawm (1994, 557 f.) and on the other Grimm (1995, 581 ff.), Habermas (1996, 185 ff.).

References

Balibar, E. 1993. "L'Europe des citoyens," in: O. Le Cour Grandmaison and C. Wihtol de Wenden (eds.), *Les étrangers dans la cité*, Paris, 192 ff.
_____. 1994. "Une citoyenneté européenne est-elle possible?," in: B. Théret (ed.), *L'Etat, la finance et le social. Souveraineté nationale et construction européenne*, Paris.
Baratta, A. and Giannoulis, Ch. 1996. "Vom Europarecht zum Europa der Rechte," *Kritische Vierteljahresschrift für Gesetzgebung und Rechts-wissenschaft*, 3. 237 ff.

252 *Welfare State and Democracy in Crisis*

Battis, U./Tsatsos, D./Stephanou, D. 1995. *Europäische Integration und nationales Verfassungsrecht*, Baden-Baden.

Closa, C. 1995. "Citizenship of the Union and Nationality of Member States," *Common Market Law Review*, 487 ff.

D'Oliveira, H. U. J. 1993. "Case C-369, M.V. Micheletti and others v. Delegación del Gobierno en Cantabria, Judgment of 7 July 1992," *Common Market Law Review*, 623 ff.

_____. 1993a. "European Citizenship: Its Meaning, its Potential," in: J. Monar, W. Ungerer and W. Wessels (eds.), *The Maastricht Treaty on European Union*, Brussels, 81 ff.

European Commission. 1996, *The European Union - What's in it for Me?*, Brussels.

Giannoulis, Ch. 1992. *Die Idee des "Europa der Bürger" und ihre Bedeutung für den Grundrechtsschutz*, Saarbrücken.

Grimm, D. 1995. "Braucht Europa eine Verfassung?," *Juristen-Zeitung*, 581 ff.

Habermas, J. 1996. "Braucht Europa eine Verfassung? Eine Bemerkung zu Dieter Grimm," in: J. Habermas, *Die Einbeziehung des Anderen. Studien zur politischen Theorie*, Frankfurt/M., 185 ff.

Hall, S. 1996. "Loss of Union Citizenship in Breach of Fundamental Rights," *European Law Review*, 129 ff.

Hobsbawm, E. 1994. "Citoyenneté européenne et citoyenneté nationale. Une solution de continuité (Contrepoint)," in: B. Théret (ed.), *L'Etat, la finance et le social. Souveraineté nationale et construction européenne*, Paris.

Mansel, H.-P. 1988. *Personalstatut, Staatsangehörigkeit und Effektivität*, München.

Marias, E. (ed.). 1994. *European Citizenship*, Maastricht.

Marx, R. 1997. "Reform des Staatsangehörigkeitsrechts: Mythische oder rechtlich begründete Hindernisse?," *Zeitschrift für Ausländerrecht und Ausländerpolitik*, 67 ff.

Menegazzi Munari, F. 1996. *Cittadinanza europea: Una promessa da mantenere*, Torino.

Messner, C. 1997. *Das Subjekt als Horizont. Zur Repräsentation von Individuum und Gesellschaft im philosophischen Diskurs*, PhD. Thesis, Saarbrücken.

Pastore, M. 1993. "Frontiere, conflitti, identità. A proposito di libera circolazione e nuove forme di controllo sociale in Europa," *Dei delitti e delle pene*, 19 ff.

Pollmann, C. 1993. "Unification des territoires et citoyenneté par la résidence: le recours collectif au droit comme stratégie," in: A. Marchand (ed.), *Le travail social à l'epreuve de l'Europe*. Paris. 221 ff.

Preuss, U.K. and Everson, M. 1996. "Konzeptionen von 'Bürgerschaft' in Europa," *Prokla*, 105, 543 ff.

Ruzié. D. 1993. "Nationalité, effectivité et droit communautaire," *Revue générale de droit international public*, 107 ff.

Sauerwald, C. 1996. *Die Unionsbürgerschaft und das Staatsange-hörigkeitsrecht in den Mitgliedstaaten der Europäischen Union*, Frankfurt/M.

Sepi, M. 1997. *La cittadinanza europea* (Ms.).

Silvestro, M. 1994. "Droit de vote et d'eligibilité aux élections municipales et au Parlement européen," in: E. Marias (ed., 1994).

Wiener, A. 1996. "(Staats)Bürgerschaft ohne Staat. Ortsbezogene Partizipationsmuster am Beispiel der Europäischen Union," *Prokla*. 105, 497 ff.

Zimmermann, A. 1995. "Europäisches Gemeinschaftsrecht und Staatsangehörigkeitsrecht der Mitgliedstaaten unter besonderer Berücksichtigung der Probleme mehrfacher Staatsangehörigkeit," *Europarecht*, 54 ff.

T - #0106 - 160425 - C0 - 219/152/14 - PB - 9781138702646 - Gloss Lamination